a book
of *KING'S*

Views of a Cambridge College

a book of *KING'S*

Views of a Cambridge College

Edited by **Karl Sabbagh**

Photography by **Martin Parr**, with **Eleanor Curtis**

KING'S COLLEGE CAMBRIDGE | THIRD MILLENNIUM PUBLISHING, LONDON

Contents

Three Windows

I look out at the chapel from a different angle,
its scaffold of continual repair
re-erecting history. Previously, high in the east
I overlooked the window,
gazed down on tourist and choir
aloft in irreverent awe.

Now I sit across the quad, thumbing an archive
in a room of cream and quiet,
books whitely labelled and leaning.
Before me in foolscap
lie the sheets another I mistyped
three decades ago.

He was pretentious. He also dared.
He knew what to think, even when wrong.
Now I, his future I,
grown ignorant with knowledge
see where he laid stones the river
still flows round, stones I still tread.

This old fool waves to that earlier fool
out from this room of simple thought,
to the window of that flat across the Parade,
where in the tintinnabulating morning
he'd dragged down the sash to the rain, scenting
white stone and forbidden lawns.

Noel Williams

Foreword

Karl Sabbagh

A hologram is a type of image with the unique property that, if you break it into pieces, each piece still allows you to see the whole image. In a way, *A Book of King's* is like a hologram. Each piece of writing reveals elements of the whole College. For each writer, the defining characteristics of King's – its buildings, its music, its individual members, its waywardness – informs what he or she has written, even if the topic is as specialized as the Collective Intelligence of the Internet or as immediate and personal as waiting on table at conferences.

The 40 or so contributors to this book were each invited to write a piece which reflects in some way an experience of King's. Some write specifically about their time at the College, as students or Fellows; others relate how people, or events, or things learned or unlearned at King's, made a difference to their later lives. Many more King's people could have been invited – some were – since the College seems to have made a practice over the years of producing a range of people who, in addition to their other abilities, can write well, and as editor of this book I want it first and foremost to be readable. The range of contributors is very wide – from established writer/illustrator Jan Pieńkowski to undergraduate writer/illustrator Anna Trench; world traveller and diplomat Sir Anthony Figgis to world traveller and primary school teacher Tansy Troy; librarian and historian Peter Jones to art historian, undergraduate and model Lily Cole; radical socialist Martin Jacques to radical Muslim Arzu Merali. The parallels and comparisons are unintended but they spring out of the rich variety of people who have passed through King's, and occasionally stayed, over the last sixty years.

One important aspect of the book is the photography. The College made the inspired decision to invite the noted Magnum photographer Martin Parr to take photographs at King's on a dozen or so occasions during the last year. His photographs provide a very personal view of King's, a view which shows that it is 'not just a pretty place'. Martin's photos are arranged principally in two picture essays and a gallery of portraits, and the choice of images is his. Only when he offered us a picture of a chair with a jacket hanging over it as a portrait of the Provost did I exercise some modest editorial control. (The picture of the chair is still in the book, but not as a portrait of the Provost.)

As Robin Osborne points out, unlike many Cambridge colleges King's is an artery rather than a heart, and Eleanor Curtis's photographs represent King's as a set of buildings and spaces where some people work and live and other people pass through. Her photographs have a different style and a very different palette from Martin Parr's, and like his they show a side of King's that is familiar to the few and hidden from many.

I should say that there is nothing 'official' about this book. It is not a history or an intellectual *tour d'horizon* or a gallery of stars or a survey of the treasures of the College. Although the College has been

Karl Sabbagh.

entirely supportive of my approach to the book it has not tried to impose any particular type of content. As a result, some aspects of King's are almost absent. There is little about sport, for example, apart from a passing reference by one of the College's leading oarswomen. (Mind you, there have been times when sport itself has been pretty absent from the College.)

Nor is this a paean of praise of the College. 'The College can make some amazingly stupid decisions,' says the Advocate General of the EU; 'I am struck by a sense of decline,' says a Professor of European Studies at New York University. But since one of the phrases frequently used about the College is 'self-critical' this is perhaps not surprising.

Nevertheless, even the occasional criticism is embedded in affectionate, grateful, funny and moving accounts of how much, and in how many different ways, King's has influenced the lives of the thousands of people who have passed through the Main Gate to spend years or decades within its walls.

Retracing some paths not taken

Samson Abramsky

Before (1967–72)

At the age of 14, I had decided, or rather it became clear to me, that I was going to be a writer.

I initially applied to King's to do Social and Political Sciences – but not with any real enthusiasm. I was doing mathematics A-level, largely out of deference to my father's wishes. But my school mathematics education was a disaster. The subject seemed totally alien to me, without rhyme or reason. In the end, I crashed out of Mathematics, and changed to English. After that, everything went swimmingly. I got an Open Scholarship in English to King's.

It seemed my course was set. My life plan was to be a writer. I was going to Cambridge to study English. What's the problem?

A week after arriving in Cambridge, I had changed my degree to Philosophy. I had already been contemplating this change, and the decision was confirmed by the first meeting of my group of students with the Director of Studies in English, a brisk lady who painted a picture of our forthcoming march through English literature: another week, another classic, another essay. I felt that this would lead to a professionalized and detached relationship to literature, rather than the intuitive, passionate engagement I supposed appropriate to the writer-in-waiting I believed myself to be. And Philosophy was making her siren call, as she does to the innocent and uninitiated: 'come to me, I am truly and uniquely fundamental; I and only I address the ultimate questions we all must ask, and seek to answer'.

Philosophy at King's (1972–5)

For most of my time at King's, there was no Fellow in Philosophy with a permanent position. So I had a succession of supervisors, among them several striking figures, including Kathy Vaughan Wilkes and, finally, Ross Harrison, the current Provost.

In my second year, I had Ian Hacking as supervisor. He has had a remarkable and highly decorated career. At that time, he cut quite a dash in the Cambridge Philosophy Faculty, with his good looks and intense manner. What was most important for me was the sense one got from him that it was perfectly natural to move easily and freely between Philosophy, Mathematics and Science. Once, as we were ending a supervision, he picked up a *University Gazette*, and idly considered which Part III Mathematics Tripos courses he might go to. In general, North American philosophers – some, by no means all – have been better able, by dint of their broader training, to engage seriously with mathematics and science than their British counterparts.

I had already begun to experience 'mathematics envy'; the sense that, beyond the toy logic studied by philosophers, there was a world of deep and precise ideas which any

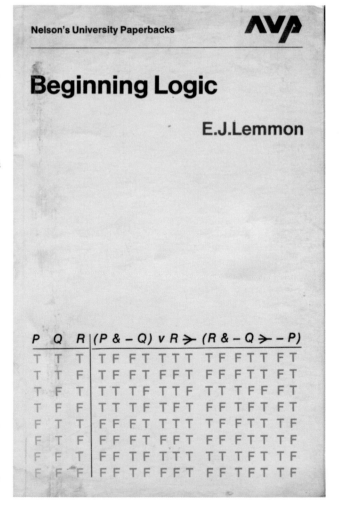

serious attempt to form theories about the world needed to have access to. My first small step into that world was, in fact, through the medium of 'toy logic'.

In my first vacation from Cambridge, I spent several pleasant afternoons working through all the exercises in EJ Lemmon's *Beginning Logic*, which has served several generations of students well. Lemmon had been a philosopher, coming from a humanities background in the British style, who had taught himself enough mathematical logic to have done some elegant work on the algebraic semantics of modal logic, and written a famous manuscript with Dana Scott presenting modal logic based on the then-new Kripke semantics. His book finished with some serious and, one suspects, heartfelt advice to the student on how to take their education in real mathematical logic further. Although it was far from obvious at the time, I had caught the bug; I was infected, I was doomed.

That first summer vacation, I faced the ruins of my mathematical education. I had no confidence in my grasp of the most basic principles of arithmetic and algebra. What were the rules? How did this game work?

I found some programmed study books in the public library: the kind where you do an exercise, turn to another page to find the answer, if you got it right you moved on to the next topic, otherwise back to more explanation and another problem. I was 20 years old, recovering what I should have known at 12. I worked quickly though these books, then American college texts on Euclidean geometry and algebra. I was, apparently, feeding a hunger.

But returning to Cambridge, I had no time to continue this self-education; there was formal studying to do. Ian Hacking did direct me to a brand new logic text, *Computability and Logic* by Boolos and Jeffrey, now a classic in its fifth edition. I devoured the first part on Turing machines and computability, then the chapters on the incompleteness theorems. I was a long way from being any sort of mathematician, but I was no longer innocent of mathematics. I knew now that mathematics did have both rhyme and reason, and I was beginning to learn some of its stories.

Ian Hacking was an inspiring and friendly figure as a supervisor. He remarked at some point: 'I think it's a good thing that you're doing Philosophy'. He meant this as praise and encouragement, but I was increasingly coming to doubt it myself. During that year, I manifested growing restlessness and discontent with the narrowness of Cambridge Philosophy. Ian was surprisingly tolerant of this erratic behaviour, perhaps because he had some confidence in me; more likely, probably, that having fallen under the spell of Michel Foucault at that time, he was somewhat impatient himself with the narrowness of the British philosophical scene, which he would soon depart. He tried to set me up with some tutorials with Imre Lakatos, but Lakatos died suddenly of a heart attack. Then he tried to set me up with George Steiner, but that didn't work out either. He put me in touch with a few other maverick philosophy students, and we formed our own little reading group. Our first text was Husserl, who truth to tell I found unutterably dull. I also read Hegel's *Phenomenology of Spirit* at that time. It has some under-appreciated comic moments. We can all find a place in our hearts for 'the night in which all cows are black'.

By the end of that year, I knew that I was not going to be a philosopher. Philosophy had questions that sounded grand, but no answers to them, just an interminable, nit-picking conversation. Crucially, I had no confidence in the *methods* of analytical philosophy. Grounding precise analysis in ordinary language was a losing game, building towers of concepts on sand. Trying to buttress natural language with flimsy bits of toy logic didn't help much either. Nor did Continental philosophy beguile me. The smell of the higher bullshit came through clearly enough, amid the posturing and dramatics. I could feel the truth of literature, and this wasn't it.

I saw glimpses, through all this, of a subject I might have wanted to do, if it only existed. It still does not exist, but is perhaps a little closer to existence now than it was then, thanks among others to a number of people who have become friends and colleagues in later years, such as Johan van Benthem, Rohit Parikh, Adam Brandenburger and Jeremy Butterfield (who had joined my little group of maverick students, and who I was to meet again 25 years later in Oxford).

Whether because I was not content with the game, or not good enough at it, I did not get a First in Part IB of the Philosophy Tripos. I was told by Ian Hacking that I had come at the top of the Upper Seconds. He left Cambridge in the summer of 1974, going to Stanford. My last contact with him was a postcard he sent me, well over and above the call of duty, expressing approval that I was learning some abstract algebra, and no doubt offering some trenchant good advice.

I wanted to get out of Philosophy, and thought about changing subject for my final year. But which subject I might want to do would have me? In the end, I gritted my teeth and went back for another year. To make the best of a bad job, I took the two most mathematically oriented courses, Mathematical Logic and Philosophy of Mathematics, together with two History of Philosophy papers: British Empiricists (Locke, Berkeley, Hume) *vs.* European Rationalists (Descartes, Spinoza, Leibniz, Kant).

My heart wasn't in it, and I didn't expect to do well. Another Upper Second in Part II, again high up in the list, but so what? I was leaving, that much was clear: leaving Cambridge, and leaving Philosophy. For all the individual kindnesses I had received, my feeling was that Cambridge as an institution had chewed me up, and was spitting me out.

A new direction (1975)

Before I had started at Cambridge, my father had not been feeling well. Cancer was suspected, and he underwent a painful biopsy, which gave him a clean bill of health. However, his health continued to deteriorate. Eventually, heart disease, already in an advanced state, was diagnosed. We were kept in hope by the doctors until a rather late stage. He died in my final year as an undergraduate at Cambridge. I had witnessed the slow, inexorable progress of his illness over the previous four years. He died aged 64, a few months short of retirement.

I had decided, in another of those moments of clarity around the age of 13 or 14, that religion was a form of wish-fulfilment. People believed because they wanted or needed it to be true; they believed what they had been taught to believe. Despite this, I had continued to live in a rosy glow of inner optimism that everything would turn out well, that somehow, secretly, the world was on my side. That daydream was no longer available to me. The world looked pretty cold and uncaring. The necessity of making my way in it somehow, without wealth or connections, all of a sudden loomed rather large.

Despite having decided that Philosophy was not for me, I was not above exploring some options for using it as a passage to the future. I applied for Fulbright and Kennedy scholarships in late 1974, the beginning of my final year. My father was still well enough then to joke a little. For some reason he wanted me to apply to Princeton, and simply used the argument: 'I like the name "Princeton".' I did apply there. I dare say I never stood a chance. Just as well: success would have been a disaster. I began to cast around for postgraduate courses I could do. I looked with a certain longing at Masters courses in Mathematics, but that was crazy; I simply wasn't prepared.

My supervisor in Mathematical Logic and Philosophy of Mathematics in my final year was Timothy Smiley, the logician in the Philosophy department. Of all the people who taught me during my time in Cambridge, he was the only one I came to somewhat dislike, mainly because of the sense he gave off that, while he would do his duty, he had a certain distaste for me. He also had the strange Cambridge habit, which I have encountered on a couple of other occasions, of apparently believing that it was ok to fart, loudly, repeatedly, and unapologetically, in the company of others, as long as one was the senior person present.

For all this, it was Smiley who played a significant part in helping me to find my next step. Perhaps he simply wanted to get me off his hands, but he made some enquiries, and told me that it might be possible for me to apply for a place on the Diploma in Computer Science at Cambridge. Computers were the big wave of the present and future in 1975. I didn't know anything about them – after three years of Philosophy, I didn't know anything about anything – but they seemed to offer scope for people with some logical and analytical skills. It was worth a try.

Two good men (1975–8)

Neil Wiseman led a Computer Graphics group at the Cambridge Computer Laboratory. He was clearly comfortable in his own skin, felt no need to show off to anyone, and enjoyed and was good at what he did. He also ran the Diploma in Computer Science, and interviewed me for a place. The course description stated quite clearly that A-level Mathematics was required as a minimum qualification for admission to the course. Whether someone had put in a good word for me, or he simply sized me up for himself, Neil decided to offer me a place. Most of my fellow students on the course had taken Mathematics or Natural Sciences degrees at Cambridge.

Neil was a much-loved figure in the Computer Laboratory, as the tributes to him when he died, aged 61, in 1995 made clear. He was a good man, and I owe him a great deal.

So I found myself hoisted up from the shipwreck of my degree, and aboard a brave new vessel, a starship no less. Many things were strange and new, and some of them disturbing. The heroes on the course were the uber-geeks, such as Paul Bond, who would later write software for Acorn. I was not one of them, but this was not the nightmare of my school mathematics either. Principles and ideas could be learned, skills could be acquired. The computer was unforgiving, but consistent, and amenable to logic. I began to perceive that there was a powerful and deep order of ideas here, a new world to explore.

I avoided the disastrous mistake that many people who have ended up in computing have made, of feeling that they are in fallen circumstances, that the subject is beneath them. Quite the contrary; I felt more in tune with what I was studying than I had since my first days in Cambridge.

My expectation had always been that the Diploma would lead to a programming job, and it did. I joined GEC Computers Ltd in 1976. I spent two enjoyable and educational years there, working on operating systems development. But during my time there, I became aware that there was an academic discipline of Computer Science which was beginning to study the very kinds of things I was working on, with growing depth. It seemed that Computer Science could be a subject where you 'did your damnedest with your mind – no holds barred', as Percy Bridgman had defined science. One of my fellow recruits at GEC, who had just graduated from Edinburgh, got their research reports, the old orange booklets. There, in 1977, I saw Robin Milner's first papers on what would become CCS, his Calculus of Communicating Systems. Robin would return to Cambridge, and to King's, some 18 years later, and I would succeed him at Edinburgh. But all that lay far in the future. What struck me now was the idea of returning to university, to do research in Computer Science.

I wrote to Roger Needham, on the flimsy pretext that he had been Chair of the Examiners when I had done the Diploma, and had been happy to give me feedback about my results (a 'high Non-Distinction', to go with my 'good Upper Seconds'). I received a response which went well above and beyond the call of duty; a typically pithy letter with a clear recommendation, that the best place for me to go to in London (I was married now, and my wife was working there) was Queen Mary College. In 1978, I started a PhD there. I had embarked on the career and the work I am still engaged in, 31 years later.

Does it matter what we do? (2009)

On a mild, rainy June day in Akademgorodok, the science city on the outskirts of Novosibirsk, Siberia, I was walking back from the conference centre to the hotel with a distinguished Danish colleague, some 15 years my senior. As we picked our way through the puddles, he was talking about his grandchildren, and eventually declared, expansively: 'Family is everything!'

I warmed to the sentiment, and my family is very precious to me. And yet I wanted to say: 'Dines, come on, you have spent the last 50 years pouring huge energies, care, passion, attention to detail, insight and wisdom into your work. Would you have even been the same person your family knows and loves without all this? Would they have had more of you, or would there have been less of the essence of you for them to have?'

Few of us can say that it matters terribly much to the world what we have spent our working lives on. We have added our bricks to the collective edifice of science, culture and the rest, but if they had fallen from our hands, others would have picked them up and added them in our place, with a different pattern here or there, but all to much the same effect.

Yet it matters terribly to us individually, and it matters terribly to the world that in each generation people, collectively, do go forth and give of their best, pour the energies of their life without stint into their work, as if it mattered terribly.

The small world of King's

Sebastian Ahnert

The Fellowship of a College like King's may seem to defy simple analysis. Its Fellows vary across so many disciplines, come from a variety of backgrounds, and range from extrovert to self-absorbed. But two revolutionary scientific papers published in the 1990s cast light on how we can look at the College as a human network and observe a certain amount of patterning in what seems a fairly random arrangement.

Networks surround us all in everyday life. We interact with others in our social network, use the Internet to exchange information, travel on rail or road networks, and use electricity delivered to us by a power grid. The new scientific research showed many of these real-world networks share common – and at the time, unexpected – properties.

The first paper recast Stanley Milgram's 'six degrees of separation' hypothesis, according to which any two people on Earth are separated by at most six links of mutual acquaintance. It did so by introducing quantitative criteria for identifying a *small-world* network, in which any two nodes are separated by only a few links. The neural network of a worm and the power grid of the United States both turn out to be small-world networks, as does the collaboration network between Hollywood actors.

The second paper revealed another property shared by a wide variety of networks in nature and society, namely that they are *scale-free*, which means that they contain many nodes with few connections and a few with many, and that this also holds true if we look at a subset of the whole network. This observation is independent of the size of the subset we choose, which is why the network is termed scale-free.

Based on the composition of College committees one can draw a collaboration network for the Fellows of King's. I have drawn such a network here, together with an indication of Fellows' election dates, and it shows how the Fellows at King's are connected through common committee membership (excluding *ex officio* members). We can therefore see which committees are – in some sense – close to others, and which ones attract newer or older Fellows. Note that several committees are too delocalized to be labelled meaningfully, but that all their links are present. Interestingly, the two largest committees –

Council and the Research committee – are separated by a noticeable gap, which implies that Fellows are interested in being part of one or the other, but not both. The – at least superficially – somewhat related Finance and Investment committees are at opposite ends of the network, which perhaps reflects the rather different sort of expertise required by the two committees – one dealing with the details of the day-to-day budget and the other with the long-term perspective of the endowment. Despite these separations, this network too fulfils the formal, quantitative criteria of a small-world network. This scientific evidence is entirely in line with my personal experience. Despite having only recently joined the Fellowship, I already feel very much part of the close-knit community – the small world – that is King's.

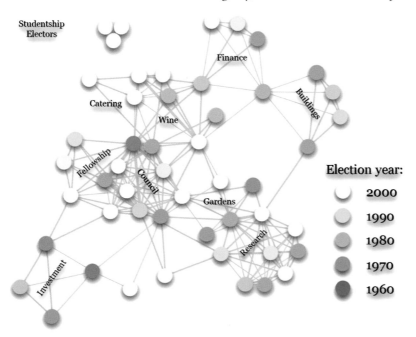

Studentship Electors
Finance
Catering
Buildings
Wine
Fellowship
Council
Gardens
Research
Investment

Election year:
2000
1990
1980
1970
1960

Art without boundaries

Stephen Bann

A roll-call of the famous musicians – instrumentalists, singers and composers – who passed through King's in the 1960s would come swiftly to most people's minds. A list of Kingsmen who played a part in the propagation of advanced visual art in that decade and after would not be so obvious. But it is worth compiling. By 1970, Jonathan Benthall had reached the last of his series of outstanding articles on 'Technology and art' for the London magazine *Studio International* – self-described (not inaccurately) as 'the world's most authoritative journal of modern art'. He would later act as secretary of the ICA (Institute of Contemporary Arts) in London from 1971–3. Charles Harrison had been appointed Assistant Editor of *Studio International* in 1967, and from 1971 onwards would take a leading role in British conceptual art as general editor for Art & Language Press. Paul Overy had published books on Manet and Kandinsky by 1970, and would proceed to be chief art critic of *The Times*. It should be underlined that none of these Kingsmen (any more than the present author) had gone up to Cambridge to read History of Art, which only just became available as a Part II subject in the early 1960s. Nor did they (or we) form any kind of group within the College. What follows is therefore a personal view of the many different opportunities for viewing and writing about contemporary art in King's, and the University as a whole, over the period.

The legacy of Bloomsbury was always, of course, highly visible in King's. Roger Fry's portrait of Keynes at work hung then in a set in the Gibbs Building, and intrigued me with the gymnastics of writing on a board laid over crossed legs. (How he would have appreciated a laptop!) The sturdy table oddly daubed in a dusky pink by Alan Clutton-

Keynes by Roger Fry.

KING'S COLLEGE CAMBRIDGE

I don't know whether you still look after the Picture Lending Library. but Art now blocks my bedroom door, and to anyone who could divert it I should be grateful. – Best wishes –
E M Forster

Frize

Brock proved a welcome distraction in the course of some tutorial discussions. In sharp contrast, Michael Jaffé had furnished his spacious rooms above the jumbo arch in baroque splendour, leaving me with the long-term ambition to scatter occasional tables with Renaissance medallions – an aim at least partly fulfilled in a contemporary mode when I became a friend of Ian Hamilton Finlay. I could not really appreciate at the time the consummate sense of style that had inclined Noel Annan to select the Italian painter Renato Guttuso for his leaving portrait. Nothing could have been more correctly attuned to the political spirit of the times than the choice of this veteran of the *Resistenza*, who was also particularly revered as a master by the Soviet Academy. Edmund Leach had a hard act to follow, but capped Noel by understatement with the fine David Hockney drawing.

Among the younger dons, Jasper Rose was a friendly maverick. He was for a time art critic of the magazine *Time and Tide* in the early 1960s, and his house in Portugal Place was full of sensitive paintings by his wife Jean. In my first year, he had the great courtesy to attend what must have been an excruciating sole performance of my one-act Pinteresque play performed in a minute study in The Drain, with Château Climens, Barsac, 1947 (*en magnum*) serving as some compensation. Luckily I had graduated by my third year to a capacious top-floor set in Wilkins, right opposite the South Door of the Chapel, where it was possible to throw a large Halloween party, with bobbing for apples. I recall that Victor de Waal, then Succentor, was rather expert at this, though my most vivid recollection is of Sandy (Colin St John) Wilson enquiring if he could use a piece of my 'chinoiserie' (actually a tea-bowl with puce transfer decoration) as an ashtray.

However it was Francis Haskell who most generously encouraged my artistic entrepreneurship. In this time before multicoloured posters had become easily available to undergraduates, the College sponsored a Loan Picture Library. Early in each term the growing collection of framed works had to be hauled out of the store and displayed in the College Hall. The charge for a term's loan was '4/- for the original paintings, drawings, etchings and lithographs and 2/6 for the reproductions'. Not surprisingly, the majority of Kingsmen opted for the reproductions of the masterpieces of Western painting at the lower charge. The many specimens of the painting of Roger Fry, admittedly rather the worse for wear at the time, habitually failed to find a taker – though I notice that some of them have now been splendidly rehabilitated, and hang in restricted spaces like the Saltmarsh Room. But some of the originals were in great demand: two spectacular lithographs by Picasso were among them, and such highly desirable works could only be allotted after a draw for priority.

My role as custodian of the Loan Picture Library involved me in one minor embarrassment, and several exciting opportunities. The embarrassment came on the occasion when borrowers were late in returning their pictures, and left them against the locked door of the store, which happened to be just next to the access to EM Forster's bedroom on A staircase. I still have the polite little message on a white card (to which I immediately responded) that said: '...Art now blocks my bedroom door, and to anyone who could divert it I should be grateful'. The opportunities were for the purchase of more pictures to be added to the stock. Francis took the enlightened view that, as I did all the administration, I should also select any new works that might be bought from the receipts. Among other paintings, I chose a Prunella Clough from a commercial show in Cambridge, and went up to London galleries to select a small Josef Herman oil of Welsh miners and a rather large William Turnbull abstract watercolour.

Towards the end of my tenure, Francis agreed with the plan of organizing an exhibition of art by members of the College in a room in the Provost's Lodge. This elicited a surprising variety of works, including a mobile encircling a Coca-Cola bottle which was submitted by Charles Harrison. Needless to say, we were all amateurs. But not long after I left the College after gaining my PhD in 1967, arrangements were being made for the appointment of the first Artist in Residence. Bob Young, then Graduate Tutor, took appropriate soundings, and Mark Lancaster was the first holder of the post.

Looking further afield throughout Cambridge during the 1960s, one could hardly fail to note the many signs of the burgeoning of contemporary art forms. The Fitzwilliam was still essentially a repository of the great works of the past, though I chose to illustrate two treasured pictures from the collection – a Courbet and a Cézanne – in my first book, *Experimental Painting* (1970). Sandy Wilson, who was teaching in the Architecture Faculty, was already by this stage beginning to form what became one of the finest collections of post-1960 British painting (now installed at Pallant House in Chichester). I attended the housewarming party given at his newly built home in Cambridge, when he introduced Peter Blake and Eduardo Paolozzi among the guests. Sandy's wife, Muriel Wilson, presided in All Saints' Passage over what was then the only Arts Council Exhibition Gallery outside London. Among the pioneering shows held there was a display by the Situation group – and it was probably Colin Renfrew's brilliant critical writing on these artists that emboldened me to buy the Turnbull watercolour for King's. I myself began to write art criticism for *Broadsheet*, a mimeographed precursor of *Time Out* of which I was co-editor, from 1962 onwards; for *Granta* (Mark Lushington of King's being co-editor) from 1963, and for *The Cambridge Review* (David Morse of King's being co-editor) from 1964. I also covered Cambridge exhibitions for the London-based *Arts Review*.

The newly created Anglia Television began a regular critics' programme in the mid-1960s, and I was ferried to their studio in Norwich to talk about such things as the epoch-making Rauschenberg show held at London's Whitechapel Gallery in 1964 (curated by Bryan Robertson, who had begun his career in the 1950s running the upstairs gallery of Heffers bookshop in Cambridge's town centre). These fleeting appearances, in which I cautiously sipped red wine with other critics on the small screen, left me with an abiding distrust for the wiles of film editors. But they culminated in a more active role in one of the editions of Raymond Baxter's *Tomorrow's World*. The Arts Council Gallery in Cambridge had mounted an ambitious travelling exhibition of kinetic art works, and I was shown wrestling with one of the Brazilian artist Lygia Clark's so-called 'animal' constructions, which took an embarrassingly long time to find its feet.

King's was my base when I assisted in running the University's Society of Arts, which had developed into a forum for stimulating interest in the contemporary scene. Colin Renfrew had been originally involved in the creation of this undergraduate society, and it then passed into the dual guardianship of two other members of St John's – the future novelist Piers Paul Read and Rackstraw Downes, who has subsequently become a well-known landscape painter in the United States. In 1962, the society was handed on to Philip Steadman (Trinity Hall) and myself. Not all the artists and art specialists whom we invited to speak at Cambridge responded positively. The abstract expressionist painter Alan Davie announced that he had 'given up all forms of lecture'. Those who did accept were, of course, entertained and put up for the night at our expense. There were a number of tense moments, as when one young painter (now a Royal Academician) chose the most expensive items on the menu at Miller's in King's Parade. My own effort to make an unprepossessing college guest room fit for the visit of Victor Pasmore could have been counterproductive as the only flowers I could find to brighten it up were vivid magenta and purple dahlias, quite discordant with his own restrained palette.

A leading specialist in graphic design started off by alienating his audience in Scroope Terrace when he explained that, having looked us over, he had decided to give the lightweight version of his lecture; he later picked a quarrel with the King's porter when claiming the key for his room and went off in a huff, spending the night playing chess with a long-suffering member of the Architecture department. The American painter, Larry Rivers, whom we had decided to treat to a home-cooked meal at our garret in Green Street, arrived in company with a young woman whom he had apparently met on the train, and announced halfway through the meal: 'Now I'm going to give myself away. Have you got any Teacher's?'

There were also high moments of a more intellectual kind. The designer and psychoanalytic writer Anton Ehrensweig (shortly afterwards the author of a classic text of the period, *The Hidden Order of Art*) gave a memorable lecture. We corresponded afterwards about the significance of Rauschenberg's show. Stefan Themerson, the film-maker, novelist and publisher who ran the Gaberbocchus Press, spoke movingly about his connections with Kurt Schwitters, and handed round the original copies of the precious collages that Schwitters had given to him. Not a promotion of the Society of Arts, but certainly memorable as an irruption of the avant-garde into 1960s Cambridge, was the impact of the auto-destructive artist Gustav Metzger. He gave two performances of his acid paintings on nylon, the first at a meeting of the Theoretical Amoralists in a medium-sized room in Trinity, and the second some years later in the large lecture hall in the Engineering Laboratory, where his gestures with the brush were controlled by a radio operator, and photographed by a royal prince. One of his ravaged nylon canvases later provided the cover image for my *Experimental Painting*.

No account of contemporary art at Cambridge during the period could fail to mention the presence of Jim Ede, who was then just beginning to open his collection of British and international art to members of the University on a regular basis. It was Jonathan Benthall, as I recall it, who first directed me along the Backs to Kettle's Yard in Northampton Street, and I made the first of many visits. At this point, Jim had no official connection with the University, but simply let it be understood by word of mouth that he would be at home every weekday afternoon in term-time, available to talk about his remarkable collection, and his view of art as a 'Way of Life'. He also lent generously from his stocks of works by particular artists, enabling me to enhance my rooms in King's with a drawing by the sculptor Henri Gaudier-Brzeska and a painting by the Cornish fisherman, Alfred Wallis. What may not always have been understood is Jim's continuing commitment during these years to assisting contemporary artists, even if they did not seem to accord with his taste. Through Jim's intermediacy, I bought my first painting of consequence in 1963 – a watercolour by the Indian artist Avinash Chandra which he had mischievously dubbed 'School of Braque'.

It need hardly be stressed that neither King's, nor Cambridge as a whole, adhered to an orthodoxy of any kind, with regard

stephen bann at home M.11 Kings

an film play

8.30 saturday 25 february rsvp

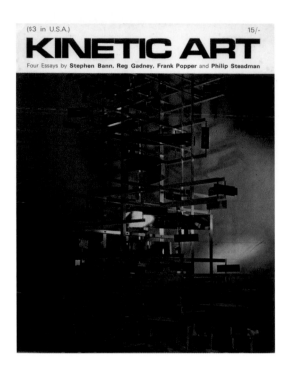

to contemporary art. Charles Harrison, who would later become a major authority on English modernism, noted in *Granta*'s 'Modern Art Issue' of November 1963: 'Jim Ede's hospitality offers a unique opportunity to see much of the very best of English painting as it should be seen'. Yet the broad scope of this issue of the magazine illustrates how many directions were emerging simultaneously at the time: beside a review by Karl Sabbagh incongruously subtitled 'Bastard of Kings', one can find my own 'Notes' on Giacometti, Robert Harvey writing on Pop Art, Jules Lubbock on Richard Robbins' figurative paintings, and Reg Gadney offering an introduction to Kinetic Art. Reg Gadney (St Catharine's) would shortly take over as an editor of *Granta*, and a year later the magazine was playing host to a catalogue for the 'First international exhibition of concrete, phonetic and kinetic poetry', held in the Rushmore Rooms of his college. Also in 1964, Philip Steadman edited the first of three issues of the London-based magazine *Image*. With the enthusiastic collaboration of Reg Gadney, Mike Weaver (Magdalene) and myself, *Image* sustained for two years a heady but slightly unstable combination of photojournalism and critical writings on the avant-garde, both historical and actual. *Image* then yielded place to a more consequential production: *Form*, a 'quarterly magazine of the arts' edited and published from Cambridge between 1966 and 1969 by Philip Steadman, with Mike Weaver and myself as co-editors.

The aspect of this period that strikes me when I look back is the sense that there were no constraining boundaries to these interests that we were developing. The notion of the 'extra-curricular' hardly made sense. In this respect, the atmosphere of King's was congenial. My History supervisor, Christopher Morris, stipulated that the first essay that I wrote should be on anything but a historical topic. I chose to make a rather laboured comparison between the treatment of landscape in the Psalms, and that in Chinese poetry as translated by Ezra Pound. We were also told then that lectures in our own degree subject were dispensable, but we should be sure to attend lectures in other faculties. I decided to attend the spellbinding series on Montaigne by Mme Odette de Mourgues. On leaving Cambridge in 1967, I was happy to sell my copy of *The Tudor Constitution: Documents and Commentary,* but retained among other things the early 19th-century edition of Montaigne that I had purchased at Heffer's. I was not to know that, a third of a century afterwards, I would be writing about the engraver of the frontispiece.

'All the bosses do is provide decoration'

Patrick Bateson

King William III tried to impose Isaac Newton on King's as the Provost. The Fellows of the time were too cunning and the sovereign's attempt failed. If Newton had become Provost he would have been the first praeposital scientist. However, the job remained firmly in the hands of the humanities – until I was elected. I was still excited by science and decided to retain my University Chair with all its obligations to teach and to continue with an active research programme. This meant that I would only work part-time for the College.

Much of my research life has been spent collaborating with scientists in fields other than my own. When I returned from the United States in 1965 with a King's Research Fellowship, even my liberal-minded College had an expectation that Fellows should dine in Hall several nights a week. Despite the disruption to home life, meeting Fellows from other disciplines was rewarding and sometimes had major benefits. It certainly did for me. One evening in 1966, by chance I sat next to Gabriel Horn whom I did not yet know. He had been working on the neurobiology of attention and habituation, but was very interested in the effects of learning on the nervous system. I was keen to bring my behavioural knowledge to bear on mechanisms that underlie learning. I had been working on behavioural imprinting, the process by which recently hatched birds, like ducklings or domestic chicks, become attached to the first moving thing that they encounter. The object of their attachment is usually their mother, but in the laboratory it can be something quite artificial. The imprinting process seemed like a very good candidate for understanding the neural basis of learning because any effects of experience should stand out more prominently in a bird that had come straight out of a dark incubator. We recognized our common interests and thus began our long and highly productive collaboration which lasted until well after I became Provost.

Later I was led in quite a different direction. One day in 1995, Professor Robert Savage came to see me in my office in King's. He had chaired a working group for the National Trust on the conservation and management of red deer on the Quantocks and on Exmoor, including the various implications of a ban on hunting the deer with hounds – a practice peculiar to that part of southwest England. Its terms of reference did not ask for any investigation of the ethical or moral issues. A prominent Methodist minister, Lord Soper, proposed, therefore, that the National Trust set up a balanced working party on deer hunting to examine issues relating to cruelty and animal welfare not addressed in the Savage Report, and led by an independent chairman. Professor Savage wanted to know whether I would chair the working party. I said that such a study would need new research and that such work could not be carried out by a committee. I would do the research if I had a free hand in carrying it out. The Council of the National Trust pondered my offer and then asked me to conduct a scientific study.

Thus began a scientific saga which took me into new territory. It would have been new for anybody because no study of what happens to a mammal when it is chased by dogs had been carried out. I was, however, deeply interested in issues to do with animal welfare. As President of the Association for the Study of Animal Behaviour in the late 1970s, I established an ethical committee and played a central part in establishing an approach that is now enshrined in British law protecting animals used for research. The principle is one of maximizing scientific and medical benefit while minimizing pain and suffering in the animals. The problem of how pain and suffering should be assessed could not be sidestepped and I suggested how the process might be made transparent. I also gave much thought to the ethical issues involved.

In my approach to the welfare issues to do with hunting, I decided to use the triangulation technique which Gabriel Horn and I had employed in our work on the neural basis of imprinting, namely to employ different approaches, each of which was associated with its own subset of ambiguities. The approaches included: assessments of the behavioural responses of the hunted deer; the physiological state of hunted deer in relation to that found in suffering humans; the physical damage to the animal at the end of the hunt; the deer's ability to cope with the challenge of a prolonged hunt by dogs; and departures during the hunt from the conditions to which the animal is well adapted. I was fortunate in being able to bring together a distinguished scientific panel covering the areas of knowledge concerned.

I reported to the Council of the National Trust in 1997, concluding that the level of total suffering of red deer would be markedly reduced if hunting with hounds were ended. Of course, scientists are beset by people who believe one or other side of an argument because of 'common sense' and both sides of this issue had its protagonists. But at the end of the study, as a result of the evidence we gathered, I was left with no doubt that the deer were forced into a prolonged struggle which in no way resembled being hunted by wolves – nor were they playing, as was sometimes suggested implausibly by the supporters of stag-hunting.

I argued that hunting with hounds could no longer be justified on welfare grounds, given the standards applied in other fields such as the transit and slaughter of farm animals and the use of animals in research. On the strength of my report the National Trust immediately banned hunting of red deer with hounds on its land. The media coverage of this work on hunting was enormous and I was vilified by those for whom hunting with hounds was their ruling passion. Every effort was made by the supporters of stag-hunting to ruin my reputation. In the middle of this I was elected Biological Secretary and Vice-President of the Royal Society which was discomfiting to my critics.

The Royal Society has a motto, '*nullius in verba*', which is an extract from a line by the Latin poet Horace. The line may be translated as follows: 'I say no master has the right to swear me to obedience blind.' In effect, the fundamental mode of conduct was to trust the authority of evidence rather than the authority of somebody's say-so. It is an excellent principle which had its place in the debate about hunting with hounds. It should have its place in academic administration, including the running of King's. In my case the benefits of being involved with the College and the Royal Society flowed both ways. At the Royal Society, among other jobs, I had to oversee the election of Fellows on the biological side. I introduced a simple expedient that I had obtained from chairing the Electors to Fellowships at King's. Members of committees will often vote in favour of their personally preferred candidate in preference to someone who had emerged as the stronger candidate. Worse, they will give greater weight to their preferred candidate by giving the stronger candidate the lowest possible ranking. They will not do this, however, if their rank-order is made public. So the solution was obvious: make known to all members of the committee how all the others voted. The effect is miraculous and virtually eliminates tactical voting.

Towards the end of my Provostship I benefited once again from working in a place like King's where one meets people from quite different backgrounds.

I have been consistently sceptical of the idea derived from folk psychology that a useful distinction exists between behaviour patterns that are innate and those that are not innate. A young philosopher of biology, Matteo Mameli, who had been elected a research Fellow of King's, shared my scepticism and we collaborated in a way that was both productive and enjoyable.

Working part-time as Provost while continuing to work as University Professor saved the College a lot of money, but some of the Fellows felt that the Provost should be around all the time and not spend half the day in his laboratory. The expectation was that the Provost should be available at all times and chair all committees. King's certainly had plenty of committees and these multiplied as time went on.

The style of running a college is very different from that found in scientific departments. Later when I was Head of the Zoology Department, meetings of committees I chaired rarely lasted longer than an hour. When I crossed the road to King's to chair a college committee, I found some Fellows dug in for a good afternoon's session of argument. Their idea was to wait until a consensus was about to form and then toss in a hand grenade that opened up at least another half hour of discussion.

During my time as Provost, higher education expanded enormously and with it a declining readiness of successive governments to pay for it. This has left its impact on senior members who are expected to be more accountable for less pay. However, the worst effects were on our students who graduate with ever increasing debts. All of this has meant that King's like every other college has moved into permanent fund-raising. In addition, we have the enormous running expense of keeping our beautiful Chapel in good order. Such fund-raising requires a great deal of time and starts to develop a life of its own. When I was on a fund-raising trip for King's in the United States, I obtained the details of many trusts and foundations. The number of administrators employed by these organizations was strongly and positively correlated with the length of time the bodies had been in existence. It has to be said that the same inexorable trend is to be found in all other aspects of university administration. A very good reason is always found for introducing another layer of bureaucracy, ensnaring the unfortunate academics who had become involved, and providing more work for those who had not.

Fund-raising was especially difficult in the United Kingdom. Alumni of British universities were not used to being asked to support the places where they spent their time as students. For all that, I saw the culture change and our non-resident members responded with increasing generosity. Of course, those who might give to King's appreciate being courted by the Provost, and it is not easy playing a part-time role in such circumstances.

One of the pleasures of being Provost, however, was that my wife, Dusha, and I could work together in ways that both of us found satisfying. Although much went on during the day, official life continued into the late evening. A substantial chunk of the job began after coming out of interminable committees and went on until after breakfast next day when the distinguished overnight guests finally departed. Apart from all the other things she did, this part of keeping the show on the road fell heavily on Dusha's shoulders.

Jack Plumb, who had been Master of Christ's College and enjoyed entertaining Princess Margaret, the Queen's sister, asked us very early in my Provostship if we would invite her to one of the carol services in King's College Chapel. After we had agreed and were firmly on the hook, he said: 'She will be staying with you, of course.' Our jaws dropped but we could hardly say 'No'. Thus began a series of visits and an exposure to a demi-monde totally unfamiliar to us. Princess Margaret liked to be treated with appropriate formality and was, I suspect, slightly ill at ease in an academic environment. However, as we got to know her, we respected her intelligence, sensed her vulnerability, and I have to say that we became increasingly attached to her. Fellows of the College were bemused by all this.

Among our many other guests we particularly enjoyed the visit of the Dalai Lama who insisted on having dinner with us rather than his two monks who travelled with him. We found him to be a man of enormous warmth, intellectual curiosity and, indeed, humour. When we asked him how he could eat what we were having for dinner when he normally abstains from food after midday, he said that he would say a prayer. At a question and answer session arranged for the students he was asked whom he admired most in the world. Without hesitation, he said: 'Gorbachev.' Later Gorbachev was due to stay with us and I was asked vehemently by a Russian dissident, who had suffered terribly during the

Brezhnev era, how I could have such a man staying in the Lodge. I was able to say that if he was good enough for the Dalai Lama he was good enough for me.

The visits of the Dalai Lama and Gorbachev demanded tight security, as did that of HM the Queen when she came for dinner after an Advent carol service in 1991. All these arrangements paled into insignificance compared with what was done for Salman Rushdie when, for the first time after the *fatwah* had been placed upon him four years before, he stood up in the Chapel and gave a public address. After the service he came for lunch in the Lodge. The police were very worried about assassins. Virtually every long curtain in the Lodge had an armed Special Branch policeman hiding behind it. Each shrub in the garden was investigated to see whether it concealed a bomb. Dadie Rylands, whose rooms looked down onto the garden, rang the Porters to say that: 'Some rough-looking types are in the Provost's garden – with dogs.'

I have to say that Dusha and I enjoyed enormously living in George Kennedy's eccentric Provost's Lodge, with its main staircase descending to within two inches of the

Chapel ceiling stone boss.

front door and its strange voids into which nobody could enter. An architect friend said that Kennedy must have been spatially dyslexic. I like to think he did his designs for the builders on the backs of envelopes and the envelopes were rather crumpled. For all that, the Lodge has some wonderful spaces and for 15 years it became our home.

As Provost I had to participate in the great tableau events in the Chapel including the famous Nine Lessons and Carols on Christmas Eve which was broadcast to 100 million people around the world. I am not a believer and some of my more militant atheist friends accused me of hypocrisy. However, I loved the beauty of those occasions. On Christmas Eve I had to read the last lesson, St John's grandly poetic version of the Creation. It starts: 'In the beginning was the Word, the Word was with God and the Word was God.' I wondered whether this poetic vision was a mistranslation. The King James version of the Bible was translated from Greek and the Greek word for 'Word' is *logos*. Now *logos* can be translated as 'idea' and so an alternative version of the Gospel according to St John, Chapter 1 might have started more plausibly: 'In the beginning was the Idea, the Idea was with God and the Idea was God.'

As I sat in the Provost's stall in the Chapel and gazed up in wonder at the wonderful vault above, I saw things that were probably never intended. Running down the middle of the vault is a series of great stone bosses. Each one was supposed to be solid and weigh half a ton but recent research suggests that they are hollow. They are certainly not keystones since the forces keeping the vault in place are taken by the ring of stones into which each boss sits. All the bosses do is provide decoration and since the vault was built at the beginning of the 16th century, they celebrate the Tudors, with alternate portcullises and Tudor roses. As I looked at a rose which I could see from its side I was sure I could see an old man with moustache and beard looking rather severely at me. So much for having rationalist thoughts in a place of worship.

New minds in old buildings

Martin Bell

I suppose it would be gracious after all these years to thank King's for giving me the best education I ever had, but it didn't. The best education I ever had was in the ranks of the Suffolk Regiment for the two years before going up. It was towards the end of National Service, and if I had done the studying before the soldiering I could have avoided the soldiering altogether. But I did not know that at the time. I would have missed a great deal if I had. And if I had passed the War Office Selection Board, the process for identifying the potential officers among the recruits, I would have learned far less. But I failed the WOSB. The presiding brigadier was suspicious, and ordered me to take it again. I failed again; and did not mind so much until I saw the cadets who had passed – as thick as two planks in my view; but, like so many apprentice Kingsmen, I was an opinionated young man.

I learned a lot in uniform that I then applied in three privileged years at King's. I learned in the Army that time spent in reconnaissance is seldom wasted: so, since I was clearly not as bright as the densest of officers and had a horror of exams, I studied old exam papers as if my degree depended on them (which it probably did) and in due course I became a master of weighing the odds and predicting the likely questions – even down to the subject of the General Essay; the Tripos Parts I and II were the equivalent of my Grand National; I wagered on them and won. I learned in the Army that you succeed together or you fail together – and then I went off into two professions, journalism and politics, which attracted the ambitious and in which people mistakenly supposed that they could only succeed at each other's expense; I consciously tried not to do that. And I learned in the Army that respect doesn't come up the line with the rations or with rank, but has to be earned the hard way.

By the time I got to King's I also had to unlearn some lessons learned at boarding school, which was also in Cambridge, at The Leys. It was another world back then in the 1950s. Diplomats, missionaries, generals and others – even colonial administrators, it was so long ago – came to lecture us about their various professions and point us in those directions. They invariably assured us that we would become leaders of men (no mention of women, in those days – and I wouldn't have minded being a leader of women). Then I got out into the real world, on active service as a soldier in Cyprus, which was then a British colony, and discovered that no one wanted to be led – at least by me. We weren't that keen on being led by our officers and sergeants either. We perfected the art of going through the motions, of appearing to do our military duty and of undetected malingering. We also grew up faster than we would have done in a more sequestered environment.

I rose to the rank of corporal. A study of German history tells us that ex-corporals can be dangerous people. To this day, having spent many of the intervening years in the company of warlords and uniformed thugs in a variety of hostile environments, I have a lot of time for soldiers but little for the *Fuhrerprinzip*. People really don't want to be led. They want to be cherished, valued, worked with, even loved – but not to be led, except only and to a limited extent in soldiering. And even there what keeps the soldiers going, in the hardest of circumstances, is not the system of discipline and chain of command, but pride in themselves, in the regiment or corps and the fear of letting each other down. It is known in the Army as 'the buddy buddy system'.

So by the time I reached King's in the autumn of 1959 I suppose that I had been shouted at so much by the sergeant major, and so much locked down in the system, that I had become a bit of a rebel. When the voice of authority said 'Jump!' my response could now be 'Why?' as a student, rather than 'How high?' as a soldier. I was a one-man awkward squad. Those who bore the brunt of this included my Tutor, George Steiner, whose knowledge of so many literatures and languages intimidated me no end. He and the sergeant major came from different planets.

I preferred his – who would not have preferred the quadrangles of King's and rectangles of Churchill (George was a Fellow of the newly built Churchill College)? But I couldn't break the habit of kicking against the people requiring me to do this or that, the academic equivalent of the officer class, who I supposed were teaching me what to think. They were doing nothing of the kind, of course. They were teaching me how to think, which was entirely different.

If set to write an essay about medieval French literature, I would argue that the study of medieval French literature was a waste of time. If asked about the moralists I would write an editorial attacking them one and all. And as for Wordsworth … I was (and still am) a minority of one who believes he is the most overrated of all the supposedly great poets. So when the learned Dr Donald Davie lectured enthusiastically about him, I repressed an urge to heckle him, but sent him instead a lengthy tract about Wordsworth's bathetic tendencies. The lecturer kindly answered it the following week. For me, academic meant futile.

In short, I was an insufferable young man. But King's was used to insufferable young men, and no doubt in due course insufferable young women, as I suspect that it still is. It worked a sort of alchemy, turning a full-of-himself 20-year-old into a rather more outward-facing 23-year-old. I entered the College like a radio set on 'transmit' mode and left it, I hope, on 'receive' mode. The change must have had something to do with the academic staff, but was also brought about by the magic of the place, its spaces and graces, its arches and architecture, its wonderful sense of being anchored in the Middle Ages and yet still taking young people in and transforming them in the 20th, and now 21st, centuries. There was something about its composure that made you think outside yourself.

Some time in the 1950s my father, who was a farmer and writer and part-time mystic, delivered a secular sermon in a church in Suffolk at which he spoke of the yearly miracle of new crops growing in old fields. I see King's in much the same light. It grows new minds in old buildings. It makes connections. One of its most famous sons – or godfathers, perhaps – was EM Forster, who was still around in my time. His celebrated dictum, 'Only connect', should be the College's motto.

Somewhere buried in its library there may still lie the yellowing pages of a piece that I entered for the James Essay Prize of 1961 – and indeed won it because no one else was daft enough to write a supernumerary essay. Whatever it was about, I don't doubt that I would repudiate every one of the opinions expressed therein (unless I got on to Wordsworth, against whom my prejudices have hardened). That is often the way with undergraduates, I believe: they are young pretenders and even impostors, embarrassing the people they later turn out to be, especially in matters of politics and fashion. If we are now who we were then, the transformation never worked and we are indeed in trouble.

I no longer view 'academic' as a term of disparagement. My view of academia has changed along with everything else. Aside from the necessary arts and sciences – and our Chapel is, among other things, a sublime expression of both – there are just two subjects of study which stand out for me now as more important than any other. And one of them was definitely not on the syllabus at King's in those days – nor is it in these. It depends on where you live. There are at least a dozen countries, from Angola to Cambodia and from Nicaragua to Bosnia, where the most important subject for the young to master is landmine awareness. If they get that wrong, they will not live to learn anything else.

For the rest of us, it is history – history, history and still more history. I do not suggest that we should be haunted by it and live our past as obsessively as, for instance, the Serbs, who define themselves by it. But we should be more aware of it than we are. This applies especially to the political class. New Labour's Downing Street appeared in these recent years to be a history-free zone, with heavy consequences at home among the families of the fallen soldiers, and abroad in the outcomes of ill-considered military interventions. We British are now fighting our fourth Afghan War. We might pause to remember who won the other three. We did not. In force levels, objectives and ferocity of combat it most closely resembles the Second Afghan War, from 1878 to 1880. We finally declared victory and left the field, which is what we usually do and will doubtless do again. It would be good if our politicians understood these things, instead of declaring that they would be happy if the soldiers accomplished their mission without firing a single shot. Kipling, who did understand his history, has a message for us here:

> *If any question why we died,*
> *Tell them, because our fathers lied.*

This leads me on, inevitably, to politics. In 1959 I spent (and in my view wasted) £20 on joining the Cambridge Union Society. I was surprised to discover so many ambitious young people using it as a climbing frame for later careers in politics; and even more surprised at the numbers who succeeded. I wondered what was the point of it if they never had a life in the real world between one set of cloisters and another. In rapid succession, these presidents of the Cambridge Union became Members of Parliament, and in due course cabinet ministers, *and all of the same political party.* This uniformity of ambition, and apparently of opinion, was surely not in the spirit of a university. It certainly was not in the spirit of my College. I even briefly joined the Marxist Society, which was used against me when I entered politics.

For many years later, in rather peculiar circumstances, I became a Member of Parliament myself. Three of those ex-presidents were still in place, exactly as I remembered them from the 1960s. One of them had achieved rather more than the others; they were all Tory grandees of a sort; but none of them seemed to me to have had much of a life between then and now. I had the good fortune – certainly in the spirit of King's – to sit as an Independent, free of party discipline and beholden to no one but my constituents and myself. I gravitated naturally to the awkward squad, those MPs from both sides of the House who were the despair of their whips and dared to apply their judgements to their votes, regardless of party. A Parliament of Independents would never have voted for the invasion of Iraq. In so far as we had a leader he was another Kingsman, Tam Dalyell, who was the longest-serving MP and thus the Father of the House. Whenever he stood up to speak one had no idea what he was going to say, except that it would be against the grain of whatever had gone before or would come later. He was never a contrarian for the sake of it. He was just plain contrary. We followed him not out of solidarity, because free spirits do not do solidarity, but out of curiosity, to see where he was going. He left a Tam-sized hole in the House on his retirement.

He had been ahead of me at King's, so I had not known him there. But we had something else in common besides being MPs. He too had failed his officer selection test as a young soldier, and he should have passed with ease. For one of his ancestors had founded the Royal Scots Greys, Scotland's original cavalry regiment, in which he served as a trooper. But one day he lost a tank on manoeuvres and was returned to his unit. Tanks were smaller in those days, but it was still the sort of irregular accomplishment to be expected of a Kingsman.

I found four years in the House of Commons a more shocking experience than any number of years in the war zones – and this was before the great storm of the MPs' expenses scandal (initiated by a Kingsman, Ben Leapman). When I am with the soldiers I have a feeling of keeping the company of the best of British. That was not how I felt about the politicians, with the exception of Tam and some others. I thought: if this is the best that we can do there must be something wrong with us. Indeed, the standard of debate was such, and its adversarial system so obviously bankrupt, that I experienced the strangest of flashbacks. Instead of the Cambridge Union seeming like an imitation of the House of Commons, the House of Commons seemed like an imitation of the Cambridge Union. Maybe it was those three ex-presidents still on their green leather perches.

As a country we face challenges which were unimaginable when I was an undergraduate: of global warming, of wars for natural resources, of the unconditional campaigns of militant Islam, of child suicide bombers, of pirates and paramilitaries, of failed states, of tides of refugees flooding across disputed borders and, at home, of a democracy in disrepute and a politics on the sick list. Our political class has even lost faith in itself. These challenges cannot be dealt with by machine politicians or ticks-in-the-boxes types of public servants applying conventional strategies. Those strategies were tried in the past and, even if they worked then, will not work now. The use of force is no longer decisive: it can as easily turn victory into defeat as defeat into victory. The beginning of wisdom is to know what you don't know. As General Sir Richard Dannatt, the recently retired Chief of the General Staff, said of the Army's deployment in Afghanistan, 'What we didn't know we didn't know, and after we got there we knew a lot less'. We need horizon scanners, crow's nest lookouts of the highest calibre and original thinkers at every level of public life. We need to be smarter, craftier, stealthier, more agile and pre-emptive, more aware of what may be lying in wait for us on the blind side of the hill. We need mind-power more than firepower, special forces more than bombardiers: 'Only connect' will serve us better than 'Death or glory'.

The Independent, Tuesday April 8, 1997.

Hence the importance of a school for free spirits. Thanks to Henry VI, and countless others, we have such a school. It is our own King's College.

Weavings

Peter Cave

'All things conspire', wrote Hippocrates, attending to the interweavings of an animal's bodily parts. More expansively – radically expanded centuries later by Gottfried Wilhelm von Leibniz, expanded beyond the wildest butterfly's wings – all events across the universe, past, present and future are interconnected. We are burdened with the past, pregnant with the future: we weave and are woven; and here, passing into grey beardedness, I muse upon some King's enhancements to a life, my life, through Fortuna, humanism and philosophy, woven with EM Forster's 'Only connect'.

Once you sense a shoelace is loose, even a little – or the bra strap tempting roving fingers – you cannot ignore the sensation. With King's connections arousing the senses, connections multiply, even around me, the 'even' well justified, for I was – as student – but a fringe, yet now within the King's tapestry, albeit still on a frayed edge.

After Philosophy graduation, courtesy of godless University College London, I meandered through research years at King's, chosen maybe as loyalty to parents who knew nothing of university save wireless broadcasts of *A Festival of Nine Lessons and Carols,* never to be missed; or maybe through awareness of the College's tolerance and radicalism; or perhaps because of the godless philosopher Bernard Williams, or the year being 1972 'bravely' admitting the first women – or simply my sensing King's great distinction, a college with an edge and on the edge. Motives are often difficult to discern, often lacking sharpness of contours.

Proust famously fell into reveries from the taste of a *petite madeleine* cake dipped in linden tea. In radically lower key, the sight of polished leather boots can, metaphorically, set me going; but here, first, is some more mundane life. Polished boots follow.

Preparing a BBC programme on John Stuart Mill, *The Utility Man*, and his impact on my life as tolerant atheistic humanist – though never tolerant of noise – brought forth images of would-be teenage rebellion, on a minor, so minor a scale. *The Prisoner* – 'I am not a number; I'm a free man' – chimed with my limited awareness of Jean-Paul Sartre, existentialism and the cry for freedom. After all, *I* did not want to be trapped like my father, cycling to work, up and then down, down and then up, the same old hill, day after day, at the same job – a joiner – for little appreciation and even less pay. He was hardly free; and his bike would never get him to London, to the world. I spoke up for nonconformity. A rebel – 'twas I. Well, not quite; but I was secretary of Northampton's Young Communists – there were three of us – and I did favour the Rolling Stones over the Beatles. Furthermore, a school friend wore a purple cloak – outrageous for 1960s Northampton – and I dared to 'practise' sex with my girlfriend.

The programme's preparations returned me to King's, to interview the splendidly beaming Ian Thompson, then Dean of Chapel – though now deceased, untimely so, because, it seems, of a cruel and judgemental world. ''Tis better to be a dissatisfied Socrates than a satisfied pig.' I quoted Mill, eager to impress on the Dean that atheists, discerning of fine values, need not swirl solely in the swill of swinish contentment. To my surprise, the Dean had a fair bit to say in support of the pig. I should have responded with Jesus who, apparently lacking such preference, cast devils into a swinish swarm, causing the pigs to fly off a cliff's edge. Consider too Jesus' treatment of a fig tree: because it was without figs – was it the fig season? – he withered it. As for the Christian attack on lust and adultery … Small wonder I embraced atheistic humanism; after all, lust is a pleasure – and often the best it gets when of a certain age. My atheistic humanism, though not necessarily its heterosexual direction, melded with some King's alumni: Forster, for example, was the British Humanists' first president.

Polished high-heeled boots, made from soft leather, figure right now. Lying on the carpet in the Keynes building, I come round from a faint, the faint of a delicate flour, plain, not self-raising: that's me. Well, I do these things when I overheat or could it be when recovering from excess wine after high-minded philosophy?

The boots are in mind – for, whenever staying in King's, I am reminded of the admirable Goldie, Goldsworthy Lowes Dickinson, don of the early 20th century. Before knowing much about the College, I read of his autobiography. It was published in the 1960s, three decades beyond his death. It would not have done for the 1930s to print Goldie's fetish for boots – boots in trampling mode, worn by male lovers. 'Polished boots moved my feelings,' he wrote.

Many years later, I happened upon a blue plaque for Goldie – 'Author and Humanist' – in London's Kensington, near Knightsbridge. Fleetingly, gazelle-like, Cambridge's Knightbridge Chair of Philosophy came to mind, the Chair so often misnamed 'Knightsbridge', as if sponsored by Harvey Nicols – an apt reflection given current commercialization dangers to academia.

Goldie sets off threads of musings, musings on how so many lives are darkened by repression, prejudice and intolerance, the darkness often resulting from old books praised as 'holy'. Goldie, with melancholy, tells how his footwear love was rarely satisfied. Later, the King's genius Alan Turing committed suicide – he ate of a poisoned apple – after being forced to undertake chemical treatment to kill his 'unnatural' homosexuality. I now redden at my unhappy 'Beware the apple' quip that once caused offence, when talking to a King's friend of Turing. Quips have a place; but that quip was so without place. Courtesy, care and sensibility are needed, fragile creatures that we are, all are.

Courtesy, care and sensibility are justly needed, but that truth offers no justification for those who, after selecting scriptures, demanded, for example, the death of Salman Rushdie, member of King's, because of certain, apparently offensive, sentences. 'To avoid offence, don't open the book,' intimated Rushdie. As a minor author, I temptingly add, 'Feel free to burn my books, so long as you buy them first.' Of course, many, many religious believers do not seek to silence others; they interpret scripture humanely. That helps to show that holy books are unreliable sources of morality: they require our interpretation. Accountable to God? Not at all. 'Accountable to humanity,' say I.

Allow me to mention another repression – of what, in some quarters, is still unmentionable, yet in which virtually all take delight. Yes, masturbation has also suffered condemnation. Goldie's headmaster and father made him feel it was so wicked – one would grow up 'ashamed in the presence of women and unable to hold up one's head among men' – that he desisted for many years. Step forth Immanuel Kant. Kant – that great Enlightenment figure, though not that enlightened – insisted that suicide and masturbation are both immoralities; but masturbation is worse. Why? – Because we gain pleasure from that latter wrong.

No fan of Kant, I embrace the toleration of Forster – of his 'only connect' motif, of 'live and let live'. Forster wrote how annoyed he was with society for wasting his time by making homosexuality criminal – 'the subterfuges, the self-consciousnesses that might have been avoided'. An image of Forster collecting his Order of Merit now comes to mind. He was heard to say, 'Had the Queen been a boy, I would have kissed her' – or maybe it was that he could have fallen in love with her.

'Fruit or nut.' I am at a graduate seminar in the 1970s, led by Bernard Williams, the then Knightbridge Professor at King's, and Professor Elizabeth Anscombe of New Hall.

'Fruit *or* nut' was printed on a chocolate wrapper. Now, we can see how the chocolate could be fruit *and* nut – or solely fruit or solely nut – but how could it be fruit *or* nut? What fact could make it true that the chocolate was fruit *or* nut?

The example fascinates, casting me back to two early 20th-century King's dons, the immensely influential Frank Ramsey and his work on truth, facts and propositions – central servings for the philosophical diet – and WE Johnson, today little known, but then greatly known as a Cambridge logician. It was Johnson who suggested truth was redundant. To say that it is true that King's Chapel is on fire is to say, with a certain emphasis, that King's Chapel is on fire. It was Johnson, his elderliness wrapped in a red shawl, who fascinated a young student, Naomi Bentwich, to such an extent that she urged him to publish. She typed as he dictated, the result being three unjustly dusty volumes on logic – and a preparedness by Naomi to give herself in marriage. It was not to be. Both families objected. Naomi turned her attentions to Maynard Keynes. That also was not to be.

'He could teach me nothing'; thus spoke Wittgenstein of Johnson. 'I could teach him nothing'; thus spoke Johnson of Wittgenstein.

These words underline the significance of context. Bertrand Russell had sent the young Wittgenstein over from Trinity to King's to learn some logic. Wittgenstein survived only one session. His comment was dismissal of Johnson as trapped in old and erroneous ways. Johnson's comment expressed exasperation at the steamrollering student, unprepared to listen. Different perspectives can lead to conflict – though not necessarily between those who possess the perspectives. Johnson and Wittgenstein became close friends, with Wittgenstein admiring Johnson's piano playing, radically more so than his logic.

Perspectives can indeed lead to conflict: witness the witnesses at a 1940s Moral Sciences Club meeting in King's Gibbs Building. Wittgenstein typically dominated proceedings, yet on this occasion the speaker was a fellow Austrian, Karl Popper, disgruntled from London, ready to hold his ground. Witnesses disagreed and raged. Did Wittgenstein raise the poker to threaten Popper or to make a point or just to poke the coals? The poker, I believe, remains in Gibbs.

'When the facts change, I change my mind. What do you do, sir?' asked Maynard Keynes, often accused of mind changes. Perspectives change: our minds may change as a result. This, though, does not cast us into relativism. As Bernard Williams would say, whatever the different accounts of the First World War, one thing that ought not to be claimed is that Belgium invaded Germany. There are facts of the matter.

There are indeed facts of the matter, but what place for facts in religions? The religious usually stick with belief in God or gods whatever the worldly disasters. They may speak of leaps of faith, though rarely of hops, skips or jumps – faith that kangaroos them beyond reason and evidence. Richard Braithwaite – another of the King's Knightbridge brigade – who hosted the poker incident, argued that religious belief, given its insensitivity to contrary evidence, was no testable belief at all, but rather commitment to a way of life, be it to promote brotherly love or kill infidels.

'But God really is an existent being,' insists the believer. 'Ah,' I reply, 'you are just stressing your commitment to brotherly love.' 'No, no, God really, really exists,' persists the believer. 'Yes, you really, really are committed to brotherly love.' And so the 'really's multiply.

Is the chocolate really fruit or nut – or not? Prejudging how sharply concepts apply to the world can lead to error, bafflement or worse. Consider: Bandit shoots Sheriff. Sheriff is rushed back to his Little Rock home and dies from the bullet wound a few days later. Bandit, though, escaped to his mountain hideaway, but was caught, lynched by a mob, dead before the Sheriff's death. When and where did Bandit kill Sheriff? When and where he shot him? But Sheriff was still alive then: a man cannot have been killed while still living. Well, did Bandit kill Sheriff when Sheriff died in Little Rock? But Bandit was himself dead by then and never visited Little Rock. Surely, a man, when dead, cannot kill someone. And yet …

And yet … is someone deceased later becoming a murderer any more curious than a woman in Cambridge unwittingly becoming a grandmother because of a birth to her

Wittgenstein.

daughter, thousands of miles away in Shanghai? Here manifest the interconnections between events that so impressed Leibniz, interconnections that paradoxically may involve no consciousness and no physical changes in the individual changed. Here threaten dangers of imposing precision – of thinking that a killing must occur at a precise time – of thinking exact measures can be given of what cannot be so measured.

Maynard Keynes, in his Fellowship dissertation, drew attention to mythical exactitude when discussing probability, using examples as diverse as the reinsurance rates for the *Waratah*, a vessel that sank in South African waters, and the probable loss to a lady beauty contestant who missed the final viewing. Frank Ramsey, similarly spirited, helped guide Wittgenstein away from 'scholasticism', of treating the vague as if precise. Wittgenstein listened. Although Ramsey lived for only 26 years, he found time for music, mountaineering and psychoanalysis – as well as his pioneering work in mathematics, economics and philosophy.

At home in Soho – this 1720s terrace was constructed when, in another world, the Gibbs Building was under way – the noise of city life, the loss of stars and sky, sit incongruously with the tranquil Cam pictured, the skies that stretch the eyes, the Chapel's spires, the muse of dons crossing the court, 'And nineteenthly …' 'And yet …'

And yet, round the corner is Kettners where Maynard Keynes and other Apostles, of that well-known secret society, would meet; a few minutes' walk north is Gordon Square, once home of Keynes and the Bloomsbury Group; ten minutes south is English National Opera, much loved by Williams, where King's Ed Gardner currently conducts and where Britten's *Billy Budd* with Forster's libretto is performed. Some minutes to the southwest locates where I am now, the Athenaeum, escaping Soho's noise.

Goldie and Keynes were of this 'owlish' club; and the eccentric Naomi Bentwich hovers again in mind, for her granddaughter, inheritor of Naomi's intriguing correspondence which requires working and weaving, first met me here, having encountered my brief encyclopaedic entries on Johnson and Keynes.

The King's tapestry highlights individuality, with muddles of reason, passion and value. Detached values of equality, fairness, impartiality compete with attached ones of loyalty, love and partiality. Witness the challenge of Forster's preference for loyalty to a friend over loyalty to country. Witness Williams' example: able to save only one person from drowning – your lover on the left or a younger unknown person on the right – does morality demand impartial judgement whether to head leftwards or rightwards? To reflect thus would be 'one thought too many'.

A colour supplement flutters, showing Williams on King's Chapel's roof, arms outstretched, the byline intent on shock: atheist commands great religious institution. Williams was, in fact, much moved by humanity, by music religious and otherwise, and by the muddles in – and beyond – morality. As once said, we think no less of painters because they have the odd evening off and get drunk; so, should we think any less of moral individuals having time off from morality?

Forster promoted the poetry – the eroticism and human conflicts – of CP Cavafy, describing him deliciously as 'a Greek gentleman in a straw hat, standing absolutely

motionless at a slight angle to the universe.' Keynes stressed the dangers of attributing an unreal rationality to human nature, his later economics explicitly heeding the undercurrents, our 'animal spirits'. King's, for me, celebrates the slants and angles, the marvellous muddles of humanity – of humanity at its best. Ramsey wrote,

'I don't feel the least humble before the vastness of the heavens. The stars may be large, but they cannot think or love; and these are qualities which impress me far more than size does. I take no credit for weighing nearly seventeen stone ... Humanity, which fills the foreground of my picture, I find interesting and on the whole admirable.'

King's, for me, displays patterns of toleration that stretch far, far back to Anthony Collins, at King's in the late 17th century, who promoted reason and fought religious persecution. And King's, for me, brings kaleidoscopic colours to the weave, colours exalted in King's music, influence, debate – and humour. Rupert Brooke's splendid *Heaven* plays the humanist humour, telling of how,

> *Fish say, they have their Stream and Pond;*
> *But is there anything Beyond?*

concluding,

> *And in that Heaven of all their wish,*
> *There shall be no more land, say fish.*

Hear now King's Choir singing *Spem in Alium*, the voices lifting us to heavens of hope, the breadth of beauty. As a humanist, I have no problem with being moved by religious music, by religious words. Yet think too of the sufferings here on Earth that challenge our humanity. What 'facts of the matter' justify our lives so flourishing, while others scrape to sustain any life at all?

How to draw the threads together, to close? Let us return to Forster's 'Only connect' – and to Goldie. Forster wrote of Goldie that he was neither a great philosopher nor writer nor successful reformer, yet his 'beloved, affectionate, unselfish, intelligent, witty, charming' qualities were fused into him, making him 'a rare being, leaving people who met him more hopeful about other men because he had lived'.

What more would you want?

The world that Turing built

Suranga Chandratillake

In 1936 Alan Turing invented the computer. Writing an esoteric paper about proving propositions within a well-defined logical system, Turing needed a model to articulate his argument. He decided on an imaginary machine that was a little like a typewriter, only equipped with the ability to read as well as print symbols and a step-by-step method of processing that would allow it to solve problems when appropriately configured. This blueprint – the Turing Machine – forms the basis of all modern computers.

In 1950, Turing wrote a very different paper. Starting with the question 'Do machines think?' he proposed a test that he called the Imitation Game. Now more widely known as the Turing Test, it pits a computer against a human judge in freeform conversation conducted blindly via exchanged notes. If the human cannot tell the difference between the machine and another human, Turing argued that it would be unreasonable not to consider the machine intelligent, conversation being the test by which we generally judge the intelligence of others. Turing predicted, with customarily casual confidence, that digital computers would pass the Test within 50 years. Nearly 60 years later this is still not the case; Turing's Machines are everywhere, but not one has passed his Test.

I read Computer Science at King's and graduated in 2000, the year by which Turing predicted his Test would be passed. It was also the year Turing was recognized as one of *Time* magazine's 100 most important people of the century and the year that the dotcom boom and related excitement over the commercial potential of the computer pushed stock markets around the world to gravity-defying peaks. As for any Kingsman or -woman pursuing the Computer Science Tripos, this all reinforced the sense that I was following in impossibly large footsteps. The College's computer room, the Turing Room, a damp, rather smelly basement affair in the Gibbs Building, had outside its entrance a large, somewhat stern portrait, with more portraits inside, and the University Computer Laboratory's own Turing Room was famous because it was home to an old coffeepot that was the target

The old coffeepot used in the world's first webcam.

of the world's first webcam. Even messing about in boats didn't provide an escape – the College IV that I coxed one term was rather wittily called the Turing Machine.

If King's 'Compscis' can't escape Turing, none of us can escape the world left in the wake of his work. In a century packed with technological advancement, the computer stands tall, a colossus of invention due to the remarkable ubiquity of its uses. In the modern world, computers do a lot of things. Behind the scenes, they control devices as simple as alarm clocks, as commonplace as telephones, as complex as jumbo jets and as critical as pacemakers. They are used to model the stock market, the weather and the spread of disease both through continents and within a single organism. IBM's Deep Blue beat world champion Garry Kasparov at chess in 1997 and, in 2009, Google's computers provided results for 293 million individual searches every single day. Turing was not blind to the commercial utility of his inventions. Writing to his mother in 1936 he described his work on cipher algorithms, suggesting that he might be able to 'sell them to HM Government for a quite substantial sum', but even he would have been staggered by the reality we live with today; in 2009 the US government alone spent $180 billion on information technology.

Opposite: On the staircase leading to the Turing Room, Turing's portrait glows.

Despite this versatility, no computer has passed the Turing Test in the 60 years since it was described in Turing's 1950 paper, *Computer Machinery and Intelligence*. Unique in its conversational style, the paper gave birth to the entire field of Artificial Intelligence and remains one of the most cited papers on the philosophy of intelligence, attracting devotees and detractors in equal measure.

Turing begins by dismissing the question 'Can machines think?' as so vague as to be useless, proposing to replace it with a test that is better defined yet closely related to the essence of what the original question seeks to capture. He then turns to the Imitation Game, describing how it can be modified to create this Test. The Imitation Game is played by three people – a man (A), a woman (B) and an interrogator (C). A and B are in a room separated from C and communicate with C only via some form of blind format (such as written messages passed under the door). C must consider A and B's responses in order to determine which is the man and which the woman. A's objective is to cause C to make the wrong identification and B's objective is to help C identify correctly. Turing then asks: 'What will happen when a machine takes the part of A in this game?' Will the interrogator make as many wrong decisions when the game is played like this as he does when the game is played between a man and a woman? These questions replace the original, 'Can machines think?'

Having described the Test in fewer than 500 words, Turing sets about creating an entire field of study with which to pass it. He outlines nine 'Contrary Views' that he expects the paper to face on publication. The rigour of his defence is such that 60 years later no real criticisms have come to light that do not fall into one of these nine buckets. While the paper may be famous for the Test, it is these arguments that make it such a fantastic read. As well as working through essentially technical arguments ('Arguments from Various Disabilities'), Turing finds space to exert his strong atheism in pointedly dismissing 'The Theological Option' and lobs more than a little sarcasm at 'The "Heads in the Sand" Objection'. Either an indication of a very contemporary obsession or yet another ironic aside, there is even an 'Argument from Extrasensory Perception' that suggests conducting the Test in a 'telepathy-proof room' to defend its validity against this particular weakness. Throughout the paper and particularly in these objections, one feels the very presence of Turing's mind – one moment the clipped and precise voice of a mathematician; the next, disarmingly human with his chatty commentary on the social sciences and the position of women in the Muslim faith.

Having defined the Test and refuted likely objections, Turing turns to helping would-be Test-takers, providing multiple constructive strategies on how one could go about building a machine to pass the Test. Finally he analyses the physical limitations of current computers, suggesting that technological progress will lead to computers in 50 years time with 10^9 bits of memory storage. 10^9 bits is approximately 120 megabytes (MB) and, to provide context, a £750 laptop today typically has over 2,000 megabytes, around 15 times Turing's imagined computer of the future. Turing then declares his belief that a computer with 10^9 bits of storage would 'play the imitation game so well that an average interrogator will not have more than a 70 per cent chance of making the right identification after five minutes of questioning.'

Turing's belief that all that is required to pass the Test is a powerful computer is an important point that ties the 1950 paper to his earlier work on the science of computability. What a computer can do is limited in two ways. As anyone who has been forced to upgrade their laptop knows, the first way a computer is limited is by its actual physical processing power. Making faster, more powerful computers is a never-ending marathon conducted in research labs the world over.

More fundamentally, however, every computer is mathematically limited by the laws of computability that Turing first addressed in his original 1936 paper. There is a certain class of problems – the non-computable – that cannot be addressed by any computer that is modelled on the Turing Machine. These problems are so complex that the universe literally does not contain enough atoms with which to build the computers required to solve them – and even if it did, these colossal, mythical machines would require hundreds of thousands of years of processing time.

But in the 1950 paper Turing states his belief that passing the Turing Test is computable and in his view, all that was required for a computer to pass his Test was a faster, more capable computer than those available in 1950. In fact, Turing's predictions were wrong. Modern microchip engineering has far outstripped his expectations and computers in 2000 were an order of magnitude more powerful at solving computable problems than he expected.

So, given the incredible success of computing in the 20th century, what went wrong? There are many views on why passing the Turing Test has been so elusive. Some in the mainstream artificial intelligence research community consider the Test irrelevant, suggesting its goal of human conversation is of questionable utility. But believers exist. The Loebner Prize Foundation awards $3,000 annually to the computer that comes closest to passing the Test, and promises a further $125,000 of prizes for the first machines to pass the original Test or a modern variant.

While it continues to struggle with artificial intelligence as defined by the Test, the modern computer has supported the growth in popularity of at least one other form of non-human, startlingly formidable intelligence. The Internet, a vast network of machines, connects not just computers, but the humans that use them, allowing thousands of people to cooperate and compete on areas of shared interest, giving rise to what is generally described as Collective Intelligence.

Collective Intelligence is not a new phenomenon. In nature, species like *Ecitron burchelli* (the South American army ant) behave collectively with a level of intelligence that does not exist in any given individual creature, allowing a colony, for example, to navigate rainforests precisely by combining visual signals seen by multiple animals into a precise, high-definition image that facilitates collective decision-making. James Surowiecki opens his popular book *The Wisdom of Crowds* with an early example of Collective Intelligence in an anecdote dating back to 1906, when the British mathematician Francis Galton was intrigued by a contest he saw at a county fair. Visitors were invited to guess the weight of a prize ox and the person with the closest guess would win the animal. Galton realized that the average weight of the combined guesses was closer to the animal's actual weight than any individual guess. The collective guess was closer, more intelligent, than the individual.

At first glance the Web itself might be seen as an example of Collective Intelligence – a vast tapestry of sites and pages, each capturing paragraph upon paragraph of human intelligence. In fact, it is not. There's nothing collective about a given Web page, as it is created by an individual and is 'read-only': anyone can look at the page but there is no provision to modify it. Collective Intelligence, in contrast, appears when multiple individuals are able to contribute – sometimes competing, sometimes collaborating – eventually giving rise to an emergent, collective answer.

A better example is Wikipedia, the user-generated encyclopedia. Unlike the read-only Internet, Wikipedia is read/write. Users can read the articles but also actively participate in their creation by modifying their contents, imparting a piece of their own individual intelligence. It turns out that with the creation and curating of encyclopedias, many cooks can be added without spoiling the broth. A 2005 study in *Nature* found that Wikipedia's scientific articles had a similar level of accuracy to those in *Encyclopedia Britannica* and contained a similar frequency of serious errors. But just being as good is not interesting. What is astonishing about Wikipedia and the Collective Intelligence that created it is the speed at which it was built – Wikipedia did not exist ten years ago and today has over three million articles in English alone. The *Encyclopedia Britannica* in comparison was started in the 18th century and today has 120,000 entries, a mere 4 per cent of the size of its younger collective cousin.

But while the creation and maintenance of Wikipedia is an act of Collective Intelligence, the end result is just a mass of information. Wikipedia on its own cannot pass the Turing Test. As Andrew Hodges, Turing's biographer extraordinaire, pointed out when discussing an earlier assault on the Test, 'This sort of mindless disgorging of information is the antithesis of what Alan Turing had in mind when illustrating his ideas with wit and humour.' Indeed, in the 1950 paper on intelligence Turing worries less about naming capital cities of the world, say, and more about whether a computer would be able to compose a sonnet on the subject of the Forth Bridge or enjoy strawberries and cream.

Wikipedia may be stumped by those questions, but another, even more familiar Web service that uses Collective Intelligence may be able to help. As the volume of information on the Web expanded during the 1980s and 1990s, the need for services to navigate it grew. For many years, Internet search engines merely 'crawled' Web pages, creating large 'indexes' that could be looked up against every time a user performed a search. The difficulty with search turned out to be relevance. There are so many results or 'hits' to every keyword, that simply being able to retrieve the list of potentially relevant Web pages for a given search is rarely useful. In 1997 two young Stanford University students launched a new search engine that changed everything. It was called Google and it was built on Collective Intelligence.

The Google method also started with an index of web pages but then took a sharp diversion. Using a technology called PageRank, Google analysed the links that exist between those pages. Links are created by the individual writers of a given page, connecting their page to related information on other pages. The simple Collective Intelligence observation at the heart of Google's PageRank is that, on balance, a page that is linked to more than others is probably a better one. The assumption is that while some (human) writers will link to the wrong pages, overall, more of them will link to the better pages. So when a user performs a search on Google, Google not only retrieves the matching hits from its index, but orders them by PageRank. The pages voted as being better appear first, above those that had fewer 'votes' or links. PageRank then adds an elegant recursive twist by conferring greater value to the links that are made by sites that themselves enjoy a high PageRank – good pages are influential pages. The result, as anyone who uses Google knows, is spectacular. Google's engine has an uncanny ability to second-guess which page you wanted to find, often before you knew the page in question even existed.

Returning to the Turing Test, the question is: can the mass of data on the Internet attached to a Collective Intelligence engine like Google yield good answers to even the most human questions? As a test, I entered a search for 'are strawberries and cream enjoyed' and scanned the first hit. Without clicking through to the underlying page, I learnt that this 'delicious snack is enjoyed all over Britain' but also that there is 'one place which is considered the best place to enjoy strawberries and cream and that is during … Wimbledon'. It seems Collective Intelligence has given us enough with which to answer the question and, especially if one uses the Wimbledon qualification, sound rather human in the process.

This example is not as silly as it sounds. Robert Ennals, another Kingsman, works on a related problem at Intel Research in Berkeley with his project, DisputeFinder. DisputeFinder uses Collective Intelligence to highlight bias on the Web. The tool operates in the background while a user browses the Web. When the user happens on a page that contains a claim that the collective DisputeFinder community considers unverified or debatable, the paragraph in question lights up. With a click, the user can then access a multitude of arguments both for and against the claim, aggregated from across the Internet.

DisputeFinder works well. People are passionate about certain topics and, as a result, the tool provides a wealth of information from all sides of an argument on subjects as diverse as the effectiveness of Keynesian economics and the appropriate point during pregnancy at which to outlaw abortion. The individual is suddenly more intelligent, equipped at the point of reading with Collective Intelligence. DisputeFinder is also interesting because it self-selects precisely the fuzzy, ill-defined areas of human thought and conversation that have proven so challenging for computers that have tried to pass the Test.

One can imagine combining DisputeFinder's approach with a form of popularity ranking similar to Google's PageRank to create a tool that mines the best or most collectively agreed-upon answer to a diverse range of human conversation topics. Such an algorithm may be able to answer the Turing Test successfully. The Test may yet be conquerable after all.

What would Turing make of all this? One suspects that Turing's original expectations for machine intelligence are those that are still followed in traditional Artificial Intelligence research – a single, large machine with the necessary building blocks programmed into it with large databanks of information. The Collective Intelligence approach is rather different. The Web and Google-like search engine technology is not an attempt at artificial intelligence; it is, if anything, an admission of the lack of artificial intelligence and instead a tool by which to supplement human intelligence. The guiding principle is not to converse with one's intelligent computer, but to use one's computer as a dumb window onto a highly accessible collection of knowledge of human intelligence. A Collective Intelligence-powered suitor to the Test would, ironically, be reflecting our own views back at us, mimicking the way we would collectively respond, rather than necessarily creating its own response. But then, of course, Turing's own name for the test was the Imitation Game, so perhaps this is not so far from the intended result.

A King's parade of lawyers

Anthony Clarke

After coming down from King's in 1964 I was sitting in the Middle Temple Library wondering what to do. Knowing no one, I wrote to Ken Polack, who had taught me at King's and he said, why not go and see Mr NA Phillips, another Kingsman? I did and he procured a pupillage for me in the informal ways of those days and since then I have been following a respectful two paces behind. I too practised at the Admiralty and Commercial Bars, sometimes against Phillips QC (with varying success). Nick Phillips became a distinguished silk and has had a stellar career on the Bench, culminating in his being successively Master of the Rolls, Lord Chief Justice and now, since October 2009, the first President of the Supreme Court. Much later I was privileged to be Master of the Rolls and am now the 11th member of the Supreme Court. I wonder what Ken would have made of two of his students being founder members of the Supreme Court.

I had matriculated (whatever that means) in 1961 and spent one of the most enjoyable and stimulating periods of my life at King's from 1961 to 1964. I am not quite sure why but I wanted to read Law and naively supposed that I would be able to read the subject for three years. Much to my astonishment I discovered that that was not permitted. When I enquired why that was so I was told that the study of Law was not an academic pursuit, or at any rate not a *sufficiently* academic pursuit. Notwithstanding that stark approach, I discovered that it was possible to study Law for one year or, at a pinch, two years. This seemed to me to be somewhat inconsistent with the underlying policy, since one might have thought that, if the study of the law was not academic or sufficiently academic, the College would not permit it at all.

In the event I decided (and was permitted) to study Law for two years. The question then arose what to study for the first year. The problem was that there were very few subjects in which Part 1 of the Tripos was a one-year course. In the event I chose Economics. King's did not disapprove of economics, whether studied for one, two or three years. It was immediately apparent to me (and I think others) that there was nothing academic about Part 1 Economics. If the College had applied the same academic test to Economics as it did to Law, it would certainly have prohibited the study of Part 1 Economics. I soon concluded that the reason that a different test was applied to Economics from that applied to Law was not based on principle but expediency.

Until the then comparatively recent appointment of Ken, King's had never had a Law don – although rumour had it there had once been such a person at King's whose books were burned by the public hangman. However that may be, by contrast with Law, King's had a plethora of Economics dons. This was because of the influence of that great doyen of economists, and of course of the College, John Maynard Keynes. Because of his influence and the importance of Economics there were plenty of Economics dons with time on their hands.

Was this policy then simply introduced to give Economics dons something to do? Was it good for lawyers and the law? In fact, the answer to the first of those questions is no. According to Patrick Wilkinson, in the four decades before the First World War about 15 per cent of Kingsmen qualified as barristers or solicitors, mostly barristers, and, together with teaching, medicine and the church, law was one of the four most popular careers. However, few of them had read Law. Taking one year at random, 1890, of the five Kingsmen called to the Bar, none had read Law. Throughout the 20th century the fixed policy at King's was that intending lawyers should read at least one Part of another Tripos first before reading Law Part II. Thus the policy pre-dated Keynes, let alone me. Wilkinson suggests that students seemed to gain, and certainly to lose nothing, professionally by omitting Law Tripos Part I. All they had to do instead was to take the crash course in the Long Vacation before embarking on Law II.

Wilkinson gives as examples (among others) Lord Parker of Waddington (1876), Sir Sydney Rowlatt (1880), Sir Thomas Inskip (1894), who became Lord Caldecote and who was both Attorney General and later Lord Chief Justice in spite of his third-class degree in Classics, and two 'scholars of law of international repute', namely Edward Jenks (1883) and Harold Gutteridge (1895).

In more recent times, but before the Keynes era at the College, there are a number of examples of distinguished King's lawyers. I mention only two. The first is Henry Brandon (1938), who became Lord Brandon of Oakbrook. When I was a junior at the maritime Bar in the 1970s he was the Admiralty Judge. He was a formidable figure who could produce fear and trembling in counsel and witnesses alike but his intellectual rigour and eye for the underlying merits endeared him to us and he made a significant contribution to commercial and maritime law. So did Roger Parker (1946) who was the grandson of Lord Parker and became Lord Justice Parker.

It seems clear that none of the above was prejudiced by the policy of forbidding Kingsmen to read Part I Law. It is also plain that, contrary to what I had thought until now, the policy was not driven by the glut of Economics dons who needed something to do. Wilkinson describes the policy thus in respect of the period 1945 to 1972:

> *Our lawyers seemed to lose nothing professionally, and to gain much educationally, by taking another subject and then diverting after Part I to Law II, possibly followed by the LLB. In addition, Keynes was passionately opposed to having a Law don in the College, fearing pedantic interpretation of our statutes; and the first and only one we have had was a King's graduate elected to a Fellowship in 1960, Kenneth Polack, who later also came to occupy Keynes' position as First Bursar.*

Wilkinson too was Senior Tutor; so he probably describes the position correctly. As to whether the policy was sound, I entirely see the force of the principle that it is desirable

The Bob Alexander Fellowship brochure.

to avoid education – whether in Law or otherwise – being too narrow, and I sometimes think that if I had my time again I would like to have read, say, Philosophy. However, that would be to have foregone the great pleasure and privilege of being taught by Ken Polack.

Ken was a brilliant and inspiring teacher. He died, tragically young, in 1995. His obituary contains detailed appreciations by many of his students who went on to achieve much in the law: notably Bob Alexander – Lord Alexander of Weedon; Nicholas Phillips; and Nick Purnell QC, a leading criminal silk who has had a stellar career. Nicholas Phillips said of Ken that he was truly an inspiration with an energy and enthusiasm for life and for the law that was immediately infectious. I entirely agree and, as they say in the Court of Appeal, there is nothing I can usefully add, save that his intellectual rigour has been something I have tried to bear in mind whenever, as all too often, I find myself engaged in sloppy thinking.

I was particularly struck by this tribute from Deborah Weich (1985):

'He was a wonderful inspiration for me, and I will always be grateful for the consistent, loyal support and encouragement he provided. Most of all he was a role model who taught by example the value and importance of maintaining your integrity in the practice of law and in life.'

King's may not have regarded 1961 as a great vintage for those destined to study Law at the feet of Ken Polack. We were few but from varied backgrounds. So far as I know, none of us had been at Eton. The most exotic was Gabriel Galindo, who is a Panamanian whose uncle was Dr Arias who was married to Margot Fonteyn. Both then and now Gabriel thinks and speaks English at a phenomenal rate and was (and is) a great entertainment for us all. He had many brilliant ideas to keep Ken on his toes. Michael Mathews was much cleverer than the rest of us. We had a competition to see if it was possible to go to the Squire Law Library without his being there. It was not. We were not surprised when he became a partner of Coward Chance and then Clifford Chance. He also became President of the Law Society. Peter Hall was a choral scholar – a larger-than-life tenor. I am sure that he would admit that his interests lay more in music than the law – and why not? Finally, Colin Garrett later founded a firm of solicitors and has now sensibly retired to make violins. Enough of reminiscence – back to Ken Polack.

Ken's inspiration has to my mind had a considerable effect on the development of the law by the effect it has had on his students who became lawyers. King's produced a brochure when setting up a Law fellowship in memory of Bob Alexander, who also died tragically young, which includes some photographs taken of some of those (including me) who read Law at King's under Ken's tutelage. They were taken when we matriculated; so a very long time ago; and they make us look very young, as indeed we were.

All of those photographed have in different ways made something of a contribution to the law and are thus evidence of the important part King's played in that. They are to my mind a powerful testament to the value of teaching Law at King's. Thus, Nicholas Phillips has and is still making a significant contribution to all branches of the law, most recently that of human rights; Patrick Elias (now Lord Justice Elias) has been the doyen of employment law in recent years; and Andrew Collins (Mr Justice Collins) has led the Administrative Court for a considerable period during which judicial review of government decisions has gone from strength to strength. Finally, Leo (Eleanor) Sharpston QC has been Ken's successor as a Fellow and teacher of Law at King's and she is of course now an Advocate-General at the Court of Justice in Luxembourg, where she is making an outstanding contribution to European Community law. It was Leo who described those photographed as the 'King's Parade'. Through her and others like her (although there will be no one quite like her) I trust that King's will continue to contribute to the law, so that it develops with clarity and vision.

Floreat King's, its lawyers and the law.

Parr's King's I

Martin Parr

New every Christmas

Stephen Cleobury

A Festival of Nine Lessons and Carols, first celebrated in King's on Christmas Eve 1918, and broadcast since 1928 (except in 1930), undoubtedly laid the foundations of the fame and reputation which the College Choir now enjoys. The beautiful and moving prose of Dean Eric Milner-White's Bidding Prayer which follows the opening hymn 'Once in Royal David's City', the first verse sung by a solo treble, introduces a sequence of scriptural readings which, in Milner-White's words, tell the Christmas story 'from the first days of our disobedience unto the glorious Redemption brought us by this Holy Child'. Each of these readings in turn shapes the choice of carols which the Organist and Director of Music makes each year. Just as the repertoire at the regular Chapel services has, over the past 90 years, been developed and expanded by successive Organists, so the range of carols has increased. This has led to the inclusion of more early music and contemporary music as well as the introduction of music from other national traditions and religious denominations.

When I came to King's in 1982 I was keen to increase the already significant commitment to contemporary music. It struck me that I could build on the work of my predecessors if I were to present a new carol annually on Christmas Eve. This would be a very good way of bringing new music to a large audience and of making a statement about the importance of nourishing a great tradition with new growth. During my time as an undergraduate at St John's, I had witnessed a remarkable exchange during a weekend seminar on modern music organized by the BBC. Pitted against one another were the composers Stockhausen, who was for a radical new start, and Dallapiccola, whose music, while highly original, was, he insisted, rooted in tradition. My sympathies were with the latter, and his image of the great corpus of music we have inherited as being a great tree trunk, with new pieces representing the new shoots, was a powerful influence on me in this connection. Not only should we have new carols for the Festival, but they should come from some of our leading composers, composers who work right across the spectrum, in chamber music, symphonic genres, and opera, for example, not just those

working in church music. As it has turned out, there has been no shirking of music in new and challenging idioms.

In the early years, the inclusion of new and unfamiliar music disturbed some, but as the practice of commissioning itself became a tradition, I began to find that people asked me in advance 'Who is writing the carol this year?' There is much appreciation and support for the new carols, although a recent caller to the BBC's *Feedback* programme (following the Birtwistle commission) expressed the view that 'whoever was responsible for the choice of the new carol should be locked up in a dark room and never let out'. That a number of the commissioned carols have become firm favourites in the world beyond King's has been very gratifying.

I have been immensely fortunate in the ready and enthusiastic response I have had from each of the composers I have approached, and it was a richly rewarding experience to come back to each piece during preparation for the recording of those written up to 2005 which the Choir made for EMI. For obvious reasons it was not possible to hold all the carols in repertoire at the same time, so they were recorded over a period of two or three years (the Choir learning them afresh because its personnel changes so quickly). A handful of the commissioned pieces was prepared in advance of each EMI recording project, so that a carol session could be tacked on to whatever else was being recorded.

I cannot claim to have had a particularly coherent plan in terms of whom to commission, having been content to allow professional contacts and, indeed, chance meetings and conversations, to lead me to invite a great variety of composers. Nevertheless it has been particularly appropriate to have had music from three King's alumni, Thomas Adès, Robin Holloway and Judith Weir, as well as from Alexander Goehr, then Professor of Music at Cambridge. Dominic Muldowney I met at the time his daughter came to King's as an undergraduate. In many cases the composer has been able to be involved in the rehearsal process and to attend the première. This has provided a fascinating insight into the way that different composers work and how they react to hearing the new piece for the first time. Often the commissioned composer has come to a rehearsal some ten days or so before Christmas Eve. By this stage I will have ensured that the Choir can give an accurate rendition of the notes of the piece, but the degree to which it been able to 'get inside' the music varies. Some composers have been anxious to move this process forward and have been a great help in doing so through quite active intervention: others have had less to say, and assumed that continuing rehearsal, and, indeed, subconscious reflection, will give that added familiarity which is needed for a convincing performance on 24 December. Some talk to the Choir about the meaning and mood of the text and the way in which the music grows out of it; others focus their comments very directly on what might be called the nuts and bolts – tempo (either I or the composer might have got this wrong), articulation, tone quality and any number of technical matters. In every case, however, the composer has found a way of encouraging and affirming what we have been doing, and so this pre-performance visit has played a vital role in helping to secure the quality of the première which we try so hard to achieve. It has also been interesting and moving to observe the reaction of each composer as the sounds of the new composition, previously in the head, are actualized for the first time. The youthfulness of the singers is seen to advantage in this context: I see it as an important part of the musical training and education that is offered to the Choir that it be exposed to new music of all sorts. One can be confident that, even if some of the choral scholars have begun to take on 'views' about contemporary music, the choristers will, like all children, be open to any new challenge, and approach it with no preconceptions. It is always, for them, an enjoyable experience to tackle a new piece, particularly when, as was the case with Harrison Birtwistle's, they were required to stamp and shout.

Discussions between me and the composer before and during the compositional process have, naturally, varied. Practical matters, such as the size and vocal range of the Choir and the way in which the Chapel acoustic changes on Christmas Eve with the capacity congregation, have to be considered, but of paramount importance is the choice of text. Some composers have turned to the rich symbolism offered by anonymous medieval poetry or the metaphysical literature of the 17th century – Bennett, Bingham, Burrell, Casken, Goehr, Holloway, Maw, Rutter and Sculthorpe; some have chosen later poetry, John Woolrich drawing verses from Christopher Smart's poem 'The Nativity of Our Lord and Saviour Jesus Christ', Jonathan Dove setting Dorothy L Sayers and Gabriel Jackson turning to GK Chesterton. Some have chosen words which reflect their own backgrounds, Peter Maxwell Davies, James MacMillan and Judith Weir, for example, selecting Scottish texts, and Arvo Pärt drawing on the Orthodox liturgy. Others have looked to contemporary poets, usually one with whom they had already collaborated, to create a fresh text, Jonathan Harvey thus turning to Bishop John Taylor, with whom he had worked on a number of pieces for Winchester Cathedral, Stephen Paulus to Kevin Crossley-Holland, and Harrison Birtwistle to his librettist, the poet Stephen Place. Giles Swayne interspersed well-known Latin words into a text of his own devising. Lennox Berkeley, the first composer to be commissioned, set a poem by Betty Askwith. The prize for the most courageous choice of text should perhaps go to John Tavener, who set 'Away in a manger'. How do you do that when the 'traditional' version is so well known? Tavener succeeded brilliantly in setting the text in the standard strophic manner, but in interpreting it in a manner by turns dramatic and serene.

The texts have in most cases dictated the musical shapes and forms; thus many of the carols are in a simple strophic form, some of these having, like their medieval predecessors, a clear refrain. Other pieces display a ternary structure and there are also some through-composed pieces. Most have been written for unaccompanied voices. Where the organ has been used, its effect has been strikingly calculated, particularly in Judith Weir's 'Illuminare, Jerusalem', where it makes three brief, but telling, appearances. In Giles Swayne's carol, the Choir was partnered by Philippa Davies, who gave a stunning account of the virtuoso flute part.

The annual radio broadcast of *A Festival of Nine Lessons and Carols* retains its primacy, but the importance of television has also been recognized, and for the last 20 years *Carols from King's* has been shown on BBC 2. This is a different, pre-recorded service, and the opportunity has been taken to vary the choice of readings and to include literature and poetry alongside biblical passages, as well as introducing some new music. The millennium was celebrated with a carol written for *Carols from King's*: 'The Shepherd's Carol' was written by Robert Chilcott, who was a chorister at King's under David Willcocks and a choral scholar under Philip Ledger, providing a happy link with my two predecessors.

In 1946 Benjamin Britten took part in the BBC Home Service series *Talks for Sixth Forms*. He has wise advice for those listening to new music:

> *Don't give up after the first hearing of a new piece. Very little music can be appreciated at once. And remember, music is not all easy entertainment. Don't just day-dream when listening to it, but listen seriously to the music that you feel one day you may like. I am afraid many people like music only for the ideas it gives them. They imagine wonderful scenes, or themselves involved in some romantic situation. They may enjoy this, but it is not the music they enjoy but the associations stirred up by this music. The fullest benefit and enjoyment to be got from listening to music is a much deeper thing – the appreciation and love of the tunes for themselves, the excitements of the rhythms for themselves, the fascination of the harmony and the overwhelming satisfaction which a well-constructed piece of music gives you. These are the things which the good composer offers you. The good listener is ready to receive them.*

Good advice for anyone approaching any new piece of music, and as the BBC repeats the Christmas Eve broadcast on Christmas Day and makes it available on 'Listen Again', anyone can take Britten's advice not to 'give up on first hearing'.

Mural in R2A

Lily Cole

Given the prospect of writing about any object of art within Cambridge, I chose to investigate a mural painted on the wall of a student's room in Webb's Court, King's. I was intrigued by its unusual surrealist content and wanted to know more about the person, the reasoning and ideas behind the mural. The mural was an enigma, a College 'treasure' with very little literature on why it existed or why it had at some point been given protected status. The work being relatively recent meant the artist was still alive and so it seemed a great opportunity to get her thoughts on the piece. Principally, I was attracted by the anarchic gesture behind the mural; that a young student – indeed in this case not even a student of Cambridge – could paint directly on the walls of the College and against all odds the work would survive 50 years. I loved the reflection that conveyed of the artist, but also of the College's liberal principles and the dialogues they allowed to happen between student and official body. Essentially I loved the possibility that the rules could be broken.

I had originally intended to write about the 1970s feminist paintings in the hallway in Keynes, the 'women's corridor', now used for storage, but discovered they had been boarded up several years ago with no archival photos made of them. The tradition of mural painting at King's went as far back as 1911 when the sitting room of John Maynard Keynes' suite, P3, became Duncan Grant's 'first experiment at domestic design', featuring a mural of grapes and nude dancers. Unhappy with the designs, Grant covered them over with standing figures painted on canvas by himself and Vanessa Bell in 1920. In 1928 Dora Carrington painted the Rylands' suite for George 'Dadie' Rylands.

However, the protected murals painted by these Bloomsbury group members in King's had all been written about and well documented. So, pointed towards the Webb's Court mural by my Director of Studies Jean Michel Massing, I decided instead to investigate the somewhat mysterious mural in R2A.

The only existing literary sources for the mural were a report filed by a previous occupant of the room, Russell Hand, made in 1985 and a letter I recovered later from the artist to Hand, written in 1983 when he had inquired into the mural. I managed to meet and interview both the artist, Irina Hale, now living in Brindisi, Italy, and the original student occupant of the room in 1956 when the mural was painted, Ronald Harrison, now living in London. With such limited primary sources, besides the mural itself, the bulk of my information came from these interviews.

A Spanish Village half an hour before the End of the World (hereafter *Spanish Village*) is as much a product of its time as it is of the soul that conceived it. Irina Hale, a half-Russian half-Irish art student living briefly in King's Lynn, painted the scene on the wall of a room in Webb's Court, between January and March 1956. The artist, who was taking weekly life-drawing classes in Cambridge, met Ronald Harrison, an undergraduate historian and occupant of R2A. The mural, 2.5 by 3.5 metres, painted impromptu and largely improvised using powder paints and an emulsion of egg-linseed oil-vinegar, was the outcome of this encounter. After Harrison graduated, the mural was allowed to remain provided that any future occupants of the room would agree to finance it being repainted if no one else would take over the room on the same basis. The painting survived these precarious circumstances for several years, with Brian Coleman and PK Pal taking over the room, before a general petition encouraged the

Bursar to declare the mural a College treasure, 'as a little hidden show piece in Webb's Court.' EM Forster was an influence in the mural's survival, having offered constructive criticism while it was painted. In 2008, the Hamilton Kerr Institute restored the mural, through a donation of PK Pal.

Irina Heard (later Hale) was born on 2 August 1932 in London to a Russian mother and Irish father. Hale's work has moved from sculpture and oil painting to media more accessible to children, illustrating storybooks since 1980 and creating shadow theatre since 1992. Her work usually dances between two rather polarized subject matters: war and fantasy. She is now, among other projects, writing 'an epic for young adults on central Asia in the 13th century' based on a fictionalized account of Marco Polo.

Spanish Village shows a village scene in Spain, set in a marketplace inside a courtyard, with stairs rising to the left and a fire-fuelled apocalypse scene above. With extraordinary articulated figures and surreal incidents, the mural is full of iconography and symbolism – the examples of sin, and of metamorphosis into the unpleasant, arguably critiquing a society felt to be wildly out of control. The many religious motifs in it move ambiguously between parodying religion and showing how the misuse of religion marks a spiritual lack in society.

Hale commented:

'Children watch a travelling marionette theatre, the puppets play the crucifixion – a tale that has lost its sacred aura and has deconsecrated itself enough to become an empty mime. The sacred element has leaked away from our lives and is replaced by a kind of theatre …'

The relativity of time is also an important theme of this mural, with activities shown in an extremely condensed and frightening form. The kinds of things that take months to process are happening in a matter of minutes, such as the wool being spun and woven simultaneously. This urgency beckons the approaching end and seems also to reflect Hale's concerns with 'modern' society. 'We don't always realize our ominous encapsulation in this speeding up of time,' Hale says, 'but it's very evident to those who have a historical perspective enough to stand back and observe it.'

The political and social context of 1956 in which *Spanish Village* was painted is crucial to understanding the symbolism in it. Hale says:

'Already one was losing faith in the concept of "progress" and had a dawning feeling that a large part of technology was somehow dragging men backward instead of forward, both as regards physical dexterity and spiritual depth and equilibrium.'

Hale links her vision of the apocalypse both to her concern with the modern 'escalation' of time, and also more directly to the nuclear threat brought about by the Cold War, a threat that arguably makes the mural still very relevant today. She tells of a 'slight air of menace' and 'end of the world-ish feeling' that inspired her to paint *Spanish Village*, caused by the memory of Hiroshima and Nagasaki ten years earlier, the accelerating nuclear arms race and increased nuclear testing, which had risen to 20 nuclear tests in 1955. In 1954–5 the US and USSR made their first deployable 'staged' thermonuclear weapon tests. There was therefore a growing public sentiment, fearful and against nuclear testing, which Hale was part of:

'In these times when a devastating apocalypse becomes ever more of a possibility, both from an overwrought earth losing its marvellous resilience to disaster – and our own being trapped in the mad machinery of "escalation" – I suppose the [apocalyptic] subject *does* become more immediate and plausible.'

Hale's vision of the apocalypse comes without the promise of salvation. Despite her Russian Orthodox background, Hale does not follow the descriptive version of the Apocalypse as found in the Bible, which includes the Second Coming, the Last Judgment, and the invitation of a new world – a New Jerusalem – as a 'holy city … made ready

like a bride adorned for her husband.' Rather more pessimistically she points only to annihilation, perhaps taken selectively from II Peter's version of Christian eschatology, 'But the Day of the Lord will come ... On that day the heavens will disappear ... The elements will disintegrate in flames.'

Frances Carey considers this understanding of the apocalypse a particularly modern interpretation, in consequence of world events:

'The events of the 20th century have conspired to ensure the survival of apocalyptic metaphor in all media as a vehicle for visions of destruction and regeneration, of nihilistic despair and futuristic fantasy; the real meaning of apocalypse as "unveiling" has been virtually extinguished by its contemporary usage as a synonym for catastrophe.'

Hale's concern with the nuclear threat only grew. Some years after *Spanish Village* was painted she became extremely phobic 'as there was a real danger of radioactive rain' and in the 1970s she did a series of 40 anti-nuclear paintings, 'almost like posters ... signalling my dawning politicizing.' Since then she has organized numerous exhibitions reacting to world wars, disasters and atrocities. The preface to *Paradises and Paradoxes,* an exhibition against the invasion of Afghanistan in 2001, read: 'Henceforth it was impossible for me to project happy and fabled pictures, as was my usual bent. Yet again the anguish of war took me by the throat, and grew like an abscess, which needs to leak out.'

Hale arranged an exhibition of documented images – 'glimpses of unimaginable realities' – she had seen in Sudan and Rajasthan entitled *Children of the World,* another exhibition for the Kurds abandoned in the Zagros mountains, others for Kosovo, for the earthquake victims of Irpinia and most recently, in 2009, for Gaza, usually using the same earthy colour scheme, and what she would class as 'poor' materials, cardboard and collage: 'an artist, what can they do except show their fist with their paintbrush?' she asks. Perhaps her politicization was influenced by her 'captor and mentor' Gustav Metzger, with whom she lived in King's Lynn in 1956, at the time the mural was painted. Metzger was an artist and political activist who developed the concept of auto-destructive art and sculpture.

In response to a shadow theatre show by Hale in 2004, journalist Adriana Notte commented:

'The artist Irina Hale has a long professional experience, aiming to try and awaken from its sleep public opinion, from her own shows to shadow theatre. All this is shown in ways accessible to children through art, in the tragic truths of poverty, hunger, wars, violence and exploitation.'

Spanish Village was certainly an early product of this compassionate, mystical, and sensitive soul, enraged by and compelled to express contemporary dramas and horrors of the world. 'I suppose as some have said, I was the very first "hippie",' says Hale, 'choosing that lifestyle before anyone else got onto it, and the mural was just one of the many things that got thrown off on the side.'

Hale's subject and style appears to be heavily influenced by the medieval artists Hieronymus Bosch and Pieter Brueghel the Elder who held up a mirror to human folly much as Hale attempted to do. Bosch used fantastic imagery to illustrate moral and religious concepts and narratives. Like Brueghel and Hale, his paintings seem to be visual translations of verbal metaphors, full of characters with moralizing, perceptive and expressive little faces. Metamorphism and monsters are important features of Bosch and are also found in *Spanish Village*. Walter Gibson wrote: 'Bosch confronts us with a world of dreams, nightmares in which forms seem to flicker and change before our eyes.'

Bosch is commonly acknowledged to have influenced Brueghel, so it is not surprising that both artists invite comparisons to Hale. She too shows an interest in peasants and village scenes similar to Brueghel's. There is a spiritual basis to Brueghel's art, as with Hale, full of imagination and wit, and often satirical, close observation of human nature. On form, 'an essential characteristic of Brueghel's art is the tendency to simplify and to reduce

steadily up the ranks, becoming editor in my third year. I have said that King's perhaps tended to look a little askance at journalism, either as a career or a pastime, but I have to say that the College looked kindly on this. When it became very clear that I was heading, at best, for a 2.2, I remember my tutor saying: 'Well, I suppose you are at least editor of *Varsity*', as if that – well, partially – made up for my shortcomings in more academic pursuits. (Indeed, although student journalists were a bit thin on the ground in King's, it is worth noting that the distinguished editor of this volume and I were back-to-back editors of *Varsity*, so I suppose they became accustomed to it.)

There was another occasion when I had to get up very early one morning to go to Bury St Edmunds where the next edition of *Varsity* was to be printed. It was so early that the College was, as it always was at that time, tightly locked up for the night, with all its inhabitants presumed to be sleeping soundly and safely inside its walls. I however needed to get out, and so made the unusual journey of actually climbing *out* of College rather than the more normal route of climbing in. I was spotted by a porter who came running over to apprehend me, no doubt under the impression that I was a particularly tardy arrival from the night before. But when he saw who I was, and which way I was going, he merely gave me a friendly salute and sent me on my way.

Perhaps the most extraordinary imposition I ever made on the College was to have a telephone installed in my room, which I am sure had never been done before, and I imagine rarely, if ever, since; though presumably now all modern undergraduates eschew the use of land-lines anyway.

The reason was this: I had, again with a brass neck that still slightly shocks me, applied to the *Time-Life* organization to be their stringer at the University. I knew of others who had preceded me in this role, and saw no cause why this vacancy should not be filled by me. It was a damned cheek, I must say, and looking back I was quite inadequate for the job, knowing extraordinarily little about journalism, or news, or indeed anything. But I applied, and in due course was appointed.

Time-Life was (next to the *Daily Express*) the journalistic organization which I most admired. Its breezy Americanism, its vast scope, its eccentric and innovative use of the English language, indeed the entire idea of a 'news magazine' (a concept often tried, but never successfully emulated in the UK) was very appealing.

In pursuit of this new challenge, I decided I would need a telephone and since, fortunately, I lived on A staircase, this posed no difficulty for the Post Office engineers to run in a line through my bedroom window. It did however require the consent of the College, and to my amazement, they agreed.

This made me immensely popular among my fellows, who could now ring up their friends and relations from the comfort of my room rather than a draughty phone box in some dark corridor or street. As a journalistic tool it was, though splendidly grandiose, effectively useless, since I was very rarely in my room when somebody called.

If *Time* needed me for an assignment, they would send a massively lengthy telegram, which gave me immense credibility in the Porter's Lodge. I was occasionally called upon to add a few paragraphs to a story being concocted in London and which needed an expert witness from the academic community, and sometimes I used the phone for those interviews, but then even dons did not always have ready access to a phone themselves, and it was generally just as easy to walk round and see them in person.

I cannot remember ever originating a story, which – considering what a hive of intellectual activity I was surrounded by – is pretty shameful. *Time* was not much interested in the activities of undergraduates, which was what I mostly knew about. There was some vague excitement, I seem to recall, when a minor member of the Royal Family turned up, probably at Magdalene – this was before Prince Charles broke the mould by himself becoming an undergraduate at Cambridge – but that was unusual and rather

unproductive, since I didn't have much access to royal circles, or indeed to the Magdalene social set.

But on the whole my contributions to the mighty worldwide empire of *Time* were, to say the least, cursory. Indeed apart from the odd quote, the only actual story I ever got into the magazine was about a black don from Canada who had arrived in Cambridge for a year as a visiting professor. That got in, complete with photograph – but only, I have to confess, in the Canadian edition, a somewhat small subset of the greater whole.

But this self-deprecation must cease, because there was at least one arena in which undergraduate life, journalism and the telephone all happily melded together. In my second Long Vac, I got as job as a holiday relief on the *Londoner's Diary* column on the London *Evening Standard*. This was a delightful job for a would-be hack, sitting on a real editorial floor in the old premises in Shoe Lane, just off Fleet Street, the newspaper presses throbbing away in the basement, and crafting little jewelled paragraphs about social and artistic trivia for the best-read gossip column in London.

Back at Cambridge for my final year, I maintained this connection, because the *Diary* – unlike *Time* magazine – was interested in the minutiae of undergraduate life, and I continued regularly to provide little titbits for them, which I sent to the copy-taker by telephone, and was able to buy the printed result in the street outside King's within a couple of hours of sending it in.

This stood me in good stead later, for when I left Cambridge I initially took a longer-term job with the *Standard*, during a glorious summer and autumn for news, which included the Profumo affair and the Great Train Robbery – two events which cemented, if cement were needed, my love affair with news.

And in the meantime, the combination of the *Daily Express, Time* magazine and the *Evening Standard* meant that I ended up as a reasonably well-off undergraduate, having started as a rather poor one. For that, and other things, I am grateful to King's – indeed I now look back at it with perhaps more warmth than I felt at the time.

Art and revolution

Michael Craig-Martin

My first memory is of arriving at the College in the spring of 1970 for my 'interview'. I had been advised that it wasn't really an interview as no one else was under serious consideration, but, because no one at King's had ever met or even heard of me, it was thought there should at least be the opportunity to say no. I was 29, and my hair was to my shoulders. To make a good impression I decided to wear my one suit with fashionably wide lapels and flared trousers.

As I waited at the gatehouse, Bob Young, the Fellow with responsibility for the artist-in-residence programme, came bounding across the lawn to greet me. To my astonishment he was wearing a long, flowing African shirt printed with a large abstract pattern in yellow, red and black, blue jeans, and open sandals. Everyone else I was introduced to was casually if conventionally dressed, but in my suit, more suitable to the King's Road than King's College, I felt a complete prat. It was a memorable introduction to the particular character of King's, and I was relieved when I learned I had passed inspection.

Bob Young, an American, was a radical social historian who had convinced King's to initiate the artist-in-residence programme, something virtually unknown in British universities at the time, though familiar on many American campuses. As there was little interest in or knowledge of contemporary art in the British academic world of those days, Bob sought advice on potential candidates from Richard Morphet, a young assistant keeper of modern art at the Tate. It was Richard Morphet who recommended me.

There had been just one other artist in the position before me, from 1968 to 1970, Mark Lancaster. As he was single, he had lived and worked at the heart of King's, in the central set of the Gibbs Building, above the arch, facing King's Parade. As I was married and we had a small child, we lived for the first year in a new bungalow in Wingate Road in Trumpington, and for the second year in a tiny house in St Edward's Passage, directly across from King's. My wife, Jan Hashey, was also an artist, a painter, and our daughter Jessica was just seven. We all greatly preferred living in the centre of Cambridge rather than the suburbs.

I was provided with a large high-ceilinged room as a studio, on the first floor of the Wilkins Building on staircase A, directly above the bar. It was fitted out specially for me with plywood-covered walls painted white, grey linoleum flooring and fluorescent lighting, and was by far the best studio I had ever had. It was my first studio in Britain that could be used all year round as it was heated.

The nature of the role and related responsibilities of the artist-in-residence at King's was unstated in a very English way. In the days before Britain became obsessed with the culture of precisely detailed job descriptions, performance assessments, and mission statements, it was normal to be given only the most sparse information about a position one was taking up, as though, like good manners, one should already know what was expected or one shouldn't be there in the first place. Though this lack of guidance could be unnerving, it meant that one had the opportunity to define the job in line with one's own interests and skills.

It became clear to me that I was simply expected to spend time working in my studio in the College during terms. I was not there to teach, but to be 'available' to any interested students or staff. I never felt I quite understood what 'available' might mean in practice, and over the next two years I alternated between thinking I was doing either too little or too much. After a few weeks I gave a slide talk about my work to introduce myself. There was a good turnout, and despite general scepticism and much bafflement, I was made to feel welcome, by both dons and students.

As artist-in-residence I had many of the privileges of a Fellow, including the opportunity to dine at high table when I chose. I usually found this experience intimidating, but the food and wine were excellent, and the atmosphere was naturally dependent on who was present. I stood out for obvious reasons and was therefore well placed for teasing, but this was preferable to the alternative of being ignored. The one-upmanship that characterized many high-table conversations meant these evenings could be both entertaining and informative, so long as one didn't find that one had been cast as fall-guy or stooge.

After dinner, drinks were served in a private dining room behind the hall. Sitting round an immense mahogany table, the conversation tended to be more mellow and less combative. There was an extraordinary silver 'train' carrying three carafes (claret, port and brandy) on hidden castors that one passed to one's neighbour on the right by rolling it silently towards them. The train did several circumferences of the table each evening.

Another privilege was the right to ignore the many do-not-walk-on-the-grass signs and take short cuts directly across the lawn of the front court. This very public privilege gave some Fellows great satisfaction, particularly when taken to task by righteous tourists unfamiliar with the rules.

I once ran into Professor Michael Jaffé, head of the Art History department, by the Porter's Lodge, who said he wanted to talk to me in private. He turned and led me to the centre of the lawn where, pacing back and forth, we conducted our conversation confident of not being overheard, despite being surrounded by dozens of students and tourists following the prescribed perimeter of paved paths.

There were certain people involved in the arts at King's whom I looked forward to meeting and hopefully getting to know. Principal among these was EM Forster, resident at King's for many decades, but he passed away in June, some months before I arrived. I did get to know Dadie Rylands, the English literary scholar and theatre director, who was as charming and hospitable as reputed.

I discovered that King's also had a composer-in-residence, the musician and composer, Tim Souster. Together with Roger Smalley, who in 1968 had been the first to hold that appointment and was now on a research fellowship, he was involved in forming the live-electronic group, Intermodulation. We were all comparatively young, in our late 20s, and got on well. We had a natural sense of aesthetic comradeship, seeing ourselves as representing similar avant garde positions in our different fields. I recall a conversation with Tim where he expressed envy that artists like myself enjoyed the recognition and support of the full range of the institutions of art, from art schools to the Tate, whereas composers like himself felt themselves to still be very much on the periphery of the institutions of music in Britain, particularly the BBC. Tim went on to work with Stockhausen in Cologne.

I also met Jim Ede who in 1966 had given his house, Kettle's Yard, and its contents including his collection of 20th-century art to the University. I loved and valued this unique outpost of modern art in Cambridge, despite the fact that its very personal mix of paintings and sculpture with furniture and natural objects – stones and shells – in more or less domestic circumstances was at odds with my own aesthetic stance. In 1970, the year I arrived in Cambridge, the first new wing was opened, making it possible to expand the gallery programme substantially to include contemporary exhibitions alongside the collection.

Of all the people I came to know at King's no one was more important to both my wife and myself than Celia Leach, wife of the Provost, Professor Edmund Leach. Edmund was well known at the time as an iconoclastic social anthropologist, because of his controversial 1967 Reith Lecture in which he had attacked the legitimacy of the nuclear family ('Far from being the basis of the good society, the family, with its narrow privacy and tawdry secrets, is the source of all our discontents').

Celia was a strikingly handsome woman, tall and thin, sharply observant and good humoured. She was a fine painter and writer, fundamentally out of sorts with what she felt was the philistine and intellectually pretentious academic world surrounding her. She was thrilled by the arrival at King's of two young artists, kindred spirits, and we became the fortunate recipients of her natural gracious warmth and generosity. We often enjoyed the hospitality of dinner with Celia and Edmund in the Provost's Lodge and came to know them well.

I believe that my time at King's coincided with one of the most confused and untypical periods in the long history of the College. I had expected Cambridge to feel stable, comfortable, and civilized in the very middle-class way I had known at Yale in the early 1960s. The comforts were there, but the self-assurance of the middle class had been shaken. Traditional values, attitudes and activities had come to be seen as reactionary and irrelevant by many of the young. I recall going to a meeting where a don was accused of being 'liberal,' which was intended as an expression of absolute contempt.

The international student revolutions of 1968 had shaken the confidence of all institutions, most markedly those involved in higher education, and had legitimized the questioning of all forms of authority. The focus of Cambridge's revolutionary moment had been what was known as the Garden House riot. When I arrived in 1970, the legacy of anger and betrayal associated with that event still persisted among many radical students.

King's had, of course, always had a reputation as Cambridge's most left-wing and radical college, and thus was considered the fulcrum of the intellectual, political and social upheavals of the times, but it seems to me to have been a hiatus, an interregnum, when no one knew quite what they should do, or how they should behave. There was a desire to identify with revolutionary change, but any clear sense of purpose or focus seemed to have been lost. Many students saw themselves as hippies, seeking to drop out from the conventional behaviour and ambitions that had been part of their upbringing: it was a time of long hair, Nehru shirts, hashish and acid. However, I suspect it was only a few years before most returned to 'normal'.

I came to know many students well during my time in Cambridge, mostly from King's, but some from other colleges, who usually sought me out because they had an interest in art. Some remain friends to this day: Richard Shone, at Clare, who became an art critic and writer, and is now editor of the *Burlington Magazine*; and Antony Gormley at Trinity, who went on to study fine art at Goldsmiths College and the Slade, and is now one of Britain's best-known sculptors. Another was the gifted King's student, Andrew Floud, who went on to study contemporary dance with Merce Cunningham in New York and later became a doctor. He died tragically in 1981, caught in a storm while piloting a small plane in America.

The person who had the greatest impact on my thinking and thus on my work was Jim Hopkins, a Fellow and Director of Studies in Philosophy at King's. Our many conversations, particularly about Wittgenstein and psychoanalysis, and his recommendations for reading, were invaluable to me in this period when I had the time for serious reflection. We became and remain good friends.

I was very happy with my studio, and my years at King's turned out to be exceptionally productive. Nearly all my work with ordinary found objects was done while at King's: lead weights *(Six foot balance with four pounds of paper)*, buckets *(On the table)*, milk bottles *(On the shelf)*, clipboards *(4 complete sets extended to 5)*, mirrors *(Forwards and reverse simultaneously)*, a glass of water *(An oak tree)*. Although this last was created in 1973, the year after I left Cambridge, it was in fact the culmination of this period of work.

Two of the most important exhibitions of my early career took place while I was in Cambridge. They were the defining exhibitions of British conceptual art, *The New Art* at the Hayward Gallery and *Seven Exhibitions* at the Tate, both in 1972. All my work for these exhibitions was conceived and produced in Cambridge. One day I was visited in my studio by the new regional officer of the Arts Council who was assisting the curator Anne Seymour

on *The New Art*. The young
man who arrived was tall
and thin, quietly spoken but
impressively well informed.
His name was Nick Serota.

During my second year
I developed an idea with a
King's Art History student,
Philip Rylands, to establish
a small gallery showing
contemporary art in the
College. At the time the
room opposite the Porter's
Lodge was rarely used, and
then only for occasional
meetings. We worked out
that it could be used as a
gallery without interfering
with this use, and that
because of its location at the College entrance and across from the Porter's Lodge, it could
be safely opened to the public.

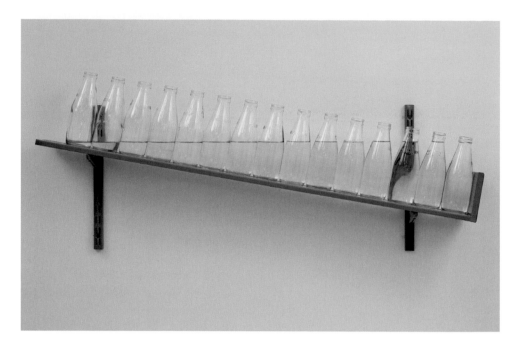

On the shelf, *1970*.

We showed the work of my contemporaries – John Stezaker, John Hilliard, Barry
Flanagan. I realize now that it must have been one of the first primarily conceptual galleries
in Britain, certainly outside London. We had a small loyal following and a visitors' book
for comments, sadly lost. The book made very entertaining reading with its outpourings of
anger and invective, usually obscene. Philip, who was the nephew of Dadie Rylands, went on
to become the distinguished director of the Guggenheim Museum in Venice.

In retrospect I think the 'impact' on King's of my presence was minimal and, except
for my contact with a small number of individuals, left no real legacy. On the other hand,
from my point of view, King's provided me with a two-year breathing space, a place to
live, a studio, and a regular income, freedom from the pressures and tedium of travelling
and teaching, time to devote myself exclusively to my work, and the opportunity to
recover my flagging self-confidence.

Despite this, by the summer of 1972 I was looking forward to returning to London.
Cambridge could often seem hopelessly inward-looking, self-absorbed and complacent – a
world unto itself. King's had provided me, as an artist, with a respite but not a context. I
needed to get back to the small but intensely stimulating London art world of the early
1970s. However, I will always be grateful to King's for its courageous and generous patronage.

One final recollection. At the Founder's Feast in 1971 I was seated at a table with seven
other men, all formally dressed. The dinner conversation was stiff and humourless, on
subjects of no interest to me, and I said very little. Halfway through the meal I introduced
myself to the small, shy man on my left, who had as yet said nothing at all. He introduced
himself and asked what I did. I replied I was the artist-in-residence. He had no idea what
that meant so I explained the position and, pleased to have found someone who showed
an interest, went on about my new work with buckets and clipboards and mirrors. I
then asked what he did. He said, 'I'm an astrophysicist.' I said, 'Oh, you look at the stars,'
and he laughed, 'Only in the garden at night.' His work, he explained, was principally
mathematical. I said, 'What are you working on at present?' He paused for a moment and
said quietly, 'I am trying to discover the origin of the universe.' Astounded and suddenly
feeling very small, I said, 'How are you doing?' He replied, 'I am very close to the answer.'

It was some years before I first heard of the Big Bang theory.

Standing up to Mrs Thatcher

Tam Dalyell

It is difficult – no, well-nigh impossible – to convey the shock to my system of arriving in King's on a Tuesday evening in October 1952, having been a member of a tank crew in the British Army of the Rhine the previous Friday. Nowadays, freshmen would generally have had a gap year, and would have been prepared for the transition from school to university. National Service was an altogether different scene. I was fortunate in that my National Service regiment had a strict, but sensible, code of discipline, and that most of the senior officers and NCOs had been together from Alamein, via Italy, and Normandy, to the Rhine Crossing. We 18- to 19-year-olds knew exactly why we were obliged to do National Service – from Luneberg, where we were stationed, Stalin's armour was only 25 kilometres across the Elbe and our firing practice took place on the Hohne Ranges, which included an obligatory tour of Belsen concentration camp. At a time when the situation in the Korean War looked ugly, this concentrated the mind. One did what one was told.

Days later, to be entering an evening meal in the candlelit Hall of King's, was a somewhat different ambience. By chance, I found myself next to two students: one was a South African scientist, the other the holder of a major scholarship in Classics. Their conversation was so glitteringly brilliant, their knowledge so wide-ranging and profound, that I wandered back to my digs in Peas Hill, saying to myself, 'What the hell am I doing in company like this?' These students were Sydney Brenner and Geoffrey Lloyd, and I was not to know that one was to win the Nobel Prize for Medicine and the other to become Professor of Ancient Philosophy and Science in Cambridge and Master of Darwin College.

I returned to my room in Peas Hill, and metaphorically wept on the sympathetic shoulder of a second-year undergraduate. He, too, was sparklingly clever, later to become a distinguished scientist and university vice-chancellor. And this brings me to the first of the great gifts that the College bestowed on 20-year-olds, many of whose feelings of near-despair were not so different from mine – really intelligent pastoral care. My Director of Studies and lifelong friend Christopher Morris had taken the trouble to send me a two-page letter, in his own handwriting, suggesting the books I should read – such as Motley's *Rise of the Dutch Republic* – during spare hours in the Rhine Army. His gentle but quizzical approach to supervisions inspired a confidence which was crucial. (If he had perceived signs of a lack of effort, any of us could have been 'sent down'). Morris cared deeply about each of his students individually, and established lifelong friendships with any pupil who took the trouble to stay in touch. He and his wife, Helen, were wonderfully hospitable in their own home, at 5 Merton Street, when such hospitality really mattered to Kingsmen.

There was something else which, glancing back over 55 years, seems to have been important. Like other King's Directors of Studies, Morris would fill undergraduates in about his own colleagues. 'You will be supervised in the next four weeks by John Saltmarsh. He is the Medieval World. He is personally acquainted with the architects who built the College Chapel. Accept his invitation to explore the Chapel Roof with him. John is *sui generis*.' Or, on account of 'flu among History dons, 'I am sending you to Adcock, Emeritus Professor,' (later Sir Frank Adcock, editor of the *Cambridge Ancient History*). 'The old pedant is worth a guinea a minute.' Adcock, who was Vice-Provost, had been the pupil of Wilamowitz-Moellendorf in Berlin, pre-1914, served in Naval Intelligence during World War One, and with his perfect German was one of the star codebreakers of Bletchley Park during World War Two. He invited me and other undergraduates to go on afternoon walks with him. 'He was worth a guinea a minute' was right. Frank Adcock bequeathed to me a deep interest in, and scepticism about, Intelligence.

Half a century later, it was this scepticism – 'Remember the false information of the Peloponnesian War,' Adcock said – which prompted me to challenge the Dodgy Dossier on Iraq (and be cartooned by Brookes of *The Times*, holding the Dossier on the green benches of the House of Commons in one hand, and angrily demanding to know why it was not shortlisted for the Booker Prize for Fiction). King's gave me, and other politicians – I think of Peter Shore on the Labour side, and Sir Ian Lloyd (MP for Havant, and Maynard Keynes's last economics student) on the Conservative side – the disposition to challenge political received wisdom.

Christopher Morris sent me to the young Noel Annan with the warning, 'Don't be daunted'. With his bow tie and imposing figure, the future Provost of King's, Provost of University College, London, Chairman of the Major Government Committee on Broadcasting, and Member of the House of Lords, was indeed formidable. Typical of King's dons, he was inquisitive about his students. Early on in my second supervision with him, he switched from German History – he was to be the author of that powerful book, *Changing Enemies* – to the subject of my origins. 'Tam, what class do you think you are?' I hesitated – 'I suppose I come from the Scottish Lairdry'. 'Oh, yes,' barked Noel in that unforgettable voice, 'I know what you mean – not quite county!' King's dons were brutally frank, and imbued many – not quite all – their undergraduates with sensible self-criticism. Kingsmen have the attractive quality of being generally unselfsatisfied.

It was also seen as a duty by Morris to expose some of his public school pupils, particularly old Etonians, to supervision by then Communist – and now venerated Marxist – historian, Eric Hobsbawm. Modest and good-humoured, though impressively focused on the topic of my essay, Hobsbawm introduced me to the working methods of central European scholars. This was a novel experience, but gave us an understanding of events. Three year later, having been allowed to do Part II Economics, I encountered the same

The Times, *Thursday September 26, 2002.*

Noel Annan.

rigour, and the same delicate, sardonic humour, in being supervised by Nicholas Kaldor.

Ten years later, as a newly elected Member of Parliament, I invited Kaldor, then ensconced in the Treasury (and unlike Thomas Balogh, popular with civil servants) to lunch, so that I could pour out my heart on the economic problems of my West Lothian constituency, where unemployment had reached what was at that time an appalling 6 per cent. Kaldor later said that it was this lunch that had sown the seed in his mind of recommending to the Chancellor and Treasury mandarins the idea of a Selective Employment Tax and Regional Employment Premium – both hugely effective and relatively uncomplicated measures in their time, which produced overall beneficial results for the British economy.

King's harboured three other brilliant economists. There was the superb and patient teacher, Robin Marris, Professor Richard Kahn, who had devised the famous multiplier-effect for Maynard Keynes as he was producing the *General Theory*, and the heavyweight, in every sense, iconoclastic Canadian Harry Johnson, later to be Professor at Manchester, the LSE and Chicago. As a tough fourth-year student I was taken down a peg or two by Johnson's reaction to my first piece of written work for him: 'Say, were you drunk when you wrote this?' It was probably for my own good. With other students such as Lal Jayawardena, later Governor of the Central Bank in Sri Lanka, or Mahbub ul-Haq, later head of the World Bank, he was infinitely gentler. King's dons tailored their teaching to what they considered to be the good of a particular student, at a particular period in his life. They were subtle.

The ethos was to live up to the idea of being a community of scholars. One manifestation of this ethos was an attitude that 'public opinion' and certainly 'public acclaim' was of little consequence compared to the discerning opinion of the cognoscenti. A personal example: I cared little that the media, in general, and majority opinion was vehemently critical of my strident opposition to the Falklands War. I was cut to the proverbial quick when Noel Annan complained to my face, 'Tam, you do not understand "the fog of war".' In vain did I try to explain to Noel that I had said that Mrs Thatcher's lie was that she did not know about the Peruvian peace proposals, which would have deprived her of the military victory which she craved for domestic political purposes, before she gave the order to sink the *Belgrano*.

In my third year, the Senior Tutor, Patrick Wilkinson, greatest of all obituarists, allocated me A9, with its beautiful view of the Chapel, on condition that I would pop my head round the corner of an elderly don on the ground floor, and an elderly gentleman on the first floor – Professor Arthur Pigou and EM Forster. Forster's influence permeated my generation of Kingsmen, and inculcated into us that relationships with friends transcended all else, and in particular our obligations to the state.

With the good fortune of being given this room – once Keynes's – and not being short of the proverbial bob or two, I used to assemble a group of my friends in King's from different faculties for tea and invite some of our teachers. One of these was Milton Friedman, bringing his vivacious wife. Later I mentioned my tea with Friedman to the first de facto female Fellow of King's, whose portrait is appropriately displayed in the corridor between Hall and the Fellows' Room, Joan Robinson. 'And what', she asked coldly, 'did Mephistopheles say to you?' This was a quarter joking, and wholly in earnest, given the tensions in the Economics Faculty. After having to cope with Mrs Robinson, standing up to Mrs Thatcher in her heyday posed few terrors.

It is the custom that by-election winners being introduced to the House are greeted by the leaders of their parties, after taking the Oath, and go to the Leader's Room. Hugh Gaitskell came to the point. 'All I know about you is that you were taught by my friends Richard Kahn and Nicky Kaldor. Who else taught you?' 'Joan Robinson.' Then a litmus test question, 'How did you get on with Joan?' – which could have been translated, 'Are you going to be a left-wing troublemaker in the Parliamentary Labour Party?' I thought it best to be candid. 'She put the fear of God into me.' Gaitskell smiled. 'That makes two of us!'

Never in my life would I be interrogated in the same depth as I was in King's. Such experience is a priceless gift and helps to avoid what JS Mill called 'the deep slumber of a decided opinion'.

Continuing contact with those who had taught me at King's was a huge gift to my political life. When I was in dire trouble, before the then formidable Commons Privileges Committee, and summoned to the Bar (the last MP to be treated thus), to find Mr Speaker putting his black cap on, in relation to my having 'leaked' a Select Committee Report on Porton Down in 1967, I received a letter of encouragement from Eric Hobsbawm on the greater importance of the issues surrounding chemical and biological weapons, to that of parliamentary 'mumbo-jumbo'.

When I led for the opposition on the Field Monuments Bill, John Saltmarsh was once again my mentor. On economic and employment matters, Nicky Kaldor, Richard Kahn, Henry Johnson and Robin Marris were at the end of a telephone. I never had (nor claimed for!) a Parliamentary researcher – the only useful advice an MP could have would come from someone who could tell me that I was wrong, or in Harry Johnson's case that I was talking nonsense – and 'nonsense' was not the word that Harry used!

King's also had a direct influence on the so-called 'West Lothian Question'. Like most politicians, I am a man of some vanity – but not sufficient to call a constitutional conundrum after myself. Twenty-two years after I had been his pupil, in 1977, at the beginning of the parliamentary process on Scottish devolution, Christopher Morris advised me sternly to read Morley's *Life of Gladstone*, depicting the problems of the 'ins and outs of Ireland'. Following Christopher's instructions, I realized the problem, and on every clause and sub-clause of the legislation, asked how, as MP for West Lothian, I could vote on education in Accrington, but not in Armadale, West Lothian – on health matters in Blackburn, Lancashire, but not Blackburn, West Lothian, on local government in Liverpool, but not Linlithgow.

I intoned, portentously, 'It cannot be asked too often.' Exasperated, the Minister on the Front Bench, John Smith, my friend, and later leader of the Labour Party, shouted out, 'Tam, it bloody well can.'

Enoch Powell rose in his seat. 'We have finally grasped what the Hon. Member for West Lothian is on about. To save parliamentary time,' Powell said, with heavy irony since saving time was the last thing he wanted to do in 47 days on the Floor of the House, 'let us give it the soubriquet of the West Lothian Question'.

Eleven days before he died of throat cancer, I went to see Powell in his home. He whispered, 'I have bequeathed to you the West Lothian Question.'

Had he known, he might have said, 'Christopher Morris, King's, and I bequeathed to you the West Lothian Question.'

King's ancient and modern

Iain Fenlon

For many, simply to name the College is to evoke the images and sounds of the Chapel Choir, above all in the broadcasts of the Festival of Nine Lessons and Carols. Despite its apparent antiquity, this service is a masterly example of tradition being invented, in this case by Eric Milner-White, Dean of Chapel; it has been celebrated annually since 1918, and was broadcast for the first time by the BBC in 1928. An adroit mixture of texts, choreography and music, astutely and sensitively drawing on both past and current, the result is a piece of imaginative ritual rich in drama, sentiment and nostalgia. Above all, the Nine Lessons and Carols is a truly grand occasion, in all senses of the word, an annual reminder that the Chapel itself, and the liturgy that is enacted there on a daily basis throughout the terms of the University year, is the only element of the original regal conception of the College itself to have been completed.

From the start there was music (as early as 1452 three books of *cantus fractus*, that is polyphony, are recorded in documents), not that it is possible to have a very clear picture of what it was or how it sounded. The Founder's Statutes, granted in 1453, provided for 70 Fellows and scholars, ten chaplains, and six clerks or singing men, placed under the overall authority of a Provost, making King's unprecedented in size among Cambridge colleges of the time. Equally unprecedented was the provision for 16 choristers, who were to be poor boys, of strong constitution and 'honest conversation', under the age of 12, and with the ability to both read and sing. Their duties included not only the daily round of Matins, Mass and Vespers, but also the requirement to wait at table in Hall. In King's, as elsewhere in Oxford and Cambridge, choristers were part of an institution rather than simply being young musicians. The pattern was to continue until the 19th century.

A King's inventory of 'pryke songs'.

While the new Chapel was being built, services were given in its predecessor, which stood on the south side of the Old Schools site, north of the present building. This consisted of an antechapel, nave and chancel, but was far from impressive. Dr Caius, the founder of Gonville and Caius College, described it as *humile et angustum* ['lowly and narrow'], and in 1536 or 1537 it collapsed without warning after Vespers; no trace of it remains. Although none of the early service books survive (presumably they were destroyed at the Reformation), some idea of what was sung by the choir can be recovered from archival records. While the earliest mention of polyphony comes from the 1440s, a remarkably detailed 'inventarye of the pryke songys' from 1529 maps out an extraordinarily detailed soundscape. From this it is clear that a substantial repertory of masses and anthems (some of it of considerable technical complexity), written by some of the most important composers of the time, including Fayrfax, Cornysh and Taverner, was being sung in King's Chapel. It seems likely that the prime mover in the promotion of music there was Robert Hacomblene, Provost from 1509 to 1528, who was himself a composer. From the statutes it is known that a polyphonic antiphon was sung in the Chapel every evening; significantly, the wording is similar to that of Eton College, King's sister college, where a votive antiphon in honour of the Virgin Mary was sung daily in front of her image. To judge from the 1529 inventory something similar must have happened at King's (though there is no evidence that the devotion was Marian), while sung masses (there is more than one 'Masse Regale' in the list) were evidently performed on major feasts.

It seems that these years were a golden age for music in the Chapel, but with the Reformation came considerable losses of vestments, plate and service books. The interior arrangements of the Chapel were now constantly under review. A high altar was put up in 1544 only to be destroyed under Edward VI, briefly restored under Mary, and removed completely in the first year of Elizabeth's reign. The Queen herself visited Cambridge in 1564, when a play was given in her honour in the Chapel, but there is no evidence of any sort of service taking place, despite Elizabeth's fondness for the pomp and circumstance of the Old Religion. Worse was to come. During the Civil War the parliamentary forces made Cambridge their headquarters, and iconoclasm was rife. William Dowsing, 'Commissioner for the Destruction of Monuments of Idolatory and Superstition', visited the Chapel on Boxing Day 1643, and ominously wrote in his diaries of the 'one thousand superstitious pictures' that he encountered there, a clear reference to the stained glass. But the fabric escaped serious damage, and almost miraculously the windows were somehow preserved. Music did not fare so well, and perhaps with good reason in view of what can be deduced about the state of things. When Archbishop Laud despatched visitors to King's in 1639, it was discovered that the choristers were ill-disciplined and that the lay clerks were unable to sing. The organ, which had been built at the beginning of the century by Thomas Dallam, a famous builder of the day who had controversially constructed a mechanical clock-organ for the Sultan of Turkey, was dismantled. In King's the changes prescribed by the government, which involved the abolition of services, may have been more gradual than elsewhere, but by 1644 the number of chaplains was down to three, and by the 1650s there were no choristers left. The Chapel fell silent.

At the Restoration a new organ was built, and the full complement of 16 choristers specified by the statutes restored, but there is no sense that the standards of the new arrangement matched those of the early 17th century. During the 18th and 19th centuries King's Chapel seems to have followed the general pattern of decline and disarray, leaving room for the reforms and revival of the late 19th century. By then conditions at the Choir School were, by all accounts, Dickensian. The traditional view is that reform, when it came, was begun by the legendary AH ('Daddy') Mann, Organist for more than half a century, from 1876 until his death in 1929. Although the present Choir School was built a few years later, it seems that much remained to be done. A recently elected Fellow in music and future Professor of Music, EJ Dent, wrote to his friend Lawrence Haward in 1909 that he had been to Chapel where he had heard 'not good' performances of Byrd, with the organ playing 'all through' and drowning out the voices, a criticism which may simply reflect Dent's interest in

AH 'Daddy' Mann on the Chapel roof.

historical performance. Mann's achievements were built upon by Bernhard Ord, known as 'Boris', on account of his enthusiasm for Mussorgsky's opera, and then, decisively from 1957 to 1974, by David Willcocks.

Dent was elected to a Fellowship in 1902, resigned 16 years later, and then after a pause returned to the College when he was elected to the Chair of Music. In his early years he had been the driving force behind Cambridge performances of Mozart's *Die Zauberflöte* and Purcell's *The Faerie Queene*. Opera was his lifelong passion, and Dent was a prime mover in the establishment of English National Opera, and in making opera more accessible through his translations of librettos; some of them are still used. In addition he was prominent on the international stage: in the 1920s and 1930s he chaired the International Society for Contemporary Music which brought him into contact with, among others, Busoni, Webern, Berg, Schoenberg and Bartok. Although for Dent scholarship was always in the service of performance, a message that was clearly heard by King's musicologists such as Winton Dean and later Philip Brett and John Butt, he brought to the task a new standard, above all in his remarkable book length treatment of Alessandro Scarlatti and his music, much of which had to be recovered from manuscripts; published in 1905, and still the only monograph in English on the subject, it is an astonishing achievement for a 29-year-old. Whether as President of the Royal Musical Association, or of the International Musicological Society, Dent moved easily in the wider world, pursuing research in libraries and archives and giving lectures; in effect he was the first great British musicologist.

In Cambridge he invested considerable time and effort in undergraduate music-making, and was equally at home conducting the performances of CUMS (Cambridge University Music Society) or the Music Club, or putting together incidental music for the productions of the Marlowe Society. Certainly he would have approved of Norman Platt, a Kingsman who came to the College at the outbreak of the Second World War, and who went on to found Kent Opera, a major touring company which lived hand to mouth bringing opera to the provinces (including Cambridge). Kent Opera proved to be the first professional experience for many young singers, including a number of King's Choral Scholars who later went on to make their careers in opera. A number formed strong links with English National Opera where another Kingsman, the Earl of Harewood, served as both chairman of the board and music director for many years. Bernard Williams, Provost from 1979 until 1987 and another opera lover, also served on the ENO board for some 20 years; his essays *On Opera*, published posthumously, would have been read with pleasure by Dent, as would the opera reviews of another King's opera lover, the author and critic Rupert Christiansen.

It was shortly after Dent's return to Cambridge that matters took a more ambitious turn when the Faculty of Music acquired a new home in Downing Place; this included a small concert hall. Here musical life thrived. In addition to the academic study of music, Downing Place also provided a focus for performance, and in particular for the concerts organized by CUMS, later to be joined by the Cambridge University Music Club, and the Cambridge University Chamber Orchestra. All this had the effect of balancing the equation, by introducing opportunities for music outside the organ loft. When the Faculty moved again, this time into an extensive modern building in West Cambridge, a large concert hall with capacity for 500 was placed at the heart of the scheme. In part this was to accommodate the needs of the Musical Society, now expanded to support a large chorus, two symphony orchestras (the second of these was normally conducted by an undergraduate) and a wind orchestra, all under the supervision of a musical director. Beginning with Boris Ord, this position has been filled by a succession of King's Fellows; from Ord the baton passed to David Willcocks, then to Philip Ledger and then, in 1982, to Stephen Cleobury. There can be no doubt that this long-standing tradition of King's involvement with CUMS has provided great opportunities for talented musicians from the College, a number of whom

Five go off in a Land Rover

Anthony Figgis

Why describe a journey undertaken 50 years ago, to a country which no longer exists, by five old codgers all now aged around 70? Because, at least in my case, it was one of the best of many good things about King's. It wouldn't have been possible without help from the travel fund at King's.

A bit pretentiously, we called ourselves the 'Cambridge-Black Sea Expedition'. It was 1961, one of the first years in which ordinary Western visitors were allowed to take cars into the Soviet Union. Ours was a battle-scarred Land Rover. Lovingly, we painted a board in Cambridge blue to announce our mission, and stuck it on top. And off we went to Leningrad, via the ferry from Tilbury to Goteborg, and on through Finland.

Few of today's undergraduates can perhaps understand the fear which existed in those days of another war in general and of the Soviet Union in particular. I've no doubt that to some of us at King's at the time, those who saw themselves as the spiritual successors of Beatrice and Sidney Webb, the Soviet military and space machine was not a threat but a glorious promise: had Gagarin not just been the first man in space? And was the Soviet Union not the answer to American domination? But for many people, certainly for me with my bourgeois background, Lenin, Stalin and now Khruschev were not names to admire. We approached the Soviet border at Viborg excited, but apprehensive. And sure enough, we felt the dragon's breath almost at once: as we drew away from the border on the Soviet side, all formalities correctly completed, a large black limousine slid out of a side street, occupied by four hefty specimens of Soviet manhood. A coincidence, surely? They couldn't be following us – we weren't that important. Or could they? Could the mighty Soviet state need to keep tabs on a ragbag of undergraduates? As the Zil behind us turned one corner after another, black and leisurely but menacing, we realized that we were indeed its prey. For the next two months an endless succession of Zils and Volgas followed us every yard of the way, through Leningrad and Moscow, to Kharkov, Rostov, the Black Sea, Tbilisi, back over the Caucasus, and out into Czechoslovakia at Uzhgorod. Always with four hefty occupants.

The trip was an introduction to group dynamics, or rather to the vagaries of human nature – seven weeks is a long time to spend all together in a Land Rover. Ours had only three seats, one for the driver and two for passengers, one of whom had the gearstick between his knees. We took turns at the wheel, though one of us less often than the others, after an accident earlier involving a hen. We had not stopped to pick the poor creature up, leaving this privilege to the four heavies in the car behind. For a few uncomfortable miles, we thought we might be the victims of a show trial for sabotaging the hen count in the Five-Year Plan. Among other things, the hen incident intensified the competition for the only good passenger seat. One of our number suddenly became afflicted by headaches when taking his turn in the back. And indeed the back was, well, different. At the start of each new day, we fashioned a chaise longue on either side on top of the camping gear and the cooking pots, facing backwards. Sleep was not possible, except at the risk of waking up with the imprint of a saucepan on one's rear, or sometimes one's trousers full of the remains of that morning's breakfast. But a ride in the back did provide light relief, thanks to the heavies. From time to time we lost our way and did a U-turn. And from time to time we just did U-turns, to see what happened. Always the heavies would pass us, still going in the other direction, affecting nonchalance, not making eye contact, and not responding to our friendly waves. Always, once past us, they would make a wild-west turn with screeching brakes, fearful of losing us as we sped away in the opposite direction.

Thanks to Peter Reddaway, who had acted as a Russian-speaking guide for British Council visitors in Cambridge, we saw sides of Soviet Russia which most visitors would not have seen. We were entertained by the Youth Section of the House of Friendship in Moscow, a hideous building where we consumed vodka and gherkins, and met the composer Khachaturian, who not surprisingly seemed bored and was clearly the duty celebrity for that day. We had an introduction to someone in the Embassy. This august personage offered us a bath, which we thought mildly offensive, and lunch, which was more welcome. But the Embassy's sausages and mash were as nothing compared to the warmth and kindness with which we were greeted by Peter's Russian friends: unforgettable meals in leafy gardens, with every treat which our hosts could afford, the table sagging with stuffed peppers, smoked meat and fresh tomatoes. Those lunches sing in the memory. Scruffy students we were, but we were regaled like monarchs. It was a wonderful introduction to the generosity of ordinary Russians.

Anyone who goes to Russia should not miss a visit to Yasnaya Polyana, the home of Leo Tolstoy. The house is not grand, and the garden not well kept, at least at that time. The whole place was like us – scruffy. But it sits in gentle countryside, unhurried, unpretentious, patient, permanent. Tolstoy's life there was sometimes tempestuous, especially his relations with his wife. But the place meant so much to him that it breathes his spirit. You half expect to see him tilling the fields in bare feet, as he did, or hear his pen scratching out another chapter of *War and Peace* in his study. We left the place feeling refreshed after the grimness of the local towns, and hoped that our accompanying heavies felt the same.

It was teasing the heavies that led us to our Lucky Escape. Or rather to our Stupid Escapade. Knowing the high cost of food in the Soviet Union, and with an exchange rate amounting to a tax on tourism of at least 100 per cent, we had tried to get sponsorship from various food firms before we set off. Only one – a manufacturer of marmalade – had responded. This meant that our campsite meals for two months consisted mostly of bread (outrageously expensive) and marmalade. Taking Soviet currency out of the country was not allowed. So when we reached Lvov on our last evening, off we went to a restaurant to spend our surplus roubles. We had a bottle of wine, probably two, possibly three. While this little celebration was in progress the heavies, all four of them, were patrolling the pavement outside. A promising situation: four of them, five of us. Why not pay the bill and then give them the treat they'd been waiting for: something not just to follow but actually to chase. So, out we went and all ran off in different directions, making our separate ways back to the campsite.

Next day we arrived at the bleak border crossing into Czechoslovakia, the original blasted heath. No one else was making the crossing, except one Russian who leapt from his car to kiss the ground as soon as he was safely back on Soviet soil. We were confronted by two privates from the Red Army, each with an automatic rifle. They ushered us inside a shed. One private mounted guard, while the other thrashed each one of us in turn – at chess. Six hours later, hungry and thoroughly frightened, we were allowed to go. Each of us in turn had been taken to a side room, interviewed by an official with a face of stone, stripped and searched. Our films were developed or confiscated and the seats of the Land Rover slit, in a fruitless search for … what? We were invited to clear off from the Soviet Union and told that we would not be welcome to return. It was only when we got to Vienna, late that night, that we heard that the Berlin wall had started to go up the previous day, tightening the screw of international tension another several turns.

We were lucky that our escapade in Lvov on our last evening, our U-turns, and one or two other misdemeanours (not to mention the hen) didn't get us into more trouble. One does not tease a bad-tempered animal. And the Soviet Union was bad-tempered. Stalin was gone. Khruschev had made his 'secret speech'. Some slight relaxation was in the air (otherwise we and our elderly Land Rover would not have been let in). But it was before the days of the Helsinki Conference or any active (and misleading) policy of 'peaceful co-existence', one year before the Cuba crisis. The memoirs of Oleg Gordievski, once the head of the KGB station in London, have revealed many things about the ruthless aggression of the Kremlin in those days and later. For anyone with direct experience of the Soviet Union, or its miserable empire in Eastern Europe, it seems a miracle that such denials of personal and national freedom can have been swept away almost without a shot being fired.

Of course, shots were later fired, especially in Chechnya. And we have not yet seen the full consequences of the collapse of the Soviet system. But the Soviet Union at the time we were there seemed likely to last, and perhaps indeed to 'bury' the Western democracies, as Khruschev boasted. When Lech Walesa was asked in an interview in 1985 how long it might be before Poland was free, he first avoided answering, then said softly 'maybe 100 years'. Four years later, the miracle had happened. So, thanks be for Gorbachev, even if he didn't at first intend all that followed.

What are the prospects for Russia now, and for its dealings with the outside world? I have not been to Putin's Russia, unlike two of our party in 1961 (Peter Reddaway, who is now Emeritus Professor of Political Science and International Relations at George Washington University and Jonathan Steele, columnist and senior foreign correspondent of *The Guardian*). The other two of us were Duncan Noel-Paton, an Emmanuel man but an honorary Kingsman for purposes of the trip, and our brilliant photographer Patrick Finn). Peter and Jonathan would be much better qualified than I am to comment on Russia's prospects under Putin. But to me, looking at the sweep of history, it is not a surprise that Russia is once again ruled by an autocrat with little time for the niceties of parliamentary government. Is Putin really such a bad thing? (This question, I realize, risks offending the political sensibilities of many past and present Kingsmen and Kingswomen.) Whatever one's answer, in spite of Putin's contempt for the liberties essential to democracy, for a free press and for the rule of law, he is genuinely popular with many ethnic Russians. (Not, of course, with the Chechens or other minorities, especially in the Caucasus.) His assertion of Russia's interests has given the Russian people a new feeling of self-worth. The collapse of Soviet communism, and of the Soviet empire, was welcome to almost everyone outside Russia. But to many inside, it was intensely humiliating. Russia after all occupies one-sixth of the world's land surface. It is more than twice as large as any other country. The cruel description of it in the dying days of the Soviet Union as 'Upper Volta with rockets' may not have been far from the mark – the life of the average Russian in those days was, and still is, far from luxurious. But the citizens of the Soviet Union knew that they had a space programme, fine scientists and athletes, and that the world respected and even feared them. To go from that to the chaos and bankruptcy of the Yeltsin era, almost in the twinkling of an eye, was bitter gall indeed. Of course, Putin's Russia is corrupt, financially and morally. Of course elections are rigged. But we should not imagine that if a truly free election were mounted in Russia tomorrow, Putin would not be likely to come out on top. He knows what he wants, and the public seems to trust him to solve more of Russia's problems than any current alternative.

And the problems are immense. An unbalanced economy, a falling birthrate, social deprivation on a massive scale, alcoholism, poor communications, corruption. But Russia also has great assets – its raw materials, its education system, the capacity of its people for endurance. Global warming and looming shortages of energy seem likely to test the endurance and capacity for sacrifice of all countries over the coming decades. Russia, it seems to me, is somewhat better placed to surmount these challenges than the United States or Britain. Whatever the shortcomings of Putin, he is not a psychopathic tyrant like

From the left: Jonathan Steele, Anthony Figgis, Duncan Noel-Paton, Peter Reddaway and Patrick Finn.

Stalin or a risk-taking adventurer like Khruschev. He is a realist, who in spite of his bluster knows Russia's weaknesses, including in the military sphere. He is also able to exploit her strengths, sometimes brutally, as Ukraine has discovered over gas supplies. Fears in Eastern Europe that a resurgent Russia might once again threaten their independence are understandable but, in my view, wide of the mark; there is no evidence that Putin wishes to take on the problems of those or any other countries in addition to his own. But as for asserting himself when he sees Russia's interests threatened, including by meddling in their internal affairs, that he will certainly do. He may be in charge in Russia in one guise or another for many years – unless of course, like so many other Russian autocrats of the past, he falls victim to an assassin's bullet or a terrorist's bomb. Russia's democratic partners in the outside world need to convince him that Russia's interests and theirs, for instance over Georgia or Iran, can be made to coincide. That will call not only for skill but patience, another commodity of which the Russians have almost unlimited supplies.

So what did King's give me, in supporting the trip? Lifelong friendships certainly, and a lifelong interest in foreign affairs. But other things too. One of those is a realization that however much we may criticize conditions in Britain, we are lucky to live in a country where one is allowed to do just that: criticize.

A naturalist becomes a scientist

Richard Fortey

During Charles Darwin's bicentenary in 2009 the Cambridge historian Jim Secord showed me a newly discovered painting of the great naturalist when very young clutching a potted plant to his bosom. From the first, it seems, the *Beagle* voyager knew exactly where his interests lay. Darwin later developed a passion for beetles, then geology, then barnacles, then orchids, and finally tried to embrace the whole biosphere. Naturalists, it seems to me, are just born ready-made. They cannot help it.

I was created that way, too. My earliest memories are concerned with trying to pick out the common British birds, using the *Observer Book of British Birds*, whose illustrations now seem so inadequate. But it got me through at least the abundant native species. I had slightly better flower books, and anyway, flowers don't hop away into the bushes, so they could be anatomized close up. A diffuse poetry seeped into me by way of the flowers' common names: forget-me-not, fritillary, foxglove, cowbane, quinsywort. My father was a fisherman, and much of my childhood was spent in what would now be termed 'species-rich unimproved meadows' but were then just fields full of flowers: with marsh orchids, meadowsweet, ragged robin. He fished, I botanized. An old photograph shows my sister with an armful of orchids – so many plucked that there would be a prosecution for it nowadays. But it is habitat change that has caused the decline in orchids in southern Britain, not flower picking. That picture now has a kind of lost innocence.

Shortly afterwards I discovered fungi. These organisms had an added esoteric attraction. Nobody else in my circle of friends knew about fungi. The test of your taxonomic powers was in the eating – there was no greater challenge. A mistake might be fatal. Pretty soon, I ran out of literature to identify the more curious species, and took to drawing them and pickling them in formalin. My interest in these organisms has persisted to the present day. At one stage I thought I might become a mycologist, and perhaps there is still time even now.

Fortunately (perhaps) fossils intervened. By then living mostly in Wiltshire, I collected from the chalk all around Marlborough. On trips to London I was off to the Geology Museum, to go raptly round the displays with my own finds in hand, trying to make the best match; sea urchins, ammonites, clams – all grist to my naturalist's mill. The older the fossils the greater the attraction; to tune in somehow to messengers sent from deepest time was exciting beyond measure. Aldous Huxley and his brother had a similar sense of wonder, and recalled the naming of ancient names as having all the formality of a holy litany. Trilobites, being the oldest of all and the most glamorous, soon became my special focus. I seemed to be torn between many things. I loved reading and poetry and took art A-level, and could not really understand why one should be 'arts or science' (I still don't). I often thought of a quotation from George Eliot that seemed to sum me up at that stage in my life: 'I flutter all ways but fly in none.' But my grammar school offered geology as an option, which was most unusual in the 1960s, so the trilobites won. I sleepwalked into King's for no better reason than that a previous pupil from Ealing Grammar School, Peter Sheldrake, had managed to go there. I knew nothing about the place. The telegram from John Broadbent informing me of my exhibition was astonishing: I don't think I knew what an exhibition was.

So this story is one of failure at the beginning. I knew nothing of what it meant to be a Kingsman. I was a naturalist, who liked and tried to write poetry, but did not have much idea about science. As a grammar school boy, the lingering public school ethos that hung over King's was dimly objectionable. Nobody in my family had ever known Dadie Rylands, and I could never quite understand why it was considered important. The Annual

Report with its interlinked list of dynasties was mystifying at best. The Provost (Noel Annan) seemed to speak a language of power and influence that had nothing to do with a boy with no money and no contacts. My friends were all English scholars, and some of them have remained friends. Maybe we were all equally confused about entering such a beautiful and mysterious place, and about being expected to be part of some kind of Establishment that we simultaneously desired and rejected. We smoked Player's Number 6 (so cheap, so awful) and vaguely tried to get laid.

But I did begin to meet College scientists. The zoologist George Salt FRS invited me home to his house in a Victorian villa towards the Chesterton edge of town – as was his practice with all new students. Although he could not have been more kind, it was an extraordinarily formal occasion. His wife referred to him throughout as 'Salty' as if he were a packet of crisps. A clock ticked ponderously in the background and I imagine that he was as relieved as I was when the occasion was over. The cake was not terribly good, either. Later, I looked at his collected reprints in the College Library and marvelled at the elegance and care of his experimental work on the ecology of insects. I tried very hard with my essays, but I suspect they were mostly routine, if assiduous. Max Walters was responsible for my botanical education. He had compiled the distribution of native plants throughout the British Isles, and was deeply committed to the Cambridge Botanical Garden, which I loved. I, too, cared about the number of species of bedstraws (*Galium*) in Britain or the subdivisions of the helleborines. Somehow I failed to convey my real passion as a naturalist, and he never sought me out. To this day I am unsure whether the failure was mine. I suppose I was trying to find some way out of anonymity. I may have felt like a Darwin without a Henslow, though I would not have known it at the time, and anyway I suspect the comparison is altogether too grandiose. Maybe it was simply that I did not yet understand what it meant to be a scientist.

However, the trilobites did not let me down. At the end of my second year, after doing respectably in Part 1b, I had the chance to go to the island of Spitsbergen in the high Arctic as part of a University expedition. WB Harland of Caius College led the assault. As a Quaker of unimpeachable integrity Harland made sure that these adventures were primed with bully beef and porridge and minimal trimmings, but adventures they certainly were. They would not now be permitted by Health and Safety legislation. Small boats dodged between ice floes to deliver nascent scientists to bits of the remote island. It was an adventure merely to get to base camp, a long and sickening boat journey across the maelstrom northwards from Norway. Seasoned sailors turned ashen at the prospect. Unseasoned sailors turned ashen from the experience. Most people arrived safely. But John Kirton had died after an accident in the field the year before, so a certain nervousness was in order.

I had been scheduled to be field assistant to Geoff Vallance, who had just completed Part II Natural Sciences. Interesting fragments of trilobites had been discovered by chance the previous year, and this was an opportunity to confirm the occurrences. Virtually nothing was known about fossils of Ordovician age from the island so it was pioneering work, of a kind that was rarely available even then, in 1967. The Beatles' *All you need is love* was top of the hit parade. It seemed that the question of what I should read in my final year had been solved serendipitously (always the best way for ditherers). It must be Geology. We eventually made the camp that was our home for eight weeks on a bleak peninsula in northern Spitsbergen. In continual daylight we could explore the strata as we wished. The fossils proved to be an unqualified thrill, as they were so obviously unnamed species. Vallance and I gave the new trilobites nicknames in the field: 'broad-brimmed Fred' and 'narrow-brimmed Fred' were two of them, but there were many more (the scientific names would have to follow). The weather was ghastly on that remote shore in northern Spitsbergen where our tents huddled on the shingle, but the rocks were superb.

We dined on dried meat bars and rice, with tinned lifeboat biscuits and margarine to follow. A day hammering rocks may seem like some kind of punishment, but to me it was an obsessive pleasure. Who knew what the next split might reveal? Five years later, 'broad brimmed Fred' became the new genus *Balnibarbi* – named after the country of eccentric natural philosophers visited by Lemuel Gulliver in Swift's famous satire.

King's had supported my trip to the Arctic, for which I had reason to be grateful forever. Not for the first time John Broadbent stepped in to offer encouragement to a diffident youth. The Supplementary Exhibition Fund made a donation that allowed me to purchase the necessary polar gear. A sleeping bag lined with eider feathers was the best that money could buy. It kept my feet warm for months. From a clothes store in Hungerford, Berkshire, I purchased long woollen combinations. The shop assistant was amazed and delighted to shift stock that had been languishing in a back room for several decades. He asked me if I might be interested in purchasing some spats as well. I told him that there was not much call for spats at 80 degrees north.

My luck redoubled for both good and bad reasons. Harry Whittington was the Woodwardian Professor of Geology in the Sedgwick Museum on Downing Street, and the acknowledged world expert on trilobites. He was the obvious person to supervise postgraduate research on the new finds from Spitsbergen. The bad side was that Vallance did not get a good enough degree to be that postgraduate. Instead, those new discoveries eventually fell into the lap of his field assistant, like an overripe plum. Chance, again, seemed to be on my side. However, while I whacked rocks on the bleak shores in the Arctic, I also had glimmers of hypotheses about the trilobites I was collecting and wrapping in old copies of *The Times*. I began to see how they might relate to developing theories of plate tectonics. I was starting to think like a scientist.

The connection back to King's at this point was through Dan MacKenzie, who is still a Fellow to this day. In the mid 1960s he was developing the mathematical model for plate movements that would make him famous. I do not believe I met him face to face during my undergraduate career, but I was allowed to admire him from a distance, as one might a special astronomical phenomenon. I timorously adopted some of the deductions that could be made about how plate movements should influence fossil faunas. I took them with me into my doctoral studies, happy to have found an occupation at last to call my own. I may not have turned into a machine for grinding out hypotheses, as Darwin famously described his mature scientific self, but a few new and testable ideas bubbled up from somewhere that at least allowed me to enter the same club. My friend the poet and classicist Robert Wells seemed to approve of my devotion to ancient fossils and what could be made of their world; it had a curious poetry all its own, he said. My contributions to the Cambridge slim volumes of verse (like the College's *Pawn*) diminished. Perhaps rather gratefully I withdrew more from College life to become a typical 'grey man' – a common description applied at that time (and maybe still) to toilers in laboratories by flamboyant students in the humanities. Ah! If only they knew … the grey men carried a jewel of unparalleled brilliance that did not require worldly display or superficial wit: the scientific method.

Having no opportunity to stay in Cambridge, I left to work in the British Museum (Natural History) – or the 'BM' as it was universally known at that time by natural scientists. A rather curiously shaped peg had found a fairly matching esoteric hole in which to fit. The next two decades were spent in single-minded pursuit of the same fossil animals I had cracked out from the rocks in northern Spitsbergen. Trilobites took me around the world, at a time when that was still a privilege: to America, China, Australia, Africa and Wales. They made me well known to a small group of specialists. Papers piled up to prove it. One did not measure success then by the number of readers (or impact factor as it might be known today) but I suppose by some sort of scholarly perfection that was never truly attainable. I joined a group of scientists in the Museum who did not

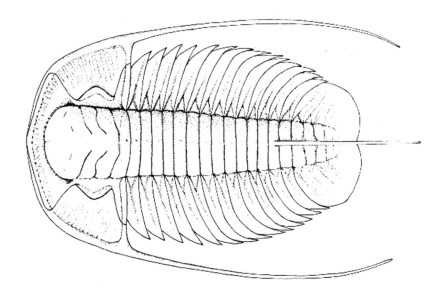

One of the trilobites discovered on Spitzbergen: Balnibarbi pulvurea, *known in the field as 'broad-brimmed Fred'.*

usually make the obituary columns, but whose determination to map the natural world may yet provide a record to tease the conscience of future generations of our own species. The world is changing fast, and museums will provide an archive of what we have done to it: a conscience, if you prefer. But as far as I was concerned, the naturalist had finally become a scientist.

Except I don't really trust this version of events: it seems too neat. The naturalist and even the poet were always trying to reassert themselves. Keeping the lid on these less disciplined *personae* in the interests of a career in a distant arm of the civil service was not easy. The trouble came with the routine of the scientific paper, where style counts for little, and only clarity is important. Many papers are written to a formula. Some scientists tend to talk about 'writing up' with a sigh, as if the important stuff has been done, and a somewhat disagreeable chunk of drudgery remains. The ideas or the data are the important stuff, and there is certainly no room for idiosyncrasy in the world of peer review. If one suffers from writer's itch, scientific writing does not provide the right kind of scratch, even though it does serve to advance the career. A kind of *samizdat* life became necessary. I wrote three humorous books under two pseudonyms to satisfy that itch. I had even previously used one of my pen names – WC Bindweed – to write funny memos that got distributed to my friends through the internal post of the Natural History Museum (as it had now become). I published a book of rhymes about dinosaurs in homage to Ogden Nash. Clearly, something had to be done.

At last, when I wrote a book called *The Hidden Landscape* (published in 1993) the naturalist and the scientist had a chance to join in writing that had some merit of its own. My exploration of the influence of geology on the British countryside brought in flowers and fungi and literature and people to provide a richer mix. In a way, I had to rediscover that omnivorous boy who had wanted to learn the whole story of *everything*. The difference between a scientist, grey or not, and the naturalist or general reader is that the former is primarily interested in theory, while the latter engages through narrative. I tried to tell the story of our islands as vividly as I could, without neglecting the scientific underpinning. Readers seemed to approve of this approach. Four books have now followed *The Hidden Landscape* exploring the history of life and of the planet, and reconciling the naturalist and the scientist between the same covers. The canvas is about as broad as can be by comparison with my years of research. But I wonder about this long intellectual journey; I wonder if, in the end, I have after all become a typical Kingsman.

'Something to be clever about'

Richard Hamblyn

A plaque on the wall of the Eagle pub on Bene't Street, Cambridge, just around the corner from the old Cavendish laboratory, records the moment, on 28 February 1953, when Francis Crick and James Watson burst into the saloon bar and announced to the bemused lunchtime drinkers that they had discovered the secret of life. Though it sounds like the opening premise of a thousand well-worn jokes – 'a man walks into a bar …' – the pair had been in earnest, for they and their co-researchers had long been aware that unravelling the structure of DNA would transform forever the understanding of all life on earth. 'Of course they never meant to call it DNA', as one of those thousand jokes goes on; 'they just ran in to the bar and shouted: "We've discovered the secret of life! Danaaaa!"'

Crick and Watson, the great double act, were inseparable during those two Cambridge years (1951–3), in the lab, down the pub, on their long daily walks along the Backs, although they fell out badly in 1968 after Watson published *The Double Helix*, much of which was written in a room in King's – 'overlooking the big green lawn that fronted Clare College', he recalled – where Watson spent his 1965 sabbatical at the invitation of the biologist Sydney Brenner. Prickly, boastful and sexist beyond parody (women are referred to throughout the book as 'popsies'), Watson's account of the great discovery was nevertheless a revelation, and did much to change the way that scientists were perceived by the wider culture. From its opening line: 'I have never seen Francis Crick in a modest mood', the book set out to expose the tensions, jealousies, intrigues and infighting that attended the most important scientific achievement since Darwin's *Origin of Species*. As Sir Lawrence Bragg observed in the foreword that he agreed to write before he'd seen the finished thing, 'those who figure in the book must read it in a very forgiving spirit.' Crick had been especially annoyed by Watson's descriptions of his manic personality and overloud laugh, for which Crick's friends blamed his perennial failure to secure a college fellowship. 'There was always King's', as Watson recalled, 'opulently nonconformist and

Crick and Watson.

clearly capable of absorbing him without any loss of his or its character. But despite much effort on the part of his friends, who knew he was a delightful dinner companion, they were never able to hide the fact that a stray remark over sherry might bring Francis smack into your life.'

In fact Crick's antipathy to college culture ran deeper than Watson realized. As a convinced atheist who detested the material trappings of religion almost as much as its mental symptoms, he hated the sight of the college chapels, especially the inescapable hulk of King's Chapel, which he and Watson passed every day during their post-lunch walks along the Backs. He thought such places incompatible with education, and even put up the £100 prize money for an essay competition on 'What should be done with the college chapels?' As he told the editor of *Varsity*, Christianity

was all very well between consenting adults in private, but it should not be taught to the young. Only a secular college would do, and in 1960 he became a founding Fellow of Churchill College which, as a specialist centre for science teaching, was to be the only Cambridge college without a place of worship. The following year, however, the Churchill trustees voted to accept a generous donation towards the building of a chapel, at which betrayal, as he saw it, Crick immediately resigned his fellowship. So it's a little ironic that one of the best-known photographs of Crick and Watson together, taken during one of their riverside walks, features the great stranded ark of King's College Chapel rearing behind them in the rain, blocking out the afternoon sky.

I often thought about Crick and Watson's collaborative adventures during the four years I spent at King's, to where I'd moved in 1990 to study for a PhD on 18th-century topography. My supervisor, Dr (now Professor) Peter de Bolla, the College's Director of Studies in English, had published an acclaimed book on 18th-century aesthetics and was buoyantly enthusiastic about my research proposal, an evasively worded document that I had attempted to reinforce with an armoury of terms – 'apprehension', 'ideology' and 'the gaze' – that I had picked up only a short time before. I was, I discovered, Pete's first doctoral supervisee – at least the first that he had taken on from scratch – so the situation was new to both of us; but little did I know, when I climbed to the top of E staircase for the first of our many supervisions in his capacious, sunlit office in the Gibbs Building, that I was embarking on a journey that would change the course of my life. That series of supervisions – at least one per month for the four years I was there – remains the most stimulating intellectual and imaginative encounter that I have ever known, an unfolding four-year conversation that centred on 18th-century books and ideas, but from which emerged new ways of thinking about historical research, about what it means to try to think about the past, about the rise and divergence of academic disciplines, and the painfully apparent distinction to be made between 'writing' and 'writing up'.

For the first few months, at Pete's suggestion, I let the direction of my research be dictated by the primary sources, and, sure enough, as I began to plough through the 18th-century holdings of the University Library's Rare Books Room, I soon alighted on a theme worth pursuing, in the form of the competing meanings that congregated around certain landscape locations, particularly those landscapes in which new kinds of knowledge about the earth were being revealed. Time and again, a handful of recurring places – the Inner Hebridean island of Staffa; the Giant's Causeway in County Antrim; the Derbyshire Peak with its geological 'wonders'; the lakes and lead mines of Cumberland and Westmorland; the smoking craters of Mount Vesuvius – seemed to preoccupy the Georgian cultural imagination, and it was the curious narrative potency of these spaces, with their layerings of human and geological history, that became my subject during my time at King's, and has remained my favourite subject ever since. I had found what I wanted to write about, but the problem was it wasn't very 'literary' – at least not in the way that English literature tended to be studied at Cambridge. I was, after all, a member of the English faculty, and although the pursuit of cross-disciplinary research was not officially discouraged, it remained the case that the single-author study was the department's dominant research model, and I was always being asked who rather than what I was working on. But though one or two of the older professors were unhappy about my proposed research (and I had to argue my case when it came to applying for faculty funding), it turned out that I had been particularly fortunate in my choice of college. King's had a long tradition of testing disciplinary boundaries, and among its recent English Fellows had been such luminaries as Norman Bryson, John Barrell, Colin MacCabe and Lisa Jardine, scholars whose research had migrated freely across academic borders, greatly influencing not only their own areas of literary study, but also those of other, neighbouring disciplines such as the history of art, the history of ideas and the history of science. Pete had himself been taught at King's by Barrell and Bryson, and was sympathetic to the idea of pursuing a non-literary subject in a non-literary way from within the confines of an English department. So my interest in the history of science was free to flourish, and by the end of my second year I was attending the weekly graduate seminars at the History of Science department on Free School Lane, just around the corner from the Eagle pub, while immersing myself ever more deeply in the arcana of scientific knowledge, in the folds of which lay hidden – as it seemed to me in that first rush of unschooled enthusiasm – the greatest stories, the greatest narratives, the greatest dramas in the world. Nothing in the literary canon could compete with the fantastical realities (and unrealities) of scientific thought, while few of the writers whose lives I had studied seemed anything like as intellectually playful, restless and alive as did many of those long-dead scientists whose works I was excitedly devouring.

The truth was, I had always regretted not studying science. At school I had drifted towards the arts and humanities for the simple reason that I liked reading and didn't dislike writing essays. I had always been interested in science and mathematics, and had chosen to study biology over classics at O-level, but by the time it came to picking a subject to pursue at higher level, carrying on with English seemed the most natural – not to mention the easiest – choice. Plus, there was a certain cultural cachet that attached itself to the arts and humanities, an aura suggestive of creativity and the complex pleasures of the imagination, as well as an appealingly urbane indifference to official forms of knowledge such as science. The arts were cool; the sciences were not. As the biologist and Nobel laureate Sir Peter Medawar famously complained in the *New York Review of Books* in 1968, 'there is a widely prevalent opinion that almost any literary work, even if it amounts to no more than writing advertising copy or a book review, not to mention that PhD thesis on "Some little-known laundry bills of George Moore", is intrinsically superior to almost any scientific activity.' And although that particular outlook is beginning to disappear – due in part to the revival of popular science writing – there remain 'two cultures', as CP Snow famously characterized them, the literary and the scientific, whose respective practitioners seem content to misconstrue one another from across the disciplinary divide.

I'm convinced that much of this mutual mistrust stems from a cultural misunderstanding of the creative nature of science. Unravelling the structure of DNA, for example, was never a straightforward matter of plodding through laboratory results, testing them against an array of hypotheses until the 'prettiest' one emerged; it was more akin to the kind of intellectual games played by philosophers or literary theorists, in which moments of insight – inspiration, even – forged esoteric connections between ideas and observations that advanced the patterns of understanding. One of the more surprising disclosures of Watson's *The Double Helix* concerned the pair's unusual work routine, which involved taking long post-lunch walks around Cambridge, talking all the while about everything and anything as they meandered through the college courtyards and out along the Backs, so that 'talk replaced work, or rather work became talk', in the words of Crick's biographer, Matt Ridley. According to Watson, this regular truanting from the rigours of the lab had been a contributing factor in their bold creative breakthrough:

'The following morning I felt marvellously alive when I awoke. On my way to the Whim I slowly walked towards the Clare Bridge, staring up at the gothic pinnacles of the King's College Chapel that stood out sharply against the spring sky. I briefly stopped and looked over at the perfect Georgian features of the recently cleaned Gibbs Building, thinking that much of our success was due to the long, uneventful periods when we walked among the colleges or unobtrusively read the new books that came into Heffer's Bookstore.'

Such youthful informality hardly fitted the popular image of Nobel Prize-winning laboratory science, and a number of reviews of *The Double Helix* expressed dismay at the candour of Watson's revelations as well as disbelief that such a pair – 'two loudmouthed young men who devoted more time to talking and drinking than to experiment' – could have brought about the greatest triumph of 20th-century science. Yet all those post-lunch peregrinations, all those evenings talking nonsense in the pub – none of it had been a waste of time, it had all been part of the creative process, and had the pair been poets or painters rather than molecular biologists, the world would have indulged them with a smile. Once again it was Sir Peter Medawar who pointed out that, in Britain at least, a teenager of Watson's imaginative gifts would almost certainly have been steered towards literary studies; but though the Cambridge English faculty of the 1950s produced a number of graduates of outstanding ability – 'brilliant, inventive, articulate and dialectically skilful; right up in the Watson class' – 'Watson had one towering advantage over all of them: in addition to being extremely clever he had something important to be clever *about*.' And that, as Medawar went on to suggest (to the immense irritation of some of his readers) is the advantage that scientists continue to enjoy over most other people engaged in intellectual pursuits: they have something to be clever about. This, of course, is not to say that one cannot be clever about Shakespeare or Kierkegaard or Morecambe and Wise; it's just that the great scientific questions seem somehow bigger, more looming, more outwardly urgent – life, the universe and everything – and, like WH Auden, who said that the company of scientists made him feel like a shabby curate who had wandered by mistake into a drawing room full of dukes, I was (and remain) slightly in awe of the territory they command.

Twenty years later, science remains my subject as a writer and historian, though I have long since abandoned the romanticized view of it that drew me towards it in the first place. I still experience the occasional moment of regret at having not pursued it through the proper channels, but there are advantages to maintaining an outsider's perspective on scientific matters, not least when trying to understand them in their wider cultural context. Climate change, for example, might have started off as a data-driven scientific concept, a hypothesis to be tested like any other, but it has since become the overarching narrative of our age, a kind of secular prophecy that feeds into a wide range of cultural anxieties about our relations with the natural world, our obligations towards developing nations, and our responsibilities to the generations to come.

It's a subject that impinges upon everything and everyone, so I'm pleased to see that King's College Library – where I once manned the desk on the graveyard shift for £2.20 an hour – has built up an important and near-comprehensive collection of

several hundred climate change publications from a wide range of disciplines across the sciences and the humanities. The King's College Global Warming Collection, to use its official title, is prominently housed in the main Library, just beyond the issue desk, where it stands as a visible reminder of the cultural and scientific challenges that face us as we head off deeper into the 21st century, as well as a symbol of my old College's continuing commitment to encouraging the variously fragmented disciplines to talk to one another across the echoing cultural divide.

Parr's King's II

Martin Parr

Battling with Nicky

Geoff Harcourt

In February 1964 Geoff Harcourt, then a recently appointed lecturer in Economics, was asked by Nicky Kaldor, the brilliant economist and Fellow of King's, to present a paper to his research students' seminar at King's. The occasion became somewhat heated, and Harcourt, who came down with mumps the following day, wrote a letter describing the seminar to a good friend at Adelaide University, Eric Russell, also a Kingsman. Harcourt was still smarting from some of the things Kaldor had said to him and 45 years later this letter conveys the spirited nature of arguments during this formative period of Economics at Cambridge.

❶ **NK:** *Nicholas (Nicky) Kaldor (1908–86). A Hungarian by birth, Nicky came to King's and the Cambridge Faculty after the Second World War. He made highly original contributions to economics, drawing on his knowledge of the classical economists and his enthusiastic adoption of Keynes's ideas.*

❷ **Luigi:** *Luigi Pasinetti (1930–). A Fellow of King's and a teacher in the Faculty from the late 1950s until the mid 1970s when he returned permanently to Italy. He is probably the last major system builder in economics.*

❸ **Hahn:** *Frank Hahn (1925–) came to Cambridge as a lecturer in 1960. He was a Fellow of Churchill. After several years as a Professor at LSE in the 1960s, he returned to a Chair at Cambridge, succeeding Richard Kahn, where he was a most important intellectual influence.*

I've at last had a face to face battle with Nicky❶ about my paper on him. I read it to his King's research students seminar last Tuesday (at his request). I think I've made an enemy for life in him (though Luigi❷ says time heals all and let things develop gradually); since, despite the ridicule he attempted to pour on me in the course of the paper, he would not speak to me afterwards (except in grudging replies to any advances I made, which soon ceased); he spent part of the week-end before the paper talking with Hahn❸ about it, and part of Monday before talking to Arrow.❹ Hahn was to come on Tuesday but his ulcers got the better of him (he lives completely on his nerves) and he had to go to bed. Luigi was there and acted as peacemaker, and fair play securer - as much as he could. Nicky's ploy was to get Hahn along before to undermine me with such remarks, + a page of equations, as - "your models under-determined, you know" (wrong, he hadn't understood it, as he later admitted), "your result is not unique, some chap in *R.E.S.*❺ gets Nicky's results without the need for your conclusions about behaviour - you haven't read this, you should have, you know". Of course, when I did look at it I found (1) I had glanced at it before and (2) did not follow it up because it made an assumption about capital - that it was flexible and in the S.R. as well as the L.R.❻ - which it was the whole point of my paper to deny and then work out the consequences for N.K's model.

Anyway, to start at official Round I, Nicky's ploy in actual debate was to keep the play in his corner by tremendous playing to the gallery - smiled asides which say "we here in *Cantab.*, know what's coming and what it's all about but look at this ignorant hick of a colonial floundering around, let's lead him on until he cuts his own throat". And N.K. being the supremely confident artist that he is, and some of the research students being the slobbering curs that they are, every time he lifted his leg at a suitable tree they barked and sniffed approvingly, or so it seemed to me and some of *my* friends there. Luigi even went so far as to tell them, i.e. the res. students, afterwards, that in future they should rally round the speaker since Mr. Kaldor was quite able to take care of himself! The meeting abounded with statements such as:
N.K.: "That's where you're wrong";
G.C.H.: "No, that's where we disagree".
But he never allowed me sufficient chance to point out the context in which the argument was set, or to explain why I made the assumption I did, or why I thought they were a fair representation of *what he himself had said*. Whenever I got close to this he took over; or tried to make me look a nana; or lead me up a false track where my head could be cut off. And while I did not give too much ground - I had not made clear certain assumptions about relative wages - I gave more than I needed, and did not always realise the comebacks that were open to me. (I have, however, written them up subsequently, so that if he replies to me in *A.E.P.*,❼ I'll really be able to go for him.) Evidently, I got a little heated in places, e.g. he said something was nonsense, I shouted that

❹ **Arrow:** *Kenneth J Arrow, at the time Fellow of Churchill College and later joint recipient of a Nobel Prize in Economic Sciences for pioneering contributions to general economic equilibrium theory and welfare theory.*

❺ **RES:** *Review of Economic Studies.*

❻ **SR:** *short run and LR: long run. Technical terms for theoretical lengths of time derived from Marshall's principles.*

❼ **AEP:** *Australian Economic Papers.*

❽ it was not nonsense, but the general concensus was that I at least held my own against unfair odds and unfair rules. Luigi said that the differences between us came out clearly in the end, and that given my assumptions I was right – and his, he was also. It boils down to 2 main points. When N.K. talks in the context of his models, of an increase in planned investment, does this mean an increase in the *value* of investment or the actual *amount* of investment; I have always thought the latter was the reasonable interpretation of what he was saying though it meant either an undefined or a zero-elastic demand curve for investment goods and leaves undertermined the split-up of current investment production. But he claims he means the former, with the implication that *after several periods*, it will lead to an increase in real capital formulation. My main point has always been that this increase had to occur within *one* period, otherwise this distributive mechanism has not worked in the S.P. – but now he won't accept my definition of period – though it is taken from *his* work. He also says he is using a one-sector model, and that a two-sector model cannot be shown on his diagrams. This can easily be shown to be wrong, but I didn't think of the obvious answer at the seminar.

The other main point is that he won't allow the equation which I give for steel prices to hold Once there is a change in investment. I have reasons (which I've put in another paper which I gave him) for thinking it wrong too, but they are *not* his. The actual outcome was inconclusive, though he rang Hahn afterwards to say that I'd admitted I was wrong. (I was about wages) And there the matter will rest for*ever*, unless he publishes something in *A.E.P.* to which, if it is what I think it is, I'll reply. All told, I thought his performance rather poor, not so much for the gamesmanship of the seminar, though you must be rather petty if you feel you have to score in front of research students by making your opponent look more of an idiot than you know for a fact, that he is; but for the petty way he snubbed me afterwards. Of course, it's not so much me he's getting at as J.R.❾ whom he seems to be jealous of (silly) and exasperated with (often understandable). She and Kahn wanted a ball by ball description which Vincent Massaro and I gave them. Kahn kept his counsel, as always, Joan seemed to think I was right, but not always, I sometimes think, for the right reasons.

One research student chimed in with a real blow below my belt which made it obvious that he'd not done his homework ; but that he would curry favour with N.K. for it. I said to him afterwards, "Look laddie, if you want to hit me below the belt in public, at least read the literature beforehand"; I got him to admit that he hadn't.

I find it a pity that I can't get on with Nicky because I like and admire him, but it doesn't worry me as I thought it would. One big question mark has been – will Cambridge be as pleasant for us when Nicky returns? Answer, yes, it'd be nice to be friendly with him but it he doesn't want to be, who cares?

❽ 'If that is what NK really meant, it is inconsistent with what he argued in the relevant papers and also is a serious flaw in his later arguments, so I believe I was right both with my definition and the consequent critique that follows from it.' **(GH)**

❾ **JR:** *Joan Robinson (1903–83). Famous Cambridge economist who was in the forefront of most theoretical developments of the first three quarters of the 20th century.*

Endnote: 'Nicky and I did become friends. Shortly before he died he wrote me an appreciative letter about the review I had written in the *Economic Journal* of his Okun Memorial Lectures at Yale, 'Economics without Equilibrium'. After he died in 1986, I wrote an obituary article and a review article on him for *Economica* in 1988 and a review article of his last book, *Causes of Growth and Stagflation in the World Economy*. In my 2006 *The Structure of Post-Keynesian Economics: The Core Contributions of the Pioneers*, Nickey's seminal contributions played a large role in the narrative.' **(GH)**

Philosopher-Kings

Ross Harrison

Philosophy feeds on a diet of puzzles but here, to start, is one that is not nourishing. Who apart from the founder is commemorated in the Front Court with a freestanding monument? Even people who know the College well think that there isn't another one. Yet it's there, a transplanted Scottish sundial, tucked away near the Chapel in the northeast corner. When you read its inscription, you discover that it's a monument to a philosopher, WR Sorley.

Sorley had one of the oldest chairs in the University, the 17th-century Knightbridge Chair of Moral Philosophy. He was the first of three holders of this chair during the 20th century who were also Fellows of King's. He had the senior University chair when the great revolution happened at Cambridge that changed the subject in the English-speaking world. But he was not part of it; it was the work of Trinity men, Russell, Moore, and Wittgenstein. Apart from his history of British philosophy, Sorley is largely forgotten. The same is not so for the other two holders of the Knightbridge Chair: Richard Braithwaite and Bernard Williams. They are the philosophers I shall consider here.

Monuments last, as do books. Monuments can be observed after death and books can be consulted all over the world independent of the existence of their authors. But the centre of philosophy in a college is life rather than death, and what gives philosophy life is discussion. It is the ephemeral accidental contact between living people that makes the subject. Conversation counts and it can be captured, if at all, only in memory rather than by looking at monuments or books.

Philosophy has been so associated with Trinity that we might wonder how King's got into the act at all. One clue is GM Trevelyan's remark that the hinge on which Cambridge intellectual life turned was that of the north gate of King's. For that gate beyond the Chapel is the shortest route from Trinity to King's. The next clue is why people move, and we can solve that by remembering discussion. Men were moving because they all belonged to the same discussion society, whose proper name was the Cambridge Conversazione Society, usually known as the Apostles. All the Trinity men mentioned so

The Sorley sundial.

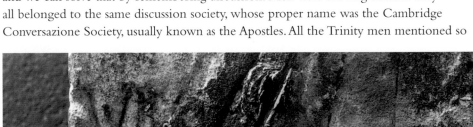

far, including Trevelyan, were members of this excessively well-known secret society. But their friends and fellow members were in King's, hence the importance of the gate.

Importance and King's gets us to Keynes. Keynes wasn't merely discussing with philosophers in the Apostles; he was a philosopher himself. He was elected a Fellow in 1909 on the strength of a philosophical dissertation. In 1912 Bertrand Russell wrote what he called his 'shilling shocker', the little book called *The Problems of Philosophy* with which so many students in King's and elsewhere have started philosophy ever since. They, quite properly, start with the first chapter on appearance and reality (the colour of the table). But if they looked at the short preface before it, they would see that Russell unsurprisingly thanks Moore. In fact he writes that he 'derived valuable assistance from unpublished writings of GE Moore and JM Keynes.' Only these two are mentioned and Keynes was there at the creation.

Once we have discussion and the Apostles as a clue, we can start to trace the apostolic succession. Keynes finally published his Fellowship dissertation in 1921 as *A Treatise on Probability* and early in the same year the Apostles elected an undergraduate King's mathematician, Richard Braithwaite. Later that year he proposed the election of another *are.*

I can't do 4 things; I doubt if I can do 3 or even 2; most people do 2; some kind of work and some kind of games; my 3 are Mathematics, Philosophy, and Political and Economic Theory – I can't manage in addition Oratory.

[...] from Braithwaite Broad Perception

undergraduate mathematician, 'Ramsey of Trinity'. (They knew each other through the Moral Sciences Club, of which more below.) Frank Ramsey was elected and the two undergraduate friends discussed philosophy. They discussed Keynes on probability. They met in Keynes's room at King's above Webbs Gate. Braithwaite consulted Keynes on whether to switch to another Part II. Shouldn't he do economics? No, said Keynes, philosophy is more difficult. And so Braithwaite switched to philosophy (or Moral Sciences, as it was then known), taking Part II in 1923.

At this time Wittgenstein was working his post-war penance as a schoolteacher in a remote part of Austria. Braithwaite and Ramsey went to see him in March 1924. Braithwaite said that he had to return to Vienna to see whether he had succeeded in the Fellowship election at King's. From that point on (or so Braithwaite told me) Wittgenstein knew that he wasn't a fully serious man. How could a mere college operation trump discussion with the master? But Braithwaite did get elected. (Dissertation on probability and induction; Keynes an elector; apostolic succession.) In the same year, Keynes further oiled the hinge on the discussion gate by importing Ramsey from Trinity to become a Fellow in Maths at King's.

King's and Richard were lucky: Ramsey was a genius. He himself was unlucky; he died, aged only 26, in 1930. But even in that short span he produced ideas and papers still influential in philosophy, foundations of mathematics, and economics. Richard, who was older, outlived his friend for a further 60 years as a Fellow of King's. A common thread about all the people mentioned so far apart from Moore is mathematics. (Russell and Keynes both read Maths as undergraduates.) If philosophy for these people starts with another subject, it is mathematics and science rather than classics or history. We get a scientific, technical approach to philosophy and a philosophical approach to science. Braithwaite made his reputation as a philosopher of science. When he was elected to the Knightbridge Chair he took more seriously than some that it was meant to be a chair in Moral Philosophy. He responded by giving an inaugural lecture, published as *The theory of games as a tool for the moral philosopher*; even in ethics he introduced a scientific approach.

No one could replace Ramsey (and Richard's first work was to edit his friend's posthumous papers). But some of the slack in discussion of the mathematical-philosophical axis was taken up by Alan Turing. No doubt embellishing the story, Richard told me how he had met Turing at lunch in King's one day in the 1930s. Turing had just run to Grantchester and back and breathlessly explained to Richard the great discovery he'd made as he jogged. 'Oh, sorry, oh,' said Richard. 'I say, Gödel, already done, last year.'

The other philosophically important discussion group during this time was the Moral Sciences Club. Unlike the Apostles it was not secret, but in those days you still had to get elected. Both Braithwaite and Ramsey were elected on the same day in May 1921. From the 1930s, for over 30 years, it met in Richard's rooms, H4 in King's (on the staircase nearest the Chapel in the Gibbs Building). It was still meeting in these rooms when I was an undergraduate. I remember on one occasion when a visiting speaker incautiously said that for action there had to be movement. Professor Braithwaite immediate got to his feet (he was a great interrupter of papers) and pressed vigorously against the wall, red-faced, straining and heaving, threatening to push out the front wall of Gibbs. 'Do you mean', he gasped as, immobile, he struggled with the wall, 'that I am doing nothing?'

A little after, he was the supervisor of a graduate friend of mine. My friend came to his room on H staircase to set out some of his philosophy of science. Richard listened, rose to his feet, extracted a chamber pot from a cupboard, undid his flies, and relieved himself. My friend suspended his exposition and it was only when Richard was sliding the pot back into its secret lair that he in turn remembered his social obligations. 'I say, I'm sorry,' he said, pausing and holding the filled chatty out to my friend. 'Do you want one?' Earlier, this same room was where the infamous incident of the poker took place at a meeting of the Moral Science Club when Wittgenstein either did or, alternatively, did not threaten Popper (who was the visiting speaker) with Richard's poker.

When I came to King's in 1975 as the philosophy Director of Studies, I started a discussion group, presumptuously called the Philosopher-Kings. It is still meeting 35 years later. I had the room that backed on to Richard's on the next staircase (G), and so forming a mirror image of his. We met fortnightly there for philosophical discussion (endless lifeblood of the subject), mainly undergraduates but including him. One evening, long before it was made famous by the best-selling book, he went through the poker incident, ignoring the symmetry by which everything in my room was reversed. 'Wittgenstein was here … Popper … and here … I was here'. (Richard's farewell paper to the Moral Sciences Club was appropriately entitled 'Egoism'.) According to Richard, as Popper talked Wittgenstein had merely been poking the fire. Violently.

Further up G staircase from where the Philosopher-Kings operated was the third King's Knightbridge professor, Bernard Williams. He shared a room with Gwyll Owen, the professor of ancient philosophy, and their common door had the philosophically puzzling notice, 'Knocking can not be heard'. This was the second of Bernard's three locations in King's. Completing the circle of this story, he started in Keynes's old room, decorated with naked Bloomsbury figures. Just like Richard before him as Knightbridge Professor, he worked from College and was still with the naked men and clothed women when I arrived. This was the time of his first books, *Morality* and *Problems of the Self*. After translation to my staircase, he wrote *Descartes*. (I remember meeting him on the stairs and he telling me that he was 'going round and round the Cartesian circle'.) While there, he was elected Provost, moved to the Lodge, and wrote the books, principally *Ethics and the limits of philosophy*, that make him still one of the most influential moral philosophers in the world.

In the first of these rooms, Bernard continued with the tradition he found on arrival of the Professor holding weekly discussions. Although open to all the University, many there came from King's. In one highly unusual session one of them took not just her grandmother but also her grandmother's new boyfriend to see the show. The presence of the unusual visitors prompted an unusual topic, the nature of philosophy. Presented with a topic, Bernard got the discussion going. It was a philosophical discussion about the nature of philosophy and, as a philosophical discussion, it exhibited typical quirks of the genre. It didn't answer the question directly, but instead talked round it, considering various possible lines of approach (how is philosophy different from science? how is it similar? is it a humanistic discipline? and so on). According to my informant, another King's student, it was the usual stimulating affair. However, it didn't satisfy the tourists. As they descended to Webbs Court, the grandmother observed loudly, 'You'd think that when he's devoted his life to the subject, he'd have some idea what it was.'

So: conversation, puzzles, performance art; philosophy lived through discussion. Through the 1930s in Richard's room, dominated by Wittgenstein, the Moral Sciences Club endlessly discussed whether King's College Chapel was on fire. Why did no one look outside and see? Later, in my room, there was a large box in the centre because I couldn't find anywhere else to put it. Lacking Wittgenstein himself, we in the Philosopher-Kings endlessly discussed his example of whether there was a beetle in the box. Why did we never open it and look?

Discussion is endless lifeblood of the subject. But one day, like life itself, it ends or at least passes as a baton to the next players. I came to the end of my time as Director of Studies, enriched with so many discussions with my students. One of my philosophical colleagues, Naomi Eilan, kindly invited all the King's philosophers to a farewell party in the Manor House at Granchester. This is a house that King's has had since the foundation, originally used as a retreat when there was plague in the city but then in temporary philosophical habitation. We talked along the river where once Turing ran and ruined their best frying pan by using it as a bat to play rounders in the garden. We sported near the Orchard where once earlier shades of King's had talked and played. All mere contingencies: accidents, conversations, philosophers, people.

conversation, representations in which it becomes both the image of a successful social order, and the means for stabilizing it.

In this now social and political sense, 'reciprocally' marks the era of coming democratization, the moment when the deferential subjects of a monarch are transformed into free citizens, active in a public sphere. It implies not just the fact of each person having the right to take a turn in the conversation, but the idea that that each turn is accorded equal value in any argument or dispute. In the ideal of fully reciprocal conversation, the force of argument is assessed by impartial reason rather than settled by hierarchy and status. This was the Enlightenment ideal of conversation; that was the practice of conversation at King's.

I took two things away with me from King's. The first was what I have tried to describe above: an abiding image of the academic life as a conversation – as interesting and as animated as it could possibly be. It meant that in missing King's, which I had been reluctant to leave, I everywhere tried to recreate its collegiality and its conversations.

The second grew out of my decision – probably the only good decision I made at Cambridge, aside from that of taking a year off – to take the Moralists' Paper. For doing it at King's turned out to mean working with a particularly enthusiastic and talented bunch of young (now not so young!) Fellows, including Colin MacCabe, John Forrester and Gareth Stedman Jones, as well as my lively and competitive peers. The work I did that year – immersed in the works of Freud, Marx and Wittgenstein, and animated by many hours of intense debate around Althusser and Thompson, Kuhn and Foucault, Derrida and Lacan, figures who formed the talking point of my generation – turned out to provide the guiding thread of my work and studies since then, however indirectly.

More particularly, it was in and through this body of work around the Moralists' Paper that Cambridge English became what some of us later referred to affectionately as King's English. King's English took the intense focus on textual analysis that is rightly considered as the heart of Cambridge English, and enriched it through the questions posed by theory and the complications offered by the contexts of history. In so doing it transformed what had started as a degree and training in literary criticism into a broader social and political criticism, a criticism of received ideas, across many different kinds of writing and textuality: political writing, the texts of everyday life, film, painting and television.

Much of this idea of King's English was epitomized in the work and in the conversation of Tony Tanner, who first interviewed me at King's. 'Why do you want to do English? Don't you want to do something else?' That was his repeated question. Was it a trick question, I wondered. How could I reply other than that I couldn't imagine doing anything else. 'Your headmaster says you are a master of the French poetry of the nineteenth century: Baudelaire, Mallarmé, Rimbaud and Verlaine. What do you think about them?' 'I think my headmaster must have been trying to impress you, or mixed me up with someone else. I don't know their work very well.' Somehow I was still offered a place.

I had elected to go to King's because Tony was teaching there, as well as because of the College's reputation as different and more radical than the other Cambridge colleges. This came through in the simple but – at the time – revolutionary fact that women were to be allowed in to the College for the first time.

I had read Tony's work *City of Words* as part of my preparation for the interview and the Entrance Exam, and had been totally blown away. Here was someone who was not only interested in contemporary writing, but also in American writing; and who not only read closely, but also brought into his reading the intellectual resources of a kind I had never come across before: sociology (Jules Henry and Erving Goffmann), anthropology (Lévi-Strauss), linguistics, psychoanalysis … everything was there. The book opened up completely new worlds to me, and conversations with Tony over the years continued to provide support, encouragement and stimulus. Like so many others, I always went to have lunch with him at King's whenever I came through.

Our final conversation, though neither of us knew it at the time, took place a few months before his death from cancer. He was very down in a way I'd never seen before, and lamented the fact that – unlike a number of his friends and peers, such as Edward Said – he felt that he had never attracted disciples. I said that he had done something far more important than that, and that was to teach people to read and think for themselves, and to take nothing at face value. He wasn't convinced, and we parted on a glum note.

To take nothing at face value; to criticize received ideas: this was the enduring lesson of King's English, and I guess of the College as a whole, just as of any successful educational institution. Among these received ideas, though, it must be said that the idea of conversation – and perhaps particularly as used here, as the frame and focus for my memories of King's – looms large.

After the grounding in ideas and analysis that studying in King's provided, what of conversation? For after Freud, after Marx, what can remain of Johnson's apparently confident appeal to reciprocity? The paradigm of conversation shifts from the easy conveyance of ideas from one person to another to a more troubled and uneasy exchange, so potentially fraught with projection and misunderstanding, that exchange hardly seems the right word.

A striking feature of the collegial conversation at King's that I've tried to describe was that – in line with the Enlightenment ideals it embodied – the real distance between student and teacher was suspended. This distance was suspended in collegial conversation. In this fluid medium, the reality of structural authority – as well as that of simple factors such as age and experience – was at least in part deferred, leaving the interlocutors free to engage reciprocally in conversation.

Like any formulation of an ideal, this idea of conversation simplifies; it emphasizes one dimension of a complex transaction, but, in focusing on this alone, marginalizes others. In reality, the mere suspension of differences and distance does not and cannot mean their annulment. In the event – the event of those formative conversations at King's – the reality of distance came through in the pressure to perform, and the real distance was present in the constant striving to overcome it.

Inside the tutorial or out, the pressure was on: to impress and to entertain, through wit and humour as well as through analysis and observation. Conversation was above all a performance of conversation, and I can still remember the almost-unconscious imitation of the speech patterns and vocabulary of my mentors that so often characterized my own performances. In that crucial year, my driving desire was to understand exactly in the way that my mentors appeared to understand, to become myself how I thought they were.

I hated leaving King's, and it was only in later years that I realized that it was only by leaving it that I was able to keep intact the ideal image of it that I had from my youthful, formative years there.

A darker side of College life only became visible from a distance and over time: how the College walls, which shielded you from the outside world, so that you could get your work done, also kept you in; how the security of enclosure also threatened closure; how what promised to protect you could end up imprisoning you. In the end, though the first word that comes to mind about King's is 'conversation', I now realize that that conversation was always more complex than I could have understood at the time.

'Please release me, let me go'

Simon Hoggart observes an Annual Congregation at King's

The old Trotskyists used to talk about the 'democracy of the committed', which meant that the people who could be bothered to turn up to meetings in the first place, and who had a very high boredom threshold, got to take the important decisions. Cambridge colleges are well aware of this problem, and so the Annual Congregation at King's College is compulsory for all Fellows. It is designed to create the democracy of the obliged to turn up.

Everyone knows that trying to persuade academics anywhere to agree on anything is like herding cats. Which is why it has to be done quickly, *en masse* and in conditions that – well, to say that it makes the Black Hole of Calcutta look like the Savoy ballroom would be an exaggeration, but not much of one. Given that this meeting is going to take some of the most important decisions facing the College, it moves along at quite a lick. Fellows have lectures to prepare, papers to write, students to teach, and even Free Cell to play on their computers.

Not that all the Fellows do turn up, thank goodness. At any one time, plenty are out of the country, or somewhere other than Cambridge, or just ill. (Or possibly malingering. Would Crick and Watson have figured out DNA if they'd been fretting about student numbers? Did Keynes spend his time dithering about underfloor heating?)

There were perhaps 80 people at the Congregation held on December 3rd, 2009, around two-thirds of the fellowship. Nevertheless the Senior Combination Room with its lurid crimson walls and portraits of great Kingsmen – normally the venue for coffee and a look at the papers, or a relaxed drink around dinnertime – was heaving, with dons perched wherever a pair of squeezed buttocks could be slotted in. It was a very King's occasion. A lack of a tie seemed to be quite as obligatory as the possession of a gown. The Bursar was the only Fellow I saw wearing anything round his neck. Ignorant of the unstated dress code I also wore a tie, so felt inappropriate, like a man turning up at a beach barbecue in a suit.

And of course my presence was noted. During the coffee break I overheard someone in the Gents say 'we ought to have a sketchwriter in every year. There seems to be a good deal less backbiting.' Obviously that was a disappointment for many people, not least me, but as any science don will tell you, the act of observing an event in itself changes the course of that event. So what follows may not be typical. On the other hand, it was the founder himself, Henry VI, who, we were told, said that it was the job of the Provost to look for consensus on major issues, and for the fellowship to avoid strife.

The Provost whose job it is to avoid that strife – you don't need to read much CP Snow or David Lodge to know how hard that can be at any university, never mind Oxbridge – is Ross Harrison. Prof. Harrison took over at a difficult time for the College but has clearly steadied the boat. He is a philosopher with, unlike most philosophers I've met, a philosophical air – firm when necessary, resigned when defeated, ready with the little joke when pleasantries might soothe a situation. He is an Ulsterman, and his ameliorative tone is very much that of the present-day reformed Ian Paisley, and the exact opposite of the old firebreathing intransigent.

The session began with a short bout of private business, after which I and the junior members were allowed in to find somewhere to sit. There followed a discussion on the role and position of junior members with which I will not detain you. Next came the Bursar's report, generally regarded as the most important event of the morning. In the past this has been quite a theatrical display – Keynes used to milk it for all it was worth – but

Keith Carne, who took over on New Year's Day 2009, is not a milker. Nor was his news liable to create whoops of joy. He had, he said, inspected the College accounts. 'There is nothing untoward in our accounting. There is rather too much untoward in our financial condition,' he said.

Stock markets had fallen around the world, though the College's own endowment had recovered somewhat from the biggest fall in January 2009. By spending no more than 4 per cent of its endowment, King's hopes to maintain the endowment's real value for future generations. But that percentage is averaged over the last three years, so even if the market rises the College faces two more difficult years, and funds would return to normal only if the markets' rise was as dramatic as the fall had been.

There was more gloom on the way. Gibbs, Bodley's and Chetwynd required 'serious work' and that was going to cost mucho wonga (I paraphrase his more technical terminology.) Everyone would be asked to make cuts. Spending on meals and entertainment would have to come down – the Bursar could promise there would be pressure on food and wine. 'Even parts of the College that have already offered cuts will be asked to make more cuts.'

It would be, he said grimly – or rather, he was too mild and affable to be described as grim; gloomily perhaps – very painful. 'There is remarkably little that the College spends on things it does not care about. That is why the cuts will be so painful.'

A debate followed on whether the cuts were needed. And if they were, where could savings be made? The College shop, in King's Parade, cropped up. This boutique sells King's memorabilia, CDs of the Choir, books by members of the College and so forth, and it needs a subsidy. Dr Carne did what academics often do when a tricky problem arises – he lobbed the problem over to a committee. 'The shop was set up as an experiment, and I hope we will set up a review committee. But if we closed the shop, we would find it very difficult to find another tenant.' It was, he thought, overstaffed. Possibly some extra income could be found by using it as a booking agent for Chapel concerts and other Cambridge events. In the meantime, it should not be losing the College money. As always, recessions create a series of interlocking vicious circles.

Then the nearest to a bit of real controversy. The topic of accommodation for graduate students came up. Traditionally, King's has offered all its graduates – generally around 250 at any one time – College accommodation. Naturally the students prefer not to live far away from King's and don't wish to pay commercial rents, which in Cambridge are stiff. But, said the Bursar, this practice was soon going to be a considerable problem, especially as the refurbishment work meant that many rooms would simply not be available. 'Reading the numbers now, we will need a dramatic reduction in two to five years' time. It might be easier to make a small reduction now, rather than a dramatic one later.'

'Are you thinking of [a total of] 200 now?' asked Ross Harrison.

'Yes,' said Dr Carne.

It would not be true to say that all hell broke loose. But for the first time at the meeting there was real disagreement about an important topic. Prof. Robert Foley pointed out that the University wanted a sharp increase in graduate numbers. If King's went in the opposite direction, other colleges would have to take them, and King's would lose ground in the University's growth area. In any case, he said, many graduates were 'deeply surprised' to be offered College accommodation in the first place. The Bursar felt that King's had done its full part.

Dr Pete de Bolla wanted the Bursar to produce a paper that would outline all the implications of reducing the number of graduate students. Dr Carne said he would try to do that, 'but it would require a lot of interpretation', which I took to mean 'most of you wouldn't understand it'. Fellows should ask if Kings' prestige as a graduate college meant that people would come even if they couldn't have accommodation.

Dr Basim Musallam, the Vice-Provost, pointed out that Harvard didn't offer housing.

The Bursar, possibly realizing that his cause was lost, said that he really wanted the fellowship to understand the risks for the future. His suggestion of a 20 per cent cut in graduate student numbers went to the vote, and not a single hand was raised. 'I think,' said the Provost drily, 'that was not really strongly supported.'

There was a short debate on the environment and whether King's was doing enough to protect it; again, I will not burden readers with details of heat pumps and oil versus gas boilers, though we did spend some time on a segment about whether students were closing their windows with sufficient eagerness and frequency.

Then the debate on education and admissions, which boils down to whether the College is admitting the kind of students who will get good results. It varies from subject to subject, of course, but the Baxter tables, which compare results from across Cambridge, have King's pretty firmly in the middle, on average at least, though unsurprisingly some subjects do far better than others. In 2008/9, for example, 20 per cent of all final students in the University got Firsts; in King's the figure was 15.9 per cent, perhaps disappointing for a college that regards itself as one of the leaders. But you could put it another way: fully 63.3 per cent of King's graduates took a First or a 2.1, compared to a University average of 54.7 per cent. Which goes to show once again that you can prove anything at all with statistics, and the education report contained many hundreds of those.

The argument, only partly aired, is about whether King's results are suffering because so many of its intake come from state schools. This has been around three-quarters recently (though it dropped to 63 per cent in the last year), partly because independent schools have come to feel that the College is not actually biased against them, and so are more inclined to encourage their pupils to apply. Meanwhile the University, under some government pressure, is trying to raise the number of students from non-fee paying schools. Dr Stefan Uhlig, the Admissions Tutor, was sceptical. 'All the other colleges seem to think they can keep edging the statistics [of state school pupils admitted] up, but everything I have read makes me think that this is a fantasy. I don't see anything happening in the UK state sector that makes me think this will be possible.'

After that bleak assessment of the condition of state education in Britain, we moved onto research and summer schools. Dr Musallam, the Vice-Provost, who is from Lebanon, spoke with a passion uncommon in British academic circles, but familiar to anyone who has watched TV coverage of the Middle East conflict. 'I cannot find a room for two months for the summer school!' he announced, waving his arms in what appeared to be considerable distress. 'We might have to close the coffee shop!'

Finally Ross Harrison made a very personal plea. As Provost, he is *ex officio* chairman of the governors at King's College School, often called – not quite incorrectly – the Choir School. It absorbed, he said in the paper he submitted, a disproportionate amount of his time, energy and concern. It was also inappropriate for him, whose experience for himself and his children had been entirely in the state sector, to be chair of governors at an independent school.

And it wasn't just for his benefit, he implied. 'By making the pain that the School has inflicted on me optional rather than inevitable, it could make the position of Provost more appealing at the next election.'

He was desperate. Why not, he said, give the job to the Dean? The job was vacant (following the tragic death of the popular incumbent). 'The advantage of [giving that job to] the Dean is that the [new] Dean is not yet here and so not in a position to refuse it.'

Surely, I thought, the Fellows must bow to this cry from the heart. I was wrong. 'It's yer job, mate,' said Prof. Simon Goldhill, cheerily, and the Fellows then voted by a large majority to keep Prof. Harrison shackled to the School. Time for a restorative lunch and a glass of wine, not least for him.

Curtis's King's

Eleanor Curtis

Learning to talk

David Ignatius

I am sitting down to dinner in Hall. In my nostrils is the smell of brussels sprouts decomposing on the steam table in the cafeteria line. It's January 1974, and I am an American research student, newly arrived, and I realize this first night that I must learn how to talk. There's too much enthusiasm in my voice when I am asked a question, and not enough irony and distance. I feel like a travelling salesman, next to these wry English undergraduates. Even if they've grown up in Newcastle-on-Tyne, they affect the sardonic manners of Lord Sebastian Flyte.

I learn to suppress and withhold. I learn not to answer questions, but to deflect them. The things I think I am good at, I learn to discuss off-handedly. My annoying sincerity begins to ooze away. I aspire to become an amateur. Mere professionalism is unworthy; it's too ambitious an ambition.

This is 1974, remember, before Maggie Thatcher and the big bang, when King's undergraduates still feel pity and incomprehension for people who are applying for jobs in banking or trade. Achievement is for losers – except, of course, for the sly intellectual form of achievement that allows the seeming dilettante to achieve a first-class degree without apparent effort.

The prodigies are in fine form each night in Hall. When we talk about Dickens, they have a precise and particular recall for all the characters in *Dombey and Son* or *Little Dorrit*. It is bad form to discuss *Great Expectations*, which is the only Dickens novel I've read. My friend Nick, from Cat's, who aspires acceptably to be an art historian, regales the table with a nonsensical account of how to catch a badger. We all think his art connoisseurship is charming; just un-serious enough. But he's another of those sneaky fellows: with the passage of time, he becomes Director of the National Gallery.

My American friend Skip over at Clare gets a summer internship with *Time* magazine in London. Dubious, that; but he redeems himself by charging to the corporate expense account the entire unabridged *Oxford English Dictionary*, whose many volumes line the shelves of his bookcase. Skip is marked for greatness, we can all see that. He gets *Time* to buy him a stereo, too: we sit listening to the Ojays sing 'Money' for hours. 'Some people, got to have it,' the song says, but we don't think so.

I am living that first year in the Keynes Building, with a view over Chetwynd Court. It is scandalous to bring women up to the room, which makes it all the more exciting; when visitors knock, we don't answer and lie in bed, giggling. What is 'right conduct'? Should I get out of a drunken friend's sports car as he drives home recklessly from a night of drinking at the White Hart Inn in Fulbourne? No, I decide. Un-cool. He almost hits a tree, but doesn't.

I have a dream, in the middle of term, in which my father tells me to switch from English literature to Economics. I wake up that morning and go directly to the Economics faculty and apply for the diploma programme. One of my tutors is an especially brilliant man named Mervyn, who has the sweetness not to make me feel like a clod for knowing so little about the subject. He talks about monetary theory with the certain confidence of a man who might be Governor of the Bank of England. That is in fact what he becomes.

I wear a black leather jacket all day, every day. I chain-smoke cigarettes. My only real aspiration is to be a bad-ass, and to play sports. I play midfield on the King's second-string football team. We have trouble, frankly, finding 11 players. Roger, the chef in the Buttery, is one of our defenders. Our best striker is an Italian busboy. I am penalized repeatedly through the season for calling 'Mine!' when I go up for a header. A very American mistake, that.

I commune with ghosts. They are all about King's in those days. One old don with a perpetual, seductive twinkle in his eye claims to have been an intimate friend of EM Forster. He regales the sweet young things in Hall with his stories. Lord Kahn wobbles around the Chetwynd Building, a living connection to the epochal days of John Maynard Keynes.

The peerless Joan Robinson haunts the courtyards. One day she humiliates a famous mathematical economist named Frank Hahn by sneaking into the back of the lecture hall in her serape and sandals and demanding to know, as he plots the graph for his 'capital theory' (whose very logic is at the heart of a then-famous debate about whether you can measure 'capital'): 'What are the axes, Frank? What are the axes?' What a taunt! He throws her out of the room, wailing, 'I told you never to come to my lectures, Joan!' The woman is dangerous.

There are ghosts in the Chapel, blessed ones. My mother is stricken with cancer my first year at King's. She is not yet 50. I go to Evensong every afternoon; some days, it seems I am the only person there, other than the Choir. They pray for me, through the ancient liturgical music. My mother is still alive as I write this; she's now 85. How can I not believe?

I move to Bodley's Court my second year. My room looks out across the Back Lawn to the River Cam and the Chapel and the Gibbs Building. I will never live in such a beautiful place again in my life, I tell myself. That turns out to be right. I stay in my room during the spring vac to study. They turn off the heat. It is so cold that I have to put my socks and shoes on when I get out of bed, so that I can walk across the frigid floor to get my trousers. I still do that, to this day. My children think it's a peculiar outfit – socks and shoes and boxer shorts. An English habit, I tell them.

I try to quit cigarettes and smoke a pipe. It looks ridiculous. I take my Economics exams and do respectably; even Mervyn King says so. I apply for a job at the World Bank but they turn me down flat, in a letter that is almost derisive. I am condemned to pursue the only thing I am remotely good at, which is journalism.

I am starving, those last weeks at King's. I have completely run out of money. I get a small grant from the Supplementary Exhibition Fund (whose name still radiates the recondite majesty of King's) and it is enough, somehow, to get me across the Channel and around half of Europe before I go back to America. I am still paying back that grant, year by year.

The King's Situation

Martin Jacques

I was a rather reluctant Cambridge student. As a school leaver, I had taken the entrance exam but decided that Cambridge was not for me. Instead I chose to go to Manchester University: I was from Coventry and preferred the idea and feel of a big northern industrial city. Cambridge was too alien, too posh, too public school. I wanted something altogether earthier. I came from a very modest background; a little interwar semi-detached house, a local grammar school, parents who were school teachers and a provincial culture in which dinner was something taken in the middle of the day and dinner parties were unheard of. It was 1964: four years later, with a First and a masters degree under my belt, I contemplated where to go next to do my doctorate. I was now, of course, a different person, worldlier, more self-confident, and more cosmopolitan.

If my memory serves me right, while doing my masters my girlfriend's history tutor at Manchester suggested that I should consider going to Cambridge for my doctorate, as he had done earlier. Somehow the idea no longer seemed so forbidding. I needed a change of environment and a new intellectual challenge: Cambridge now seemed the right place. Nor did I have any difficulty in deciding which college to apply for. I was on the left and King's reputation as a hospitable environment for those of a liberal and left persuasion was well-known to me: Eric Hobsbawm had been a Fellow, Keynes the Bursar, and I recalled that Brian Pollitt had been an undergraduate there. For me it was an obvious choice.

I can't say that my first impressions of Cambridge were encouraging. I found it very difficult to identify with what struck me during my first few weeks as an overbearing Cambridge-centric mentality on the part of dons and students alike. They seemed to believe that Cambridge was the centre of the universe yet to me, respectful as I was, Manchester felt like a far more real place. Even then, with four years of university under my belt, Cambridge still represented a big culture shock; the feudal trappings of college life, the cosseted privilege of the students, the deferential attitude of college staff, and the effortless confidence bordering on arrogance that seemed to inform so many people's attitudes.

Slowly, however, I began to adjust. I got to know the place, with the newly familiar slowly eroding my previous sense of alienating distance; I met people, I started to make friends, I got involved in student politics (this was 1968 after all). Cambridge gradually began to grow on me. I came to appreciate the beauty of the place. This was an entirely new sensory experience for me, having previously spent my life in Coventry and Manchester where beauty and the built environment were mutually exclusive concepts. At first, I found the student left-wing political scene insufferably indulgent. A small group of Situationists, who believed in the paramount importance of the 'situation', would hijack every meeting of the Socialist Society, insisting that whatever was on their mind should be the subject of discussion. And even when the left was not being plagued by the Situationists, there was an air of unreality which compared very unfavourably with my experience in Manchester. But with time I came to recognize that frivolity, self-indulgence and a frustrating incomprehension of the real world were only part of the story. There was an intense seriousness about many students, a commitment to knowledge, learning and understanding, which I found most engaging. They were often gifted with unexpected skills coupled with an imagination and ability to think out of the box. The Situationists too had an abundance of imagination, organizing a demonstration against exams in 1969 – the March of the Academic Cripples – whose participants wore bandages and slings, limped along with walking sticks or were pushed in wheelchairs.

So what of King's? I hadn't helped myself initially by choosing to live outside College. It was a decision based on ignorance: I didn't want to live in something like a Manchester hall of residence, not realizing that college life is a different matter altogether. I came to regret not spending my first year living in King's. The life of a research student contrasts strongly with that of an undergraduate. There is little connection with the College; indeed, there may be hardly any involvement at all with the College. That was true in my case, but somehow King's slowly became a bit like home. I got to know and enjoy the company of some of the younger dons. The College had a disproportionate share of the left-wing students and, as a consequence, more than any other college at the time, it was the place they gravitated towards. And the College, in various ways, provided them with a sympathetic environment. During my time at Cambridge, King's was without doubt one of the key centres of university student life.

For me one of the attractions of Cambridge – certainly compared with Manchester – was that there was plentiful interaction between students and dons. Whereas at Manchester, staff and students barely ever met outside the formal surroundings of the teaching environment and faculty buildings, the College acted as a meeting point for dons and students. This contact flowed over into other arenas: younger dons like Bob Rowthorn and Paul Ginsborg would regularly attend meetings of the Socialist Society, help with the *Shilling Paper* (which was briefly to usurp *Varsity* in its influence and circulation), and participate in demonstrations, including that against the Greek military junta in 1970 which led to the arrest of a number of students. This had been virtually unheard of at Manchester: for me it was one of the great attractions of Cambridge, hugely enriching student life, intellectual discussion and engendering an air of informality. I loved it.

I should perhaps explain a little more about my political involvement. On going to Manchester, I had joined the Communist Party. By the time I arrived in Cambridge being on the left was deeply fashionable, being in the Communist Party deeply unfashionable. The University branch had a tiny membership which seemed to live in a state of splendid isolation from the tumult that was convulsing the student body in 1968: it was a profoundly unattractive – not to say boring – institution. But such was the disarray among the student left at the time, there was clearly the potential for a very different kind of organization to make a huge impact. And so it came to pass. By the time I left Cambridge in 1971, the CP branch possessed over 40 members, a diverse bunch of extremely talented students plus a handful of dons. It was a privilege to be associated with such an extraordinarily bright group of people – among whom, incidentally, King's was well represented – who came to exercise a major influence on the wider student body during this period.

There were two sides to my intellectual life in Cambridge: my formal role as a doctoral student and the broader politico-intellectual involvement I have been describing. To be candid, I did not particularly enjoy my research. This was partly for very personal reasons. I had gone straight from school to university and by the time I went to Cambridge I really needed a break from academic study in order to gain some distance and recharge my batteries: it was not to be. It took me over a year to settle on the subject of my doctorate and even then it never really animated or inspired me. The life of a research student is a lonely one at the best of times and this hardly helped. My research was interesting but, alas, not interesting enough. At that stage, I needed something different from a 100,000-word dissertation based on original historical sources. My mind was whirring, Cambridge – not least King's – had exposed me to all sorts of new ideas, scholars and writers, and the world of the late 1960s was novel and compelling: what I really required at that moment was not a dry ultra-academic tome, otherwise known as a dissertation, that absorbed all my time but a way of exploring and expressing all these new thoughts that were whizzing around my head; for example, by writing six 15,000-word essays. That was not the system.

I finished my dissertation – assisted by a generous grant from King's for my third year (to supplement the three years I had already received from the British Academy) – and was duly awarded my PhD; my heart, though, was never completely in it and my mind was frequently somewhere else.

By my third year I was very happy in Cambridge and was possessed of many good friends. Nonetheless, I decided not to seek a research fellowship but instead applied for lectureships elsewhere. Much as I loved Cambridge's intellectual atmosphere, and much else besides, I was concerned that I might never leave the place. Cambridge is a very seductive and comfortable environment in which to live, but I did not want to become a Cambridge person, someone who stayed and never quite managed to leave; that I was certain of. I had friends to whom that seemed to have happened and I did not want it to happen to me. So reluctantly and with a heavy heart, I left King's and Cambridge during the summer of 1971 and took up a lectureship at Bristol University. After Cambridge, Bristol was mundane and boring: I sorely missed the intellectual excitement and stimulation of my Cambridge life. But if I missed Cambridge, and, of course, King's, during my six years at Bristol, in the long run I did not. I was not cut out to be a Cambridge person: I was too worldly, too cosmopolitan, too political and too practical to spend my life there.

I look back on my life at King's and in Cambridge with great fondness. Cambridge was to mark the beginning of a new intellectual and political journey for me which, during the course of the 1970s, led to a growing critique of the left, recognition that the latter was in decline, and a very early realization that Thatcherism represented something quite new and powerful. An old mould was being broken but what would the new one look like? I neither accepted the ultra-leftist explanations that were in vogue at the time nor the traditional answers offered by Communist Parties. I was in the process of discovering the Italian Marxist, Antonio Gramsci.

In 1977, I gave up my lectureship in Bristol and became editor of *Marxism Today*. At the time it was both an eminently sensible and an utterly foolhardy decision. In the event, it was to prove an inspired choice. Poverty-stricken and hugely overworked though I was, it proved the perfect vehicle for continuing those wonderful discussions – albeit in new forms and in very different times – that had so illuminated my time at Cambridge. From the late 1970s until its closure in 1991, *Marxism Today* was to become highly influential not only on the left but also the right, in fact by far the most influential political publication of its time: my three years at King's made a singular contribution to that. I look back on my days there with gratitude: they were enormously important to me. I learnt so much, made wonderful friends, and formed relationships which in some cases lasted a long time, including to this day. King's helped shape my worldview.

Medieval Wiki

Peter Jones

American undergraduates, who now fill the seats in King's College Library in the summer, often tell us how delighted they are to work in a place made up of small rooms linked and stepped, with hidden corners and surprising views out. They want to know more. They ask who is pictured in engravings on the walls, or sculpted in busts in the window bays. They discover the Archives reading room and want to know if they can look at the oldest book in the Library or the records of who ate what in the 1450s. This curiosity comes as a surprise because we are not used to our own undergraduates asking these questions. The locals are more interested – for very good and urgent reasons – in what the Library has that otherwise they might have to go find elsewhere in the University, than they are in what the Library has squirrelled away that can't be found anywhere else.

Of course the curious stuff was not always squirrelled away. As late as the mid-1980s you could walk into the Library off the open D staircase in King's and see in front of you waist-high bookcases receding into the distance packed with valuable old leather-bound books. Some of them looked a bit battered, but that really only whetted the appetite for opening them up and peeping inside. Now, 20 years on, things have become more secure but less tempting; you have to ask to see and handle such books, although you can catch a tantalizing glimpse of some of them on the glassed-in shelves of the Library Seminar Room.

Well, you might say, what does it matter, surely most of these old books can now be consulted online anyway? True, and without even entering a library. But what you do not get online is the experience of handling something that is so ancient, and you will not find the evidence of ownership, reading and use that makes each copy of an old book different. You will not find the copy of Aristotle on animals in Greek (1498) that Desiderius Erasmus read and annotated himself; or the copy of Isaac Newton's *Principia* that Edmond Halley the astronomer marked up for a second edition; or the copy of Ariosto's *Orlando Furioso* owned by Jane Austen, later bought by Virginia Woolf and given by her to Maynard Keynes. All these are locked away at King's but can be fetched out.

So, these books are high spots that would impress any visitor, good things to produce for distinguished company in the College, or for the Fellows' summer supper party, or for

the curious American undergraduate. But most of the other books do not have such glamorous tales to tell, right? Well perhaps, but even books that have been here a few hundred years and not attracted much attention can suddenly spring a surprise or two. King's College Manuscript 16 is a good example.

It's a handsome-looking thing, bound in a reddish tan leather by a skilful modern binder working in the medieval style. Laid flat, the first thing you notice about the closed book is that someone has written in large letters on the fore-edge 'IO. COKIS'. More on that name later. Opened up, the leaves of the book are made of parchment, with the flaws in the original animal skin still visible. The handwriting is that of a professional scribe, two columns per page, writing in a disciplined 15th-century English book hand – but writing in Latin. Each leaf is brightened by initial letters illuminated in red and blue, and paragraph marks too. But if you turn over several leaves you notice that a very different later hand appears occasionally, on paper leaves that have been inserted among the parchment ones. The same 16th-century hand, writing in English, appears to have written on many of the margins of the 15th-century work. Both scribes break up the text with headwords for each section – and these are the names of diseases ('Frenesis' or 'Frenzy' in the illustration here). It must be a medical book.

If this 15th-century book was noticed by anyone before our Provost MR James at the end of the 19th century, we do not know about it. What he noticed while cataloguing the King's manuscripts was that this book had actually been owned from 1574 until his death by the London-based astrologer and medical practitioner Simon Forman (made famous by AL Rowse for the records Forman kept of his sexual exploits with female clients). Before Forman got his hands on it, the book had evidently been in Oxford; on the face of it, it might even have been written there sometime around 1470, since both texts in the book mentioned an Oxford medical practitioner called John Cockis. It's his name on the fore-edge of the book. Once Forman had bought it there he started writing in the book himself, not just in the margins but on extra sheets of paper he inserted among the parchment leaves and bound into the book.

All this was sorted out by MR James. The nature of the medical texts in the book Forman had bought was not something James could do much with. In 1976–7 Mary Edmond examined the book at King's and found that much of what Forman wrote in the manuscript was copied from a printed book, Andrew Boorde's *The Breviary of Helthe*, which ran through many editions from 1547 onwards. She also discovered that when Forman was examined by the College of Physicians in London in the 1590s he had claimed that this very medical book, now King's MS 16, proved that he knew enough learned medicine and was no mere quack. The examiners for the College of Physicians begged to differ, and condemned Forman for his ignorant and unlicensed practice of medicine, banning him from any further practice – a ban he simply ignored. Two books on Simon Forman written recently by Barbara Traister and Lauren Kassell put this King's medical manuscript and Forman's brush with the College into the context of his extraordinary career as a successful astrological doctor.

One day in 2006 I was looking at the King's manuscript because I wanted to use Simon Forman in a lecture to show how medieval medical manuscripts were still in use long after printed books became available in large numbers. After all, he had copied *from* a printed book into King's Manuscript 16. Why did he copy from *The Breviary of Helthe* into the margins of our manuscript? The disease headings in *The Breviary of Helthe* corresponded with headings in the manuscript, which were alphabetically ordered. It was unusual for medieval medical texts to be ordered alphabetically, as diseases were usually listed in an order based on the part of the body affected, running from head to toe. I began to read more closely and I noticed that in the medieval text there were also many names, far more than was usual for Latin medical writings. I began to list the names and saw that many of them belonged to the Dominican or Franciscan orders, to judge by the use of 'Brother …' as a title.

The mendicants were known to have introduced the use of alphabetical order into their handbooks on preaching to make them easier to consult. Perhaps the Brothers had something to do with the authorship of this medical text, also alphabetically ordered. The names were of English brethren. I looked them up and found a few of these names were known to have practised medicine in the 15th century.

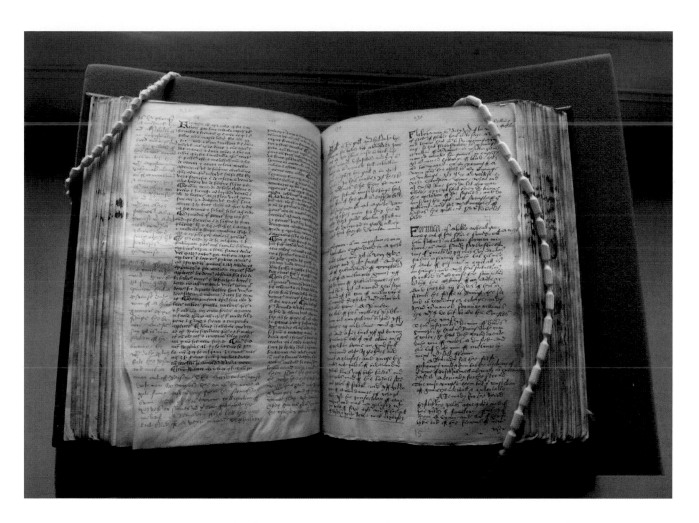

Maybe there were other copies of this text in manuscripts in other libraries? I found one that looked it as if it might be related to ours in a catalogue of the manuscripts at University College, London. My next trip to London put me in front of another 15th-century manuscript, and it did not take long for me to see it was indeed the very same text. But there was one surprising difference. In between the alphabetical entries in University College MS 11, gaps in the text had been left by the original scribe, and in those gaps later hands had entered other remedies for the same disease. But in the King's manuscript there were no gaps, yet the same added remedies were present in the text. The only possible explanation was that the King's manuscript had been copied either from University College MS 11 or from another manuscript that had already incorporated into the text the new remedies added to University College MS 11. What is more, the original scribe of University College MS 11 must have left the gaps deliberately for other remedies to be added later. The big prize was that this manuscript had a sentence at the end not present in the King's manuscript saying that the text was called the *Tabula medicine* ('Table of Medicine') and that it had been written in 1416–25.

Later, I found some manuscripts in other collections with the same medical text and the same curious feature of gaps left for remedies to be added. What we had in King's was once a kind of medical Wikipedia of the 15th century, designed to be improved by its readers and users. The fact that it had taken nearly a decade for the text to be written could be explained by the fact that the authors were compiling their book in this collective way, with different hands adding new remedies over time. I have never heard of this way of operating in the compiling of any medieval text, although we seem to have rediscovered it in the age of the Wiki.

By separating out the names of the original compilers from other later added names it became apparent that the original exponents of the Wiki concept were either Dominicans or Franciscans, or a team from both orders. The names that were added afterwards were mostly MDs of the later 15th century who were not mendicants. These later MDs were credited with remedies too, and by an extraordinary coincidence I found that one of them was Dr John Argentein, Fellow of King's College, later a doctor in the royal household, and Provost of King's. Argentein was the writer in the 1470s of a manuscript now in the Bodleian Library, Ashmole MS 1437, which was his own medical remedy book. It was also alphabetically ordered by disease and I found that the first entries under each heading were copied by him directly from the *Tabula medicine* itself. Then he left the rest of the page free to add other remedies later – exactly the method of composition used to put together the *Tabula medicine*, though in his case he did it alone rather than as part of a team. So he had borrowed the Wiki concept from the Brothers as well as a good number of his favourite remedies.

The remedies Argentein borrowed from the *Tabula medicine* include a number that show an interest in the use of alchemy for medical purposes that he shared with the Brothers. The quintessence of wine, a herb or human blood is the most unusual ingredient they called for. This 'fifth essence' was obtained by fractional distillation, many times repeated. It was particularly effective against diseases that were thought to involve poisoning of an organ or the whole body, or where the patient was in imminent danger of death. One potent variation on this theme was the quintessence of the blood of a young man, recommended for use in the treatment of ulcerous wounds, on the authority of Brother Robert Winstanton.

Still more alarming is a recipe that Argentein claimed was promoted by the Greek Patriarch and Cardinal Bessarion (whose library is now in the Marciana in Venice), a recipe Argentein presumably copied during his time as a medical student in Italy. The recipe calls for the beating for three hours of a young man, already condemned to death, with rods dipped in salt and vinegar. This is not made any more humane by the amount of wine the victim is to be plied with (which may not have been meant as an anaesthetic but as part of the distillation process). Then he is hung by the neck until dead, the blood is drained out of his body while it is suspended upside down, and then distilled up to six times. We are told that the distilled quintessence of his blood will be good for old people, and for those suffering hectic or quartan fevers.

Despite his fondness for alchemy, astrology and charms, Argentein was no benighted amateur as a doctor. He served as physician in the household of Edward V, who died in the Tower of London in 1483. After Henry VII seized the throne Argentein became physician to his first son Arthur. Despite the unfortunate end of both these royal patients, the doctor was not held responsible in any way, and on the basis of his service to the Crown he became Provost of King's in 1501 (he died in 1508 leaving the College a substantial sum for use in emergencies and a silver basin and ewer, later melted down). His beautiful brass monument is in one of the side-chapels to the Chapel.

Sadly we do not know how the manuscript containing the *Tabula medicine* and owned by Simon Forman found its way to King's. Since John Argentein clearly knew the text well, it is tempting to think that King's might have had a copy of the *Tabula medicine* once – and King's did manage to lose all but one of its medieval manuscripts by 1570. So it is just conceivable that Simon Forman bought in Oxford in 1574 what had once been a King's College manuscript, and that somehow, after his death in 1611, the manuscript found its way home to King's. But there is no evidence for this in the book itself. It is probably just a coincidence that the College of which Doctor John Argentein was once Provost now owns one of the few remaining copies of this Wiki-built medical text that served him so well.

Talking about my generation

Tony Judt

I came up to King's in 1966. That is not a random piece of information: ours was a – perhaps *the* – transitional generation. We were past the mid-point of the 1960s – the Mods had come and gone, the miniskirt was old news and the Beatles were already recording *Sgt. Pepper* – but the King's into which I was matriculated in October 1966 was still strikingly traditional. Dinner in Hall was formal, be-gowned – and required. Undergraduates took their seats, awaited the arrival of the Fellows, then rose and watched as a long line of elderly gentlemen snaked past them on their way to High Table.

Elderly here is no relative term. Led by Sir John Sheppard (born 1881), the Emeritus Fellows typically included Sir Frank Adcock (born 1886), EM Forster (born 1879) and others almost equally venerable. One was made immediately aware of the link between a generation of young men born into the post-war welfare state and the world of late-Victorian King's: the age of Forster and Keynes, exuding a cultural and social self-confidence to which we could never aspire. The old men shuffling past our benches seemed to blend seamlessly into the fading portraits on the walls above: without anyone making a big point of it, effortless continuity was all about us.

And yet, we were a path-breaking cohort. In the superficial sense, to begin with: gowns, caps, gate hours and a whole rulebook of minor regulations – all of them in place when we arrived – were the object of amused nostalgia by the time we graduated. In my first term, as an enthusiastic if mediocre rugby player, I took the team coach to Oxford to play (and, as always, lose to) New College. We got back late, courtesy of a half-successful attempt to dismantle one of our host's urinals and a rather more serious problem of late autumn fog. I arrived at the entrance to Market Hostel: it was locked – and I had no 'late pass'. A succession of stones flung at his window succeeded in waking up JR (Len) Shackleton, who came down utterly petrified: 'Don't let the warden hear you!' It goes without saying that this story would be hard to explain to a King's student today; but the point is that it would have been equally implausible to someone who arrived two years after us. The change came suddenly.

Of course, part of the self-image of King's was precisely the enthusiasm with which it purported to embrace both change in general and radical disruption in particular. The Senior Tutor of the day, John Broadbent, made a point of explaining to freshmen that locked gates and disciplinary regulations should be regarded with a nod and a wink. Even at the time this seemed a little rough on the porters, hostel wardens and bedders who were responsible for enforcing these rules – an early introduction to the subtlety of social rank at Cambridge: middle-class bohemians themselves, in outlook if not lifestyle, most college officers smiled benignly upon breaches of the rules they were expected to enforce.

Broadbent was also responsible for the appalling new bar installed shortly after we arrived. Convinced that the College must keep abreast of contemporary style and taste in all things, he approved a design that resembled nothing so much as the departure lounge at Gatwick Airport – and was chosen for just that reason: King's, Broadbent felt, should not dwell on its heritage, especially now that it had so many young men for whom the upper-middle-class milieu of Oxbridge meant nothing. Speaking as one of those 'new' Kingsmen, the first person in my family to complete secondary school, much less attend university, I can say that I would have far preferred the stuffed ambience of a 19th-century gentlemen's club to the *ersatz* classlessness of Broadbent's ideal.

Fortunately, the bar – though it symbolized King's uncertainty in the face of unprecedented changes – was not representative. In most of the ways that mattered, the

College maintained sufficient self-confidence to offer its students a reassuring sense of continuity and identity. Amusingly, this was most in evidence in its attitude to sex. By reputation at least, King's was widely known for its long-standing tradition of transgressive sexuality (albeit hitherto of the homoerotic variety). For all I know, in circles of which I was altogether unaware, this tradition was maintained through my years. But my generation was conformingly and assertively heterosexual.

Thus most of us at one time or another had a girl in *de facto* residence (occasionally serial girls, though not everyone was so blessed): sometimes a fellow student from one of the three women's colleges, sometimes a trainee teacher or nurse from the city, not infrequently an import from our hometown. Without anyone overtly acknowledging the fact, this seemed to be accepted practice by the late 1960s. Near the end of my undergraduate career, King's voted to go mixed – one of the first three colleges to do so (when I matriculated, women were only allowed to dine in Hall three times a term, whereas by the time I went down they could eat there any time they chose). Anglia Television eagerly seized the moment, set up a camera and microphone outside the College gate and began interviewing us. One young woman, the long-time live-in concubine of the same Len Shackleton, was asked whether she thought that a 'co-educational' college would face distinctive challenges: 'Oh no', she replied. 'I've been living here for a year now and everything's been just fine!' Reluctantly constrained to acknowledge the fact, the College Council voted to ask the young lady to leave.

To me, a south London boy who had never been north of Leicester, our generation of Kingsmen was not just socially mixed but geographically heterogeneous. For the first time I met boys from the Wirral, Yorkshire, Tyneside, East Anglia and the Celtic fringe. To a remarkable degree, they were – like me – the upwardly mobile products of grammar schools and the occasional direct grant establishment: we all had the 1944 Butler Act to thank for our presence in Cambridge, although for some of us the social gulf to be bridged was very substantial indeed. The mother of John Bentley, a close friend and the first boy to come to King's from a comprehensive, explained to my parents at our graduation party that whenever people on her street asked where John was and what he was doing, she was tempted to reply that he was 'back in Borstal': a more convincing and ultimately respectable answer than confessing that he was punting girls around on the Cambridge Backs.

I have no doubt that, somewhere else in the College, there lurked communities of public schoolboys; perhaps they were in the majority? But I only ever became closely acquainted with one such person – my neighbour Martyn Poliakoff: great-grandson of the Poliakoff who built the Russian railways, a spiky-haired eccentric out of Westminster School who went on to secure a CBE, a Fellowship of the Royal Society and deserved renown as a popularizer of chemistry to young people. Hardly your typical public-school oik.

For the rest, my King's was the very incarnation of meritocratic post-war Britain. Most of us got where we were by doing well in exams and, to a striking extent, we pursued occupations that reflected our early talents and interests. I have done a little research into this and discovered that the cohort of Kingsmen who came up in 1966 stand out in their choice of careers: more than any group before or since, we opted for education, public service, the higher reaches of journalism, the arts and the unprofitable end of the liberal professions.

It is thus altogether appropriate that the most promising economist of our King's generation – Mervyn King – should have ended up as the Governor of the Bank of England, rather than an investment banker or hedge funder. Before our time, talented Kingsmen certainly took comparable paths. But a glance at the obituaries reveals just how many of them returned after Cambridge to the family business or to the traditional professions of their fathers and grandfathers.

As for those who came after, it is depressing to record how quickly and in what numbers the Kingsmen and women of the 1970s and since resorted to the world of private banking, commerce and the more profitable reaches of the law. Perhaps one should not blame them: we were fortunate, jobs were plentiful and we could still bask in the last glorious rays of post-war confidence. All the same, it's very clear that our elective affinities lay elsewhere.

I used to ask my contemporaries why they opted for King's. A surprising number had no clear response: they just picked it by name, because they liked the look of the Chapel or because it sounded distinctive. A handful – mostly economists – said it was because of Keynes. But I was directed to apply to King's for very specific reasons. Something of a rebel at school – I never completed my A-levels and dropped out in the second year of the sixth form – I was tartly assured by my teachers that no other college in Oxbridge would give me the time of day. But King's, they seemed to feel, was sufficiently oddball in its own right to find me a congenial, or at least compatible, candidate. I have no idea whether any other college would have considered my application; fortunately, I never had to find out. But I did arrive at King's with a very strong prejudice in its favour.

I have never had cause to revise that opinion. I don't know how well I was taught, but I do know that I was taught in a way that few young people ever are. Most of my teachers – John Saltmarsh, Christopher Morris and Arthur Hibbert – were quite obscure, known only to generations of Kingsmen. But thanks to them I acquired not just a patina of intellectual self-confidence – whatever else I had upon arrival in Cambridge, I certainly lacked that – but abiding respect for teachers who are indifferent to fame (and, it goes without saying, fortune) and to any consideration outside the supervision armchair.

In contrast to certain neighbouring colleges, we were never taught to the Tripos. My supervisors, some of whom had first been supervised in turn by men who arrived at King's in the 1880s, were supremely uninterested in public performance of any sort.

John Dunn.

I don't mean by this that they did not care how one did in exams; rather, that they took it for granted that our natural talent would carry us through and that the point of a supervision was something quite different. It's hard to imagine such people today, if only because they would be doing the College a profound statistical disservice in the face of the Research Assessment Exercise (RAE).

Without ever making a thing of it, I think the College was well aware of its responsibility towards a generation of young men for whom Cambridge was an entirely alien world. And if the College was not aware of it, then Kenneth Polack, Broadbent's successor as Senior Tutor, most certainly was. Ken, I believe, intuitively grasped the brittle blend of surface intellectual sheen and deep social insecurity that marked so many of us in our early years. He never directly addressed the point, but I know that in more than a few cases he gently encouraged undergraduates to discuss both their fears and their practical (material) dilemmas with him. We were made to feel that, although it would be absurd to pretend that King's was 'our' College, or that he and the Fellows were all 'just like us', we had a place there and not just on scholarly sufferance.

My greatest debt, though I did not fully appreciate it at the time, was to John Dunn: then a very young Research Fellow, now a distinguished Professor Emeritus. It was John who, in the course of one extraordinarily over-extended supervision on the political thought of John Locke, broke through my well-armoured adolescent Marxism and first introduced me to the challenges of serious intellectual history. He managed this by the simple, albeit time-consuming, device of listening very intently to everything I said; taking it with extraordinary seriousness on its own terms; and then picking it gently and firmly apart in a way that I could both respect and accept. That's teaching for you.

It is also a certain sort of liberalism: the kind that engages tolerantly with dissenting (or simply mistaken) opinions across a broad political spectrum, and takes utterly seriously its own proclaimed concerns and values. No doubt such tolerant intellectual breadth was not confined to King's. But listening to friends and contemporaries describe their experience in other Cambridge and Oxford colleges, I sometimes wonder. Supervisors and tutors in other establishments often sounded disengaged and busy; or else obsessed with the sort of professional knowledge and bibliographical information more commonly associated with American academic departments at their least impressive.

I fear that there is more of this today in King's than there used to be: a pity. As in so many other respects, I think our generation was extraordinarily fortunate. Promoted on merit into a class and culture that were on their way out, we experienced Oxbridge – or at least King's – just before the descent into testing, ideological comprehensivization, bureaucratic interference and RAE. We got the best of both worlds.

As I think about it, I may not be best placed to recall and assess the 1960s in King's. I went on to do graduate work there and held a Fellowship for six years, before decamping for Berkeley in 1978; so some of my memories are side-shadowed by later developments. The King's of Noel Annan (Provost from 1956 to 1966) was giving way to that of Provost Leach (1966–79). The unmediated self-confidence of the Annan generation ('Our Age') would be replaced by a certain ironic distance: you never quite felt with Edmund Leach that he cared deeply or believed implicitly in the College as a repository of everything that was best in Edwardian liberal dissent. All of *that*, he seemed to suggest, was just another myth ripe for the unravelling.

But what Leach did stand for – perhaps even more than Annan and certainly more than the intellectually undistinguished Sheppard – was pure smarts: an emphasis further accentuated when Leach in turn was succeeded by Bernard Williams. I served on the Fellowship Electors with Williams, Dunn, Sidney Brenner, Frank Kermode and Geoffrey Lloyd and I have never lost the sense that being clever – witty, quick, wide-ranging and able (as Forster put it in another context) to *connect* – was what King's was about. I don't know that I would say of all my contemporaries, as Raymond Aron said of his fellow *normaliens* in 1924, 'I have never met so many intelligent men gathered in such a small space.' But they were a pretty impressive bunch.

On my occasional return trips to King's, I confess I am struck by a sense of decline. I most certainly don't mean by this that the College does worse than it used to in the examination tables – though it is telling how much this particular change seems to obsess people I meet. Nor am I speaking of the quality of Fellows and students: I am in no position to judge. But what began as ironic self-mockery in the 1970s ('Here at King's we don't take our own rules or traditions very seriously, ha! ha!') has become genuine self-doubt.

The earnest self-interrogatory concern with egalitarianism or moral transparency that we encountered in 1966 appears to have descended into a predictable and demeaning striving after the cutting edge of political correctness: the College seems unhealthily obsessed with the need to maintain appearances as the sort of place that would *never* engage in elitist selection criteria or socially distinctive practices of any kind.

I'm not sure that there is anything to be done about this. King's, like much else in contemporary Britain, has become a heritage site. In King's case, celebrating an

Edmund Leach.

inheritance of dissidence, un-convention and unconcern for hierarchy: look at us – aren't we *different*. But you can't celebrate these negatives unless you have a living grasp of what it was that they stood against. The free-standing trans-valuation of values only works at a metaphysical level. Institutions need substantive traditions, and sometimes one fears that King's has lost touch with its own.

Sadly, I suspect that all this began precisely in those transitional years of the mid-1960s. We, of course, understood nothing of that. We got both the traditions *and* the transgressions; both the continuities *and* the change. But what we bequeathed to our successors was something far less substantial than what we ourselves had inherited (a general truth about the baby-boom generation). It is one thing for a Senior Tutor to acknowledge the existence of age-old rules and practices, only to authorize with a wink their occasional violation. It is quite another to run an institution on the basis of the proclaimed absence of any such rules and practices, and to congratulate yourself for so doing. I don't suggest that this is what has happened at King's; but how far is it from the truth?

Liberalism and tolerance, indifference to external opinion, a prideful sense of distinction allied to progressive political allegiances: these are manageable contradictions, but only in an institution unafraid to assert its particular form of elitism. Absent that, you have hypocrisy: and worse (from the point of view of institutional stability), hypocrisy under constant challenge. In my generation we thought of ourselves – to the extent that we paid the matter any attention – as both radical and members of an elite; as critics of the status quo embedded in a tradition we had (most of us – there was the occasional exception) no desire to undermine.

If this sounds incoherent, it is the incoherence of a certain liberal descent which we intuitively imbibed over the course of our College years. It is the incoherence of the patrician Keynes establishing a Royal Ballet and an Arts Council for the greater good of everyone, but ensuring that they were run by the cognoscenti. It is the incoherence of meritocracy: giving everyone a chance and then privileging the talented. It was the incoherence of our King's and we were fortunate to have experienced it.

Curiosity, precision and confidence

Ben Leapman

When I sent a tersely worded letter to the House of Commons in 2005, asking for details of the expenses claims submitted by six MPs, I knew that I was on to something. But I did not anticipate the size of the can of worms I was opening.

My request and those of two other journalists, all made using the Freedom of Information Act, were resisted by the Commons authorities. A legal battle ensued, which carried on until we won our test case in the High Court three years later. That verdict forced MPs to admit defeat and begin assembling the 'Expenses Files' for publication – the files that were eventually leaked to the *Telegraph* before their planned publication date. The result was what Prime Minister Gordon Brown called 'the biggest political scandal of the last 200 years'.

As the revelations about moats and duck houses unfolded in that summer of 2009, politicians became an object of scorn, derided and lampooned to a degree extraordinary even by British standards. As for me, I found myself in the unusual position of receiving fan mail from readers of my *Sunday Telegraph* articles – journalists are accustomed to hearing only complaints – and I was able to reflect that I had played a part in uncovering something which the public felt was really rather important.

My letter in 2005 was not the first time I had asked elected representatives impertinent questions about their finances.

Fifteen years earlier, as news editor of *Varsity*, I had shone a light on pay increases for the elected sabbatical officers of Cambridge University Students' Union. By changing the formula used to calculate their pay they had awarded themselves a rise of 40 per cent, in a year when Margaret Thatcher's government had frozen the student grant. This seemed scandalous at the time. The man we held responsible for the decision was the CUSU Treasurer, who was himself one of the recipients of a bumper pay rise. *Varsity* splashed on the story with a picture of the Treasurer captioned 'Laughing all the way to the bank'.

I now think that we were slightly unfair to the Treasurer, a Liberal Democrat whose salary was a mere £3,397 a year before the pay rise – pitiful even by the standards of the day – and who has gone on to lead a blameless life as a senior public servant. But the episode provided me and my *Varsity* colleagues with a training ground, a chance to test our mettle and learn lessons which I would find invaluable when I locked horns with the Westminster Establishment 15 years later.

In interviewing a series of King's alumni who have reached the top of their professions – from Supreme Court President Lord Phillips to satirists Bird and Fortune – I have pondered why the College in particular, and Cambridge generally, produce so many high achievers in all walks of life.

A large part of the explanation, no doubt, is the rigorous competition which ensures that only high-attainers are admitted in the first place. Part, perhaps, is the networking potential which means that even mediocre graduates are likely to have successful friends. But part, I am sure, is the opportunity in College life to hone one's skills in one's chosen field, as a big fish in a relatively small pond. And it is a pond that is teeming with other very clever pond life, to collaborate with and on occasion to clash with.

I went up to King's intending to carve out a career as a research scientist, but I was soon attracted by journalism. It was my father's trade, so I was familiar with the concept, but I had never written a news story. At College, I wrote for a King's magazine, wittily entitled *Red Dragon Pie* after a dish served in the canteen; for the *Cambridge Political Review*; and for *Varsity*, where I was entrusted with the role of News and Features Editor, deciding

what went into the front section of the weekly paper in conjunction with two job-share colleagues. Since I graduated and went into 'real' journalism, it has taken me 20 years to reach an equivalent-ish position on a national newspaper newsdesk.

Lord Phillips, who had already decided on a career at the Bar before he arrived at King's, told me that he was inspired at the College by his Law supervisor, Ken Polack. John Bird and John Fortune gravitated to Footlights, where they had the opportunity to work with other rising stars including Peter Cook.

Would such talent find its way to the surface regardless of where such individuals had spent their undergraduate years? I suspect that in some cases the answer is no, it would not. All the advantages, from the chance to bounce ideas off other brilliant young minds, to inspiration from leading academics, to mere 'friends in high places', must surely make a difference.

Winning a place at King's (or, let's be honest, any Oxbridge college) boosts a student's life chances. So it matters who is admitted. It matters that, while King's has pretty much the best record, the products of our public schools are hugely over-represented at every college. It is why I took part in the Target Schools programme during my undergraduate days, visiting comprehensives which had seldom sent pupils to Cambridge, to talk to their sixth-formers and encourage them to apply.

In my own case, I would put what journalistic talent I have down to having retained, to varying degrees, a student's inquiring mind, a scientist's grasp of detail, a statistician's love of numbers and a politician's joy at framing an argument. None of these emerged anew during my three years at King's, but all developed there.

When an MP told me, in 2004, that he had recently moved his 'main home' to the Isle of Man so that he could claim expenses on his 'second home' in his London constituency, I was curious enough to probe further. When the Commons, in 2004, issued the first list of MPs' second-home expenses claims totals – without any detail – I was precise enough to spot the discrepancies. And I was confident enough to tell my Editor that these things warranted further investigation.

Curiosity, precision and confidence are qualities that could be found in most 18-year-olds. The role of a higher educational establishment is to recruit bright talents from the broadest spectrum of society, and nurture them, with the aim that they will make their mark. My time at College helped me, I think, to make my mark.

Portraits of King's

Martin Parr

Martin Rees

An undergraduate at Trinity before arriving at King's as a research Fellow in 1969, Martin Rees's Cambridge career has straddled the two colleges. After two stints as a King's Fellow, during which time he served on the College budget committee and as a fellowship elector, he moved back to Trinity as Master in 2004. His wife, the anthropology professor Caroline Humphrey, remains a Fellow at King's. A pillar of the UK scientific establishment, Rees was appointed Astronomer Royal in 1995, ennobled in 2005, and became president of the Royal Society in the same year. He even has an asteroid named after him.

John Bird and John Fortune

*Bird, from Nottingham, and Fortune, from Bristol,
were both grammar school boys who benefited, according
to Fortune, from an 'an extraordinary window of
opportunity' which, he fears, risks being closed if
undergraduate tuition fees are increased any further.
Fortune recounts his family's reaction when he won his
place at King's: 'My mother said "I want you to go and
see our family doctor." So I went to see him and he said
"John, I understand you are going to King's College,
Cambridge." I said "Yes". He said "I just want to
tell you that King's College, Cambridge, is the world
headquarters of homosexuality".' Fortune met John
Bird at King's, where they both read English and were
involved in student theatre. Bird, the elder of the two,
dropped out of a PhD course in European drama – 'I
was told I would have to learn Russian to quote Chekov,
which I thought was quite reasonable, but then I was told
I would have to learn Norwegian to quote Ibsen.' With
three years between them, they didn't meet on stage until
another Cambridge contemporary, Peter Cook, recruited
them to work at his Establishment Club in Soho, at the
forefront of a new wave of comedy in the early 1960s.*

Eric Hobsbawm

'I was the token Red', says Eric Hobsbawm of his time as an undergraduate at King's. He came up in 1936, having embraced Communism as a fourteen-year-old schoolboy in Berlin before his family, who were Jewish, emigrated in the face of Hitler's rise to power. Despite extensive extra-curricular activities, Hobsbawm secured a First in his History Part II – in part because, he says, 'The Party encouraged us to do as well as we could.' After graduating he returned to the College as a Fellow, teaching economic history. He had adjacent rooms to Prof. Frank Adcock. 'He thought I was going to overthrow the system,' Hobsbawm says. A leading Marxist historian, Hobsbawm remained a Communist Party member right up to the collapse of the Soviet Union, although he now concedes that 'the project has demonstrably failed, and, as I now know, was bound to fail' .

David Willcocks

War broke out just as David Willcocks arrived at King's in 1939, and he was offered the chance to defer his call-up until May 1940. As an accomplished chorister and organist he struck a deal with the Vice-Chancellor who let him sit the Bachelor of Music exam, provided he told no one. He earned a Military Cross in Normandy, before returning to college in 1945 to complete his BA. He eventually succeeded Boris Ord as Director of Music, serving until 1974, and establishing the King's Choir on the international scene. Willcocks admits there were 'tensions' with Fellows who wanted more state school pupils in the College. One Admissions Tutor said to him: 'All your people come from private schools.' Willcocks said: 'Private schools are the places where they sing Te Deum *and the* Magnificat. *I don't want to have to start teaching what a* Te Deum *is.'*

Nicholas Phillips

As the first President of the UK's Supreme Court when it was created in 2009, Lord Phillips has a unique place in legal history. He read Economics on arrival at King's in 1958, then changed to Law at the end of his first year. Today, Phillips says, 'I remember [Ken Polack] saying to me after I got a 2.2 in Economics, "Nicholas! What went wrong?" in acute distress that anybody who might become one of his students should have got such a miserable degree.' Phillips gained a First in Part II Law and went on to become a Law Lord, then Lord Chief Justice, before his promotion to the new Supreme Court role. He was in the King's rugby first team, and the Chetwynd Society drinking club, but always studied hard – 'I think most of us who had done National Service were quite prepared to settle down and do a bit of work.'

John Galbraith Graham

John Graham is crossword-setter 'Araucaria' for The Guardian *and* Financial Times. *He went up to King's in 1939 to read Classics, but left in 1941, to join the RAF, flying as a navigator in Italy and earning a mention in dispatches. When, unlike many of his friends, he was lucky enough to return to King's he took up theology, living in Gibbs and worshipping regularly in King's Chapel. He was then ordained and spent 30 years in the clergy, which allowed him enough spare time to begin compiling crosswords in the 1950s. When he was divorced in the 1970s and consequently lost his livelihood as a vicar, he became one of Britain's leading crossword compilers. His fans particularly enjoy his inspired discoveries of anagrams, such as 'orchestra' as an anagram of 'carthorse' and 'Manchester City' as an anagram of 'synthetic cream.'*

Judith Weir

Judith Weir, the composer, spent her undergraduate years studying Music at King's. She played oboe and took an active part in the musical life of the College and university, composing in her College rooms in her spare time. In her final year, 1975/6, she had a grand room on A staircase with a view over Front Court to the Chapel. In writing operas and orchestral pieces, she has worked with her King's contemporaries Susan Tomes and Michael Chance, but her strongest association with the College has been through Stephen Cleobury, the Director of Music. She says: 'I have worked with Stephen a lot; he has been a fantastic supporter. Hearing my work performed by the Choir is a marvellous thing.'

Zadie Smith

When Zadie Smith, newly arrived in Cambridge, handed in her first English composition Pete de Bolla's verdict was blunt: 'This is not an essay.' Smith recalls: 'Oscar Wilde and Virginia Woolf appeared in it as characters. I had to learn, otherwise I would have gone through three years thinking it was good to write flowery nonsense.' A short story she wrote in her final year, 1996/7, became White Teeth, *the best-selling novel which launched Smith's career as a writer of award-winning fiction. She also knuckled down to her studies and achieved a First in Part II English, having performed disastrously in her second-year exams. Most of her friends were in College and her regular haunt was King's Bar – 'You could smoke in there, it was still fun.' No longer – on a recent trip back to College she had to retreat to King's Parade to enjoy a cigarette.*

Charles Clarke

Charles Clarke arrived at King's as a 'broadly Labour' eighteen-year-old in 1969. But he missed taking part in the radical riots outside Garden House Hotel in February 1970 in a protest against the Greek military regime because 'I preferred to attend a lecture at King's on the structure of the University grants committee.' He rose from a KCSU committee post to the presidency of the National Union of Students, and 30 years later joined Tony Blair's Cabinet. While Home Secretary he was nicknamed 'two pizzas' by lobby journalists, on account of his healthy appetite. As Education Secretary in 2003, Clarke questioned the purpose of subjects like Classics, declaring that 'education for its own sake is a bit dodgy' and asking why the modern state should fund 'the medieval concept of a community of scholars seeking truth'. He left Parliament in 2010.

Stephen Poliakoff

Stephen Poliakoff passed his Cambridge entrance exam at 16 and was told to take two years out before coming up – but by the time he arrived in 1971, he says: 'My academic side had shrivelled and my interest in the theatre had grown vastly.' His first act at King's was to tell the College that he was 'going to go back home and finish my play'. The work, Pretty Boy, was put on at the Royal Court at the end of his first year. He read History which he found 'fairly awful', with huge swathes of the past covered in too little depth, so he ignored the syllabus and spent a whole term on the French Revolution, ending up 'hopelessly out of sync'. He founded a successful society called Feast, with writers, musicians and singers performing their own work in King's Cellars on Saturday nights; but the lure of a professional career proved overwhelming and he left at the end of his second year without completing a degree.

H staircase, Gibbs

Colin MacCabe

I think of Tony Tanner often. In fact I'm not sure that I don't think about Tony whenever I'm reading. Cancel that. I don't think about him when I'm reading pulp fiction or newspapers for he had no time for one and little for the other. But whenever I am reading the greatest writing, whenever I am trying to follow form and meaning with real intensity then Tony is there, if only as a perpetual encouragement and a perpetual model. He was quite simply the best close reader I ever encountered.

I first heard his name in Trinity where I was an undergraduate studying philosophy. My friends Piers Gray and Adrian Poole were standing in front of me in the lunch queue; high on a lecture that they had just come from by a junior lecturer called Tony Tanner. I fear that both my young friends were then prone to that lugubrious Leavisite mood which had so limited undergraduate reading for decades and which favoured the frown and the smirk, and above all, the self-satisfied scowl. Frown, smirk and scowl were banished. They were laughing and exclaiming; energized by the preposterous meanings that Tanner had teased out of *Madame Bovary*.

To think of Tony is to think of King's. He loved King's so much that he couldn't leave it. A fact he proved to himself the hard way. It would be difficult to place Tony directly in King's most public intellectual tradition: he had no interest in Keynes or economics. Keynes's Deputy Bursar, however, was Dadie Rylands and it is not impossible to understand Tony as Dadie's academic heir. Rylands is of course justly famous for his extraordinary role in the history of English theatre in the 20th century. The whole of the early history of the Royal Shakespeare Company could – through the figures of Peter Hall, John Barton and Trevor Nunn – be traced back to Dadie and his Marlowe Society productions and this lineage has received due acknowledgment, although it is my own personal surmise that the full history, if it is ever written, will make Dadie's role ever more central. But there are very few indeed who think of Dadie as a major academic figure. He was of an age where one wrote a book only if one had made some earth-shaking discovery. What Dadie did was to teach, to direct plays, to talk but above all to read. It was in Cambridge – and Richards and Empson are the key theoretical figures – that close reading was developed as a central academic practice. Leavis was to try to arrogate the practice to himself but in fact it was what defined the whole of the Cambridge English School.

Tony himself was trained at Jesus by Rossiter, one of Richards's most reflective disciples, and by Brockbank, who went on to become a leading Shakespearean scholar. From there he went on a Harkness to America in the late 1950s and discovered the extraordinary range of post-war American fiction from Kerouac to Bellow, from Mailer to Burroughs, and he came back bearing the good news to Cambridge. It was at this moment that he became a Fellow of King's. Of course by coming to King's as he did in 1960, he was for the Leavisites going into the very belly of the beast. King's was always the enemy for Leavis – full of people too concerned with the social whirl of London, an outpost of upper-class Bloomsbury in the Fens. Not serious enough, not moral enough and, though this was not the language used, full of screaming faggots.

The very great period of King's came of course at the turn of the 19th century when the College was opened to non-Etonians and the names of Forster and Keynes stand as the exemplars of that moment. Dadie was a direct link to that period and served for Tony as his ideal of life and scholarship. The College that Tony entered as a Fellow was in the full tide of what might be called its second wave. Noel Annan as Provost combined administrative skill of an unusual order with the very highest of academic ambitions. In this atmosphere Tony

and King's English thrived but always at his back he heard the whisper of America. I suspect from the minute he returned to England, certainly from when I first met him in 1970, he agonized about whether to leave Cambridge and his beloved King's for the endless promise of the United States. Finally the decision was made and at the beginning of the academic year 1976 he set off for Johns Hopkins. Scarcely there and he was plunged into the deepest of depressions and when two months later his job in the Cambridge English Faculty was advertised he applied immediately. In a very uncharacteristic moment of generosity, the English Faculty did not hesitate to reappoint him. But for Tony a job in the English Faculty was only the necessary condition for his real desire – to rejoin the Fellowship of King's. This was a little more difficult because on Tony's departure the College had appointed no fewer than three people to fill his place – myself, Norman Bryson and David Simpson. To argue for yet another English Fellow was more than difficult but King's, in a characteristic moment of generosity, welcomed him back. And so there we all were with John Barrell as our chief. Difficult to imagine such a carnival of criticism but it happened.

And so he returned. As Dadie waspishly put it, 'Ah yes, Tony went to America – the first time came back with a beautiful American wife and wrote a book called *The Reign of Wonder*, went off a second time, came back without the wife and wrote a book called *Adultery and the Novel*.' Indeed the Tony who returned was in many ways a depleted figure. The loss of balance which rendered him an increasing invalid and the trauma of this second American sojourn deepened in the early 1980s as his second marriage failed and many of his closest friends left both Cambridge and King's. His savage drinking, which almost certainly was the major factor in his loss of balance, now developed into debilitating alcoholism and his case seemed hopeless.

I remember sitting with him in the Octagon on one of my rare visits to Cambridge. Tony was hopelessly drunk, in floods of tears and incontinent. For the only time in my life to date, I wished for a friend an early death. There was, however, a miracle. Tony stopped drinking and reinvented himself as a bachelor college don, resumed his incredible productivity as writer, teacher and lecturer and entered on what was perhaps the happiest phase of his life. He even, after a few years, began to drink again without lapsing into chronic alcoholism. His rooms were a centre of talk and laughter, of work and writing, of teaching and learning.

Tony was of that generation of Cambridge English when to be a teacher of English was to teach the whole period of English literature. If American literature was his speciality, he was as happy writing about Pope as William Burroughs, about Jane Austen as Henry James. And in his final years hour and man were matched as he wrote for the Everyman library prefaces to every one of Shakespeare's plays. It has taken more than a decade to gather them together into a single volume but this year Harvard University Press has brought out the collected prefaces. They make a companion volume to Dadie Rylands' celebrated Shakespeare anthology *The Ages of Man*. Together they perhaps define King's English in the 20th century.

When I became a Fellow of King's in 1976, I moved into Tony's old rooms in the Gibbs Building (H4), which were positioned just above Peter Avery's. Peter I have to say had been a legendary figure when I was a student, an openly homosexual don some time before anybody had talked of 'coming out'. Indeed there were always young men in Peter's rooms, some aiding him with the transcription of a Persian medieval text, some making tea and carrying drinks, and some just there. Peter, who presented a very grand front, simply introduced them and then continued with whatever conversational topic seemed most appropriate. He was a chain-smoker and a heavy drinker but above all he was a great talker. We talked often of English literature about which, particularly modern poetry, he was very knowledgeable and we also talked a great deal about Persian literature. But in the period where I was his neighbour we talked most of Iranian politics. I surmised, and the obituaries seemed to bear this out, that Peter had been a spook in Iran and Iraq in the post-war era. What is certain is that he was extremely knowledgeable, extremely well connected and extremely astute. The result was that I received the highest-level briefings on the coming Khomeini revolution long before news of it began to appear in the newspapers. I remember in particular Peter, in considerable distress, telling me of some Iranian provincial governor who had telephoned him desperate to know how to prepare the Western food that the Shah had demanded for a forthcoming visit. For Peter this contempt for his own culture meant that the Shah was doomed, as indeed he was. Even more presciently Peter told me that the first result of the Khomeini revolution would be a war between Iran and Iraq, as Saddam Hussein would attempt to annex Khuzestan. Whenever I visited Cambridge after I left in 1981 my first port of call was H2 Gibbs and the first topic of conversation would be the current state of politics in Iraq and Iran. Peter undoubtedly maintained contacts in the Foreign Office and possibly with the Secret Service and I know that he exercised whatever influence he had in order to forestall the absolutely disastrous invasion of Iraq in 2003, whose effects he foresaw fully and in detail.

But truth to tell in later years we talked less and less about politics (too depressing) and more and more about literature and history. In his retirement he produced his major translation of Omar Khayyam and then finally his magnum opus on his much-loved Hafiz. Peter was both a Tory and an Anglican but he was the most open and tolerant of men. Perhaps this was due to his sexuality rather than his religion (he once told Tony Tanner, '... between my religion and my sexuality I seem to spend a lot of my time on my knees') or perhaps his time in the Middle East, or perhaps it was part of King's best traditions. Whatever the cause, I could bring any visitor to King's of any age, of whatever education, from any part of the world to Peter's rooms and they would be listened to, entertained and attended to. He was the most hospitable of men.

When I was asked to write this contribution I immediately thought of both Tony and Peter, and of the H staircase in Gibbs. If I had thought of the Hall and the Senior Combination Room and my life in King's for the five years I was a Fellow then there would have been other names and other conversations: Bob Rowthorn and Bernard Williams, Geoffrey Lloyd and Caroline Humphrey, Martin Rees and Ken Moody, Frank Kermode and Stephen Hugh-Jones. There was also Dadie Rylands himself but to do justice to Dadie one would need both the length of a book and more knowledge of the theatre than I possess. But in the 30 years since I left it was to Peter and Tony that I always returned when I visited King's and with their deaths the King's that I knew has receded into history.

Were they typical of King's? It is certain that in any other college they would probably have found their life more difficult. There is in King's a tradition of tolerance which may have pre-dated Keynes and Forster but which any intellectual historian would link both to their names and to the Bloomsbury group which was so important to both King's first and second waves. Tony and Peter both smoked and drank to excess, but that was not typical, certainly of the King's of my day, and my guess would be that it is even less typical now. They were both men who took enormous risks with their lives and in that also they were unusual.

Perhaps more typically of the King's fellowship, they were both convivial men who talked as well as if not better than they wrote and conviviality and conversation were values of the College that I was proud to join in 1976. I hope such virtues still endure. Above all, however, they were men of immense learning and here I think I can find something that links them both and links them to a tradition that is identifiably that of the College of Keynes and Rylands, of Annan and Williams. For both Tony and Peter's learning was exercised in the world. Neither had much time or inclination for the groves of academe. It was John Milton in his famous address to the Parliament of 1643 who said that he could not praise 'a fugitive and cloistered virtue' that 'never sallied out'. Both Tony and Peter lived in cloisters but they sallied out with their learning both in print and in person, and when they returned to the cloisters they brought the world with them to better teach and educate their students. In this they represented that aspect of King's that I most valued.

An anthropologist at King's

Alan Macfarlane

When I first arrived as a Senior Research Fellow in History at King's in 1971, I felt that culture shock which many anthropologists have reported when they visit remote tribes in the Highlands of New Guinea or the foothills of the Himalayas.

Partly it was the grandeur and beauty of the College. I felt so small amidst the lofty buildings and beneath ancient trees of what seemed like some combination of a great stately home and ancient monastery. I had never lived in such a beautiful man-made environment.

Partly it was the presence of illustrious ghostly ancestors in the portraits and the stories I was told. I shared a set with the philosopher Richard Braithwaite and he described the days when the Cambridge Philosophical Society met in Gibbs H3. He demonstrated with Popper's poker the attempted attack on Wittgenstein which Braithwaite himself had managed to deflect.

Partly it was the arcane rituals: the candlelit admission to the Fellowship with Provost Leach's hand on my head as the gowned Fellowship stood around; the special oaths and graces and little significant gestures that punctuated most days and seemed to betoken a special sacred and guarded world.

I had leapt from impecunious research student to Fellowship in a few minutes. Though I had been at Oxford for six years, two years at the London School of Economics and over a year of fieldwork in a remote mountain village in Nepal had again made the whole Oxbridge world strange.

My sense of strangeness has continued over the 40 years since then. Whenever the rituals and buildings and social world begin to become invisible through over-familiarity I go for field trips to distant lands – over 40 to Nepal, India, Japan, China and Australia. Each time I am away, King's seems like a mirage. Each time I return, for a few days at least, it is again a shock.

Towards the end of my time as a teacher in the Department of Social Anthropology, I decided to write down what I think is special about King's and Cambridge, trying to distil a little of the essence of this College as it has stood for the last 570 years.

Anthropology is a comparative discipline. It seeks understanding by setting the particular within the comparative context of the general. As I proceeded through the years at King's and tried to explain it to myself and to new generations of students and visitors, I did so by comparing it to the wide diversity of cultures in the past and present. There are certain distinct similarities between King's and the tribal worlds described by Meyer Fortes, Edmund Leach, Stephen Hugh-Jones, Caroline Humphrey and the other distinguished Anthropology Fellows of King's. The experience of living for a total of three years in a tribal village in Nepal over the same period of 40 years makes it tempting to compare these worlds.

The essence of tribes is that there is no instituted leadership or formalized political system. There may be chiefs, but they depend heavily on consensus and loyalty and many tribes are acephalous or headless. What holds tribes together is not instituted offices and the engines of the state – courts, police, bureaucracies – but rather a common sentiment of 'we' or belonging, combined with unity through structural oppositions expressed in constant feuding and competition for power and resources.

All this reminds me of King's. It is a big College and has no army or police force. The 'College Officers', Provost, Vice-Provost, Bursar and Dean have little formal power. They can only cajole, encourage, arbitrate and mediate. The College has always been full of latent tensions and factions, made manifest in periodic battles at the time of

Provostship elections. It is held together to a certain extent by these very contradictions and oppositions. Yet above this rises a strong sense of identity, 'We, the Provost, Fellows and Students'.

A tribe is usually based on kinship groups who each hold their property as corporate and undivided. The idea of corporations was largely developed by Sir Henry Maine of Trinity Hall and elaborated by Meyer Fortes and his colleagues. Corporations never die. They combine individual rights with communal property in such assets as land, animals and people, songs and myths and intangible knowledge. All of these belong to the group. They should be passed on undiminished by the present to the future. The living members are only trustees in a long chain of being.

This is exactly how King's works. It has continued since 1441 as an undying corporation and the hope is that it will last for many more centuries. The major tangible assets, such as the Chapel, School, Library, Dining Hall, Gibbs, lawns, Fellow's Garden, silver, wine and paintings, are not owned by any particular Fellow, but by all of them, and to a certain extent by the students. The intangible property in the Carol Service and reputation of the Choir, the beauty of the Backs, the rights to be called Fellow, the rituals and ceremonies, are also communal.

Above all, the essence of a tribe is that it is a total, multi-stranded world where the divisions of modern life, the penetration of the State, the Market, the Church and Society in its atomistic forms, have not occurred. This is to a certain extent what I have felt in King's. It is not now as extreme as in some places. In a recent interview with the historian Sir Keith Thomas, he described how in the early 1950s the students were welcomed by the Master of Balliol with a speech which emphasized that they had not come up to Oxford, but to Balliol. Yet in the past King's must have been close to this since its original statutes were unique in protecting it against the intrusions of the Church and the University. Only after 400 years of existence, from the later 19th century, did King's students need to take a University examination in order to obtain their degree.

King's has changed, yet it still has that sense of community which I have witnessed in the Nepalese village where I work. One gets to know people in various contexts and enters into a series of overlapping relationships with them. When an old Kingsman dies and I see the flag fluttering above Gibbs, or hear the bell tolling, I remember John Donne. I know that the death has diminished me, for I am not an island but part of a continent. The bell tolls for me as well. The solemn ceremonies of the memorial service affect me, and watching the recent procession to the gate of King's after the service for Peter Avery reminded me strongly of the death rituals of the Gurung people of the Annapurna Mountains.

There are very few places in the west where the different aspects of life are enclosed within walls – eating, teaching, praying, studying, playing, and performing. It is an intense and meaningful experience. I had known it before in two boarding schools, but that it should continue for 40 years in adult life strikes me as extraordinary.

The great differences between King's and the tribal worlds of anthropological exploration are also worth stressing. King's is an oral culture, full of memories and customs passed on by word of mouth and gossip, as in most tribes. Yet somehow this exists alongside a huge amount of literacy, writing and emphasis on books. Somehow the two co-exist.

King's has the sense of being a family or kin group, that is something to which one belongs and may continue, as in my case, until death us do part. Yet it is a family which chose me, and which I chose and which I can leave. It is more like adoption, or the fictional and artificial lineages called *ie* in Japan. A distant great-uncle, the Provost and ghost story writer MR James, stares down at me in an avuncular way in the Dining Hall. Yet he is my only real ancestor on the walls.

Being elected to King's is based on achievement rather than ascription. It is, in Sir Henry Maine's sense, a world based on contract rather than status or birth. Yet it feels like a real community (blood, place, sentiment) in the sociological sense rather than an association based purely on contract or artificial devices created by the human will. This mixture means that King's falls outside the normal classifications of anthropologists. Like Japan, which I have lived in and studied alongside King's, it is anomalous. It breaks our normal categories of understanding. It is an impossible place, something out of Alice's adventures. It is both within the modern, industrial and capitalist world, but also at an angle to it.

King's shares a physical space with the modern world. It is possible for people to walk through it or sit in its great Chapel. Yet it feels to me a separate and set-apart space, and in that sense 'sacred' in Durkheim's definition. It feels in this age of CS Lewis and Harry Potter to be some kind of portal into another reality.

Likewise it shares physical time with the wider world. Yet the rhythms of its year are non-industrial and give a quality to time which is largely lost in the secular world outside. It is set apart and special, yet in many ways prosaic and humdrum. Although the Chapel makes it clearly something special, the more hidden and enduring structure is easily overlooked and soon overlaid by familiarity.

This College, alongside other colleges in Cambridge and Oxford, has survived against all the odds, and in a way unparalleled in the world. It has managed to change very rapidly and yet to maintain a distinctive core, 'the changing same'. It is an illustration of something much larger than the College itself and has rightly become an icon for those living in an old country.

The mystery of King's and Cambridge is elusive and has to be approached not only from an anthropological but also historical direction. The greatest historian in Cambridge was FW Maitland, Professor of the Laws of England at Downing. I believe that Maitland more than anyone else provides a key to understanding King's through his brilliant insights into the mixture of status and contract in the growth of the institution of the Trust.

I cannot elaborate Maitland's insights here, beyond saying that he understood more deeply than anyone else the nature of Fellowship and the curious institutional hybrids which provide the most important feature of modern democracies and their civil society. Yet I believe that Maitland's description of the Commission of the Peace, or Magistracy, is worth quoting as a perfect epitaph for the College I have known and felt deeply privileged to belong to for over half my life.

'Certainly to any one who has an eye for historic greatness it is a very marvellous institution, this Commission of the Peace, growing so steadily, elaborating itself into ever new forms, providing for ever new wants, expressing ever new ideas, and yet never losing its identity … We shall hardly find any other political entity which has had so eventful and yet so perfectly continuous a life. And then it is so purely English, perhaps the most distinctively English part of all our governmental organization.'

'Are you being served?'

Lucy McMahon

Commodification: 'The action of turning something into, or treating something as, a (mere) commodity' (Oxford English Dictionary).

King's as a conference venue is an all-inclusive prettily packaged commodity, complete with revered history and top-of-the-range service provision. The picture is of fuchsia pink-suited events organizers striding strikingly past the Chapel, of the Hall roof lit with a flare of bright purple light; of Powerpoint with the backdrop of the Library columns through the window. The commodification of King's modernizes the ancient, the embedded, and could even fetishize the cobwebs on the gateposts, should that be required.

But is this so different from the use to which generations of students put the College? Again and again the student papers scrutinize the marketization of education; for £2,600 a year (College fee), students get the de luxe conference package at a bargain:

- All the porters recognizing you and asking how you are – £200
- Having the chance to read the Old Testament, melodramatically, in one of the most famous landmarks in the world – £100
- Meeting a stranger in the bar after formal and having a long discussion about the architecture of early 20th-century film – £100
- That feeling when you walk over King's bridge in the springtime –£100

I could go on, but it is clear that the costs are irrelevant, a poor means of valuation. Perhaps the students get the intangible, priceless elements of King's for something other than money, or maybe the idea of equal exchange in itself is inappropriate; perhaps King's is something with no exchange value. So is the holiday conference season an aberration?

In my first-ever supervision, I sneaked a look out of the window of the Gibbs Building, pretending to be lost in a stream of thought that stretched out over the back lawn and bounced off the river. Where once maybe there was a bustling market, there are beautiful lines, blocks of colour, empty sky, thinking spaces. Nine months later, I was out on that lawn, the sunshine burning the wasps into a frenzy over the shrimps dipped in honey on the trays I wobbled around between the members of the McKinsey Junior Management team. No money, no job in my home town, a boyfriend who had left me for France and – yes – a love of King's College and a desire to overstay my termly welcome – had led the catering manager to take pity on me and offer me a job in conference catering.

King's was fully booked that summer. The evenings rolled over in high-strung rhythms, pauses as the courses were consumed, and then robotic power drives to clear plates, fill glasses, serve with a slick invisibility which I never quite managed. The night always ended in the stench of the huge trough of unconsumed alcohol we decanted from lipstick-smeared glasses. Tania and I would be working on those same glasses the next day, in the quiet tension of a typical summer afternoon in King's Hall. This is when the silver is polished, butter patted, and starched serviettes are made into crowns. Tania always clocked on early, and was always the last to leave. Working three jobs and handing most of her pay to her mother, she was the slickest and most invisible of us all. Others had different techniques: Marneo was a charmer; whisking a select party into the Saltmarsh suites, he would close the door on their immaculately laid-out supper in order to pounce on their coats, inspecting every detail, because, he said, he used to work as an Italian fashion designer and could tell true quality when he saw it. To his dismay, most guests seemed to buy their coats from Marks and Spencer.

Marc and I would sometimes sit for hours behind an empty bar, talking about Polish politics and listening to endless repetitions of Rhianna's 'Umb-er-ella', until the guests burst

out of the Hall to swarm round the thousand pounds left behind the bar for their post-dinner consumptions. I did once consider applying for an internship for one of the companies who held their summer event at King's, but after a night serving their men (and they were men) at the bar, I was put off for life. Mostly they seemed to want me, rather than a drink, to come out from behind the bar, and this was when Marc, or any of the others I worked with never ceased to be brilliant: evading disaster after disaster that loomed from my severe lack of diplomacy.

The (preferred) job of serving the Fellows at high table meant being cocooned in the wine room, away from the mad mass-catering in the Hall. The late Dean, Ian, would always thank us by name. Sometimes, before the conferences hit the bar, a small group of Fellows or graduate students would cluster in, slightly spaced-looking from spending too much of a sunny day reading. Who knows where they vanished to when the paying guests swarmed? About half a year later, I would be in that same wine room – now as KCSU President – where the College Catering Committee had a vigorous dispute over the question of these corporate invasions. It was only here that I realized how the traumas caused by these paying guests spread beyond the stresses of the serving staff.

We were a strange lot, dressed all alike in white and black, but each with our own reasons for being there. There were local sixth-form students, who knew the Cambridge college bars better than I did; Spanish, Italian, Polish and Sri Lankan holiday workers, who bonded over cigarettes and hand gestures; and the King's regular staff, who managed to speak all our languages and know exactly when we were about to make the catastrophic mistake that thanks to them never came. There were jokes, backbiting, fighting, laughter – and sadnesses too. That was the summer of fires on Gran Canaria, and I watched as a friend read in the paper about the ravaging of his childhood spaces. He had to leave the island to get a job, and that's how he came to be at King's.

Interaction with the worldly banality of money is necessary for most of us, even at the expense of the invaluable. The credit crunch did not render the commodification of King's obsolete: its conference earnings remain considerable, and that figure is set to increase with the refurbishment of Market Hostel. So rather than dismiss the conference season as an aberration to the College's integrity, perhaps we can reconceptualize its contribution. King's will remain ever poised on the brink of different identities, as it is manipulated, commodified, lauded, iconized. None of those identities can be encapsulated in a price or a wage, a degree certificate or a wedding photograph. But if these things are just passwords for a hybrid, dynamic reality, surely no Marxist could complain?

First ladies of King's

Alison Maitland

Peering at the faded King's College 'Freshmen' photograph of 1972, it is hard to tell that a sexual revolution is taking place. The long hair worn by many of the men makes it more difficult to distinguish gender, and the year group gazes placidly at the camera as if unaware it is making history.

Yet this was the moment when 500 years of male academic exclusivity were swept away by the admission of the first Kingswomen. The decision by King's, Clare and Churchill to take the lead as the first Oxbridge colleges to go co-educational was a momentous one, not least for those who experienced it at first hand.

Susan Tomes, then a music student and now a renowned pianist and member of the Florestan Trio, was one of the first 30 women undergraduates to arrive at King's that year. She remembers it as a bittersweet experience. 'It felt ground-breaking, but not at all easy,' says Susan, whose daughter Maya Feile Tomes is now a Classics scholar at King's. 'I had a very strong sensation of the College being divided in its attitude to women coming in. There were people who were thrilled, but probably a larger contingent of older students and Fellows who were not pleased and tried to pretend we were not there.'

Some male traditions adapted more slowly than others. 'The porters used to call me "Sir" because they were so much in the habit of doing so.' She recalls being either loved or hated during her first year. 'There wasn't very much normality in between. Each of the women had a coterie of admirers or supporters, but there was a large number of men who would look the other way when passing the women.'

That early scrutiny was no doubt intensified by the initial restriction on the number of women undergraduates. The limit of 30 was one of the measures agreed by the co-ed colleges to placate the all-women colleges, which feared that King's, Clare and Churchill would cream off the best female candidates.

Susan Tomes (pictured top left), the first woman in the Chetwynd Society, a year after women were admitted to King's.

The decision to admit women was motivated by egalitarianism and self-interest. 'There was a feeling that there were a large number of very talented women not being given the chance to come to Oxbridge, while colleges were admitting less-talented men,' says Dr Tess Adkins, former Senior Tutor and Vice-Provost of King's, who was appointed Tutor responsible for the new women in 1972. 'So, one aim was to improve our academic results, which we succeeded in doing for a large number of years.'

Professor Jim Turner was Admissions Tutor at the time and sums it up like this: 'It was mainly a feeling that in the modern world it was better to educate men and women together; women would help create a more natural environment. Moreover, we hoped to attract some very able students, which would be good for the academic record of the College.'

This was pretty enlightened thinking for the early 1970s, given that the Equal Pay Act of 1970 had not yet come into force and the Sex Discrimination Act would not be on the statute book until 1975. Yet today's students would probably be surprised such arguments had to be made.

Jim and the senior tutors at Churchill and Clare had the job of working out the admission process. 'The overwhelming problem was to persuade the women's colleges to negotiate about the means,' he recalls.

'The discussion was extremely complicated. Since we had no idea how many women would apply to the three men's colleges, it was very important that any woman applying to the three would be considered by the women's colleges if the three had no place for her. The task of talking to the women's colleges fell largely to me, and I spent a lot of time talking to both Cambridge and Oxford senior staff. They were very keen to increase the number of women in Cambridge, but were worried that we would attract the brightest women.'

The first women candidates were an amazing group, he says. 'In the autumn of 1971, Geoffrey Lloyd (then Senior Tutor) and I interviewed a large batch of talented women for admission in 1972. Each seemed to be bright, to have travelled extensively and to possess a sophistication lacking in many of the men applicants.'

Part of the deal to protect the interests of the women's colleges, which he admits still embarrasses him, was a promise to restrict entrance scholarships to male students. Susan Tomes was one of those who should have had a scholarship. 'I was told I could go as a commoner to King's, but if I went to Girton, Newnham or New Hall I could have a scholarship,' she says. 'I didn't hesitate to go to King's because of its reputation for music. The scholarship went to a boy. Strangely enough, I thought that was just fine – that was the way the world worked. I didn't think of kicking up a fuss.'

The headmistress of her school, George Watson's Ladies' College, and the headmaster of its counterpart for boys, George Watson's College, did kick up a fuss, however. They wrote a letter to *The Times* saying that discrimination in the award of scholarships was wrong in an age of equal opportunities.

The start of emancipation at King's coincided with great political turmoil overseas, including the struggle against apartheid in South Africa and the unfolding Watergate scandal in the US that brought down President Richard Nixon. For many students, this was a time of political awakening. There were torchlit protest marches down King's Parade to demand that other men's colleges accept women – and there was a student rent strike to persuade the College to disinvest from South Africa.

Dr Charmian Kenner, who arrived in the first year of women and became Secretary of KCSU, recalls the excitement of that time. 'Those were heady days,' she says.

'We were welcomed in the College, but there were still a few people outside who hadn't caught up yet. I remember having to sign up for lectures – you had to put name and college, so I wrote "King's", and the man at the desk said, "But that's not possible!" and I said, "Well, it is now!" That was a very satisfying moment.'

Then she began to realize that 'storming the citadel hadn't changed the world' for women. 'It probably should have sunk in on day one when I was writing my election manifesto for becoming Secretary of KCSU, and I had to include my typing skills in order to get elected. But I was too excited to notice.'

Charmian, now a lecturer at the Centre for Language, Culture and Learning at Goldsmiths College, University of London, remembers attending a Cambridge Students' Union meeting about apartheid in South Africa. 'At the end of the meeting, one of the Students' Union officers, who was a woman, got up and asked, "What about the situation of women in South Africa?" and she was booed by most of the audience, who of course were mostly men. You can't imagine it happening now, but I've never forgotten it.'

In her third year, she attended her first Women's Liberation meeting in Cambridge.

'I remember standing at the edge of the room, not sure if I wanted to be involved. Then I heard someone say, 'The women at Cambridge are being educated to be the wives of the men at Cambridge', and this struck me like a thunderbolt. It resonated with something I had sensed deep down and I knew it to be true. We were expected to grow up as intelligent companions – and bring up intelligent children – for the men who would go out into the world and have the Real Careers. It was the view of society in general, and simply by being the first women at King's we couldn't walk away from that.'

The radical campaigns of the time gave Eleanor (Leo) Sharpston – subsequently the first British woman to be appointed to the European Court of Justice, where she serves as an Advocate General – a chance to show her mettle at the very start of her King's career.

Her 'non-subject' entrance interview was brutally tough. The questions included whether she would accept a theoretical invitation to do a lecture tour to racially segregated audiences in South Africa and whether the Chapel Choir should be mixed. Then one of the interviewers said, 'I suppose you're in favour of Women's Lib.' Convinced that things had gone badly, she felt she had nothing to lose. 'If you mean "Do I burn bras?" then no,' came her withering response. 'With my bust size I find them comfortable. If you mean "Do I want to be treated as a second-class citizen?" then it has never occurred to me that what would matter would be my genitals rather than my brain or my character.'

She was, in fact, just the kind of bright 'survivor' that King's was looking for in its early female cohorts, though she didn't know it then. Back home in Vienna, her damp spirits were lifted by a message from Girton offering her a major scholarship if she changed her mind and went there.

'I went for a long walk in the Vienna woods and concluded that I would see Girton in hell and would wait for King's,' recalls Leo, who came up in 1973. 'I assumed from the offer that I'd done well in my exam papers.' In fact, she had come top of Classics in the whole University, though she too was denied the scholarship she had earned because of the deal with the women's colleges.

As she waited, another offer came from Lady Margaret Hall, Oxford. There was still no word from King's. Eventually, a scruffy brown envelope with a second-class English stamp arrived in Vienna on 5 January 1973 with the message: 'Dear Eleanor, We are happy to offer you a place. Please let us know by 6 January.' Her family dashed to the post office to send an acceptance telegram before it closed for the Epiphany public holiday in Austria. Leo's early loyalty to the College, where she studied Economics, Languages and Law (while doing a lot of sport, student politics and journalism), has continued in her subsequent career, combining the Bar with lecturing in European law and a Fellowship at King's since 1992.

The arrival of women at the College posed some interesting questions for the senior staff. How should they be accommodated: in separate areas, or all mixed up with the men? What about washing facilities? In the event, the women were housed in blocks in Garden Hostel and Keynes for their first year, after which there was a room ballot and they went their own ways. Some contemporaries recall that the accommodation was far from ideal, while others say the women at least benefited from relatively up-to-date bathroom facilities.

Rumours that tutors debated whether to provide long mirrors and sewing machines for the women are sadly untrue. However, the College sought advice about potential problems from other universities with mixed halls of residence. 'I do remember that one Hall said to beware of men taking advantage of women in such matters as the darning of socks!' says Jim Turner.

Not surprisingly, there was considerable media interest. The admission of women made the national news and Jim was interviewed on the radio. The more salacious and moralizing sections of the media were keen to sniff out 'scandal'. On one occasion, this was provided by the installation of condom machines in the ladies' lavatory, at the request of female students (contraceptives were already available in the gents).

'I arranged for it to happen, then got myself into deep water with the press,' recalls Tess Adkins. 'I stupidly sent round a note saying "I've put this contraceptive machine into the women's loo" and one of the assistant women staff picked this up and must have sent it to the press.' The *Daily Express* launched an unpleasant personal attack on her.

In 1975, after the first year of women had graduated, the journalist Tina Brown arrived at King's to investigate co-residency, causing senior staff another headache. *Stop Press with Varsity*, the student newspaper, reported in January 1976 that 'a certain Miss Tina Brown' was causing outrage among students with her probing questions into their sex lives. The subsequent *Sunday Times* article by the young Ms Brown tried hard to be provocative. The female students in the King's bar 'are characterized by a delinquent cool,' she wrote. 'They wear short denim jackets or crotch-hugging velvet jeans and stare at you combatively.' Her article claimed that intrigue was rife at King's and affairs between students were short-lived, but she gave surprisingly few details of the 'sexual action' she alluded to. 'She was looking for gossip and couldn't find much,' says Tess.

Women's experiences inevitably differed. Tess remembers that a few found it very tough and there were 'one or two who left'. Others settled in quickly and either encountered few difficulties or just ignored them.

The women did have an effect on the men's behaviour, at least to begin with. Dr Sally Millership, a medical student who matriculated in 1972, says the male students were 'terribly polite' for the first three weeks. 'They opened doors and offered us chairs. Then they decided we were honorary men – familiarity breeds contempt! It just seemed quite normal after the first few weeks.'

Sally joined the College Boat Club, becoming the first woman to cox the men's first VIII. This breakthrough did not stretch to the Amateur Rowing Association, however, which told the King's captain that mixed crews 'would never do'.

Now a medical consultant on communicable disease control with the Health Protection Agency, Sally regards her time at King's as 'the best three years of my life' and keeps in close touch with the College as co-representative of her year group. 'I never got involved in Women's Lib,' she says. 'I was just having too much fun.'

Fitting in could involve going to extraordinary lengths. Susan Tomes wanted to join the Chetwynd Society. After she had attended some meetings as a guest, the exclusive debating club eventually decided to elect her – the first woman to be admitted – but insisted on referring to her as 'Mr Tomes'. As a musician, she says, being at King's was an unbeatable experience, benefiting both from the long tradition of exalted music in the Chapel and from meeting so many interesting people who were experts in their field. However, the first women also used up a lot of energy working out how to be part of a man's world. 'Perhaps it was not necessary and maybe it held us back that we were trying to work out how to be honorary men.'

In her experience, the first Kingswomen displayed little sisterly solidarity, partly because many had come from single-sex schools and were meeting men as peers for the first time. 'Women in the first year were not particularly friends with each other,' she says. 'We were entering a College with 400 men and 30 women. Finding oneself with so many men, you tried to be one of the boys, to be accepted. Looking back, that was a shame. We could have supported each other. Now there are all kinds of women's solidarity groups.'

As several of the women pointed out, the next generation finds it hard to believe some of the obstacles women were up against 40 years ago, let alone 500, and we should celebrate the part that King's played in helping to break these down. History has to be retold, over and over, or it is quickly forgotten.

'Today's Kingswomen take it so much for granted that they have a right to be there,' says Susan.

When the College put on a Women's Dinner last year, I was astounded to hear one of my daughter's female friends, herself a Kingswoman, asking why on earth women should have the privilege of an exclusive dinner. She said she thought it was unnecessary, and unfair unless the College also put on an exclusive 'men's dinner'.

My daughter, who has been forcibly educated by me about the history of women in the College, told her friend that there had been nothing but exclusive 'men's dinners' for 500 years before women came along in 1972!

Washing a 'Free Mandela' slogan off the side of the Chapel, 1964.

The road to radicalization

Arzu Merali

2009. It is the Annual Al-Quds Day pro-Palestinian march in London. Nazi salutes greet us as we walk as Muslims, Jews, Christians, atheists, and more denominations and beliefs, divine, sublime – all transformative in their mix, but united in cause. Last year a group of racists stormed the family section of the march, populated mainly by women with young children. This year, as last, flags of Israel, the Shah of Iran and Iranian communists fly against us with abusive slogans. They are joined by the Green 'reform' group in Iran. The English Defence League is the most vociferous this year, shouting 'Pakis go home,' and 'Muslim scum off our streets!'

It is 20 years and a bit more since I set foot in King's. The time for radicals is upon us again, but are we ready to accept where that mantle has fallen?

1989. 'An overview of College applications suggests that King's politics has turned green over red.' Thus spoke Senior Tutor Tess Adkins as we sat through some matriculation event. Still radical though, still cutting-edge politics, still in the face of the Cambridge establishment, the conveyor belt of governance, the great and the good. Didn't it occur to anyone that when political extremists hail from the same bastions as the pillars of the establishment, maybe they're not so radical? And maybe the mainstream is, well, all of the stream?

2010. I am a radical. I'd like to think so anyway, but my badge of honour is somewhat tainted. No ministerial position, peerage or alternative comedy show appears on my CV, despite those being typical career paths of the politically extreme once they've graduated and got 'proper' jobs. Back in 1989 my dress – long, flowing black coats and headscarves – defined me as a Muslim fundamentalist. These days I'm defined as worse. The accusation of being a potential terrorist is the least worrying. What's most disturbing is being labelled as the unruly and ungrateful guest, the 'you got it better here than your own country' line, the introduction to *Newsnight* that asks if the age of Muslim privileges over the 'host' community must end. I am many things, and I may be alienated. But I am not an alien, and I'm not a parasite.

Yet my road to radicalization – to political Islam, supposedly – and to becoming an unwitting, unwilling and still unqualified spokesperson and activist for beleaguered (mainly Muslim) communities, also began in earnest at King's.

This is my story of two and a bit years. Of how Muslim politics, feminism, the dying left and an ebullient King's English team, informs the work of Muslim civil society. Not the benign civil society that blights minority existence – where 'leaders' go cap in hand for a meet and greet with Ministers, tea and biscuits and a photo op – but the world where activism is deemed inimical to wider society, the damn-ye-with-fire-and-brimstone and *Sunday Express* headlines type. It's the story of how King's English paradoxically and inadvertently shaped my understanding of anti-Muslim hostility and restored my faith in a world that seemed to grow ever more distinct from me the further within it I progressed. Above all, this piece is a justification of why radicalism in all its forms is still a good thing.

1976. I find myself reviewing life for many reasons – therapy being one. 'Why', I recently mused, 'did the infant school teacher who referred to me as a wog, and my friend Strelli a nig-nog, stop doing so as we got older?' Mrs B of a North London school didn't stop being nasty to us or to Strelli's brother Peter or the handful of non-whites at school. It was just the name calling that stopped. Rather slow, I now realize that 1976 was the year of the Race Relations Act – a piece of legislation that, ironically, in recent years I have found myself railing against because it doesn't cover religious minorities (thus allowing, among other things, a great big British National Party-sized loophole).

At the end of my time at King's, I presented my thoughts on how, despite the very recent furore over free speech, when it comes to minorities they have none, except to speak what they are expected to say in the public realm, and then keep their own thoughts to themselves. Had I been at another college, I might well have been laughed out of the tutorial. Instead I was introduced to the idea of 'muted group theory' and its advocate. Many years later, working in human rights research, that theory surfaced again, and has become an important tool in advocating for minorities in many contexts.

As an activist from various marginalized and minority groups (women, Gujerati, Muslim), I analyse and am the subject of analysis. But being in charge of the process rather than another victim of anthropology can in some ways be traced to both good and bad experiences in these somewhat formative years.

As a result, in 1997, and as a way to obviate the increasing internalization of negativity around being a Muslim, with several of us like-minded Islamists (in the days when that wasn't such a bad word, though still ridiculously ambiguous), I helped set up the Islamic Human Rights Commission (IHRC). A little dabbling in law and then journalism led me to believe that rather than becoming a cog in the wheel or endlessly pontificating about how bad the world is, maybe I should do something to change it.

IHRC moved a long way from a group of do-gooders trying to change the world and better the lot of oppressed people, in what we soon realized was a very middle-class and, on occasion, patronizing way. We none of us would have classed ourselves thus, but for me at least a dose of the reality check I got at King's regarding class, aspiration and belonging happened all over again at the outset of this organization.

Back in Cambridge, one of the many surprises at King's was the continued mistaking of my heritage and nationality. Born and brought up in North London, from parents of Indian heritage, I was routinely asked about life in the Middle East, and a one-night trip home was reported to College officials by one tutor as a week-long sojourn in Dubai, from whence I supposedly hailed. So there I was, no longer on the periphery but firmly inside the Centre, ie King's – but King's or not, it was understood that I did not belong there. Was I surprised? Not really. Disappointed? Perhaps.

Yet this reality check on the slow and insidious journey into the middle class was worthwhile and necessary. At the inception of IHRC, my Cambridge degree had helped me climb establishment ladders without even realizing it. And suddenly I realized that I was in danger of neglecting the grassroots I claimed to care about. 'It's great you're taking on that case in Turkey, Nigeria etc.' people would say, 'but did you know that this happened to me here in London?' We were receiving increasing requests for help from Muslims facing discrimination, harassment and various forms of hatred in the UK.

Then they started – reality checks galore. That's what happens when you start asking beleaguered communities what they think, rather than impose your own beliefs on them regarding the need for their emancipation. Above all, you realize that the privileges in your life were not actually the top-notch education you had, but the opportunity of having people who face routine discrimination and hatred tell you from their heart what they really believe in and what they want for a better society for everyone.

I remember my embarrassment on reading one respondent's answer to the question: 'What are your expectations of the British government with regard to law?' It went: 'I expect the government to embrace Islamic shariah, because that is the only way to guarantee equality between black and white, men and women, for everyone to be equal.' I was embarrassed because that was my view also, but I had not expressed it.

1989. Events which had a profound impact on my political radicalization – the Lebanese civil war, the Iran–Iraq war – were now over. And there I was, all in black, standing as a woman, as a person of Gujerati heritage, in the grounds of King's. Eighteen months previously, I had been miniskirted and Marxist. It was at King's I found myself an out-and-out Islamic revolutionary.

I smile now to recollect how many battles I thought I had won by getting to that point. At the same time I was sure that the institution I stood in was an obstacle, not a vehicle, for my world view. I would be a truly different radical. A super-combo of Islamic, feminist (because to my mind, then and I guess still now, only Islam really understands standpoint feminism), and socialist (which still meant something back then) radical. My very existence would destabilize cruel and oppressive power (smile). Friends and family will attest I am still a big-headed pain in the butt but I am no longer 18 years old, and I know, in my case at least, resistance takes more than just breathing.

Back at the age of 18, though, that was the world of Thatcher, and the insidious notion of the state as individual selves had permeated most polemic. King's English taught me the profound connection between free speech, power and injustice. I learned then – though perhaps deep down I already knew – that the aspiration of many of my parents' generation was an illusion. They had come to the UK to be educated and better their opportunities, but I could see that becoming a part of this society would take more than simply joining in.

King's English, or some aspects of it, understood about structure and canon and power. Those whose work has kept the idea of 'canon' in its place as power broker but not all powerful, include my tutor Peter de Bolla and my peer Angie Sandhu. It was a clarion voice that clamoured to be heard – and was heard by some at least in the wider university community. Maud Ellman gave lectures to packed-out halls; the arrival of Edward Said for one evening saw doors locked to keep out the hordes.

Through that voice I came to know that there were other forms of racism I had not experienced. My first experience of one – something that today is loosely defined as 'Islamophobia' – was at King's and its effect remains.

1991. It was my last year at King's when, in a joint session with second years, our Director of Studies started talking about how, however much we might protest, we had all been brought up in the same culture and imbued with its canon. Of course, he said, there is one person here who hasn't, but has done an amazing job of understanding despite the cultural difference. Back then, I wondered why the second years were looking at me as he was speaking. Now, I wonder whether any of them were embarrassed by their assumptions, when he pointed out that he was referring not to me, but to a student born and raised in continental Europe.

So reviled are we, that in today's society veiled women are paradoxically denounced as both subjugated and threatening at once. We are not considered to be part of the society we were born and brought up in. You realize that when you are quite young. Many of us spend formative years trying to be accepted and then finding some self-worth in the realization that it is not your own personal failure but racism – whether it is putatively about ethnic or religious heritage – that prevents you from 'fitting in'. Some of us never get that far.

You realize it too as a woman. You can't climb, because not only is the world male dominated, but also male structured, and there are sisters as well as men, trying to drag you down. As a non-white woman, you begin to see that while your understanding of patriarchy across cultures is the same, maybe your white sisters don't recognize this equality of oppression. No matter what level of discrimination they face, they perceive your state to be worse. When I donned the hijab, I thought I was proving otherwise by doing so as an expression of claiming the public space without being subjected to the male gaze. Over 20 years later, when British cabinet minister Jack Straw lambasted face-veiled women as 'disturbing' and received support, it showed just how little has changed, and that maybe things have actually become worse.

The biggest challenge, though, is not law or law enforcement, it's still all about words and the power they convey, and the power they deny, when democracy means the rule of the majority and the permanent marginalization of minorities.

Looking back, I can't but enjoy the reputation that King's has for radicalism. I remember a group tutorial where we met with students from other colleges for a seminar on 'Tragedy'. The result was an almighty clash of civilizations. The tutor (non-King's) described her summer teaching inmates at a nearby prison. She was so happy, she said, to be back teaching people who really understand. The leader of a King's revolt in this seminar stated that he was only studying the tragedies at hand because he had to, and not because they had intrinsic worth. His heretical claim provoked accusations (including from one traitorous Kingsman) that the 'King's group' were (predictably) a bunch of Bolshies.

My favourite recollection of that confrontation was the remark from one of 'our group': 'If our Director of Studies heard that we had been labelled with some sort of corporate identity he would fall on the floor and piss himself laughing.' Her point ended there, but mine continues, because that is the point. When you are seen as radical you are demonized for it, but also your act of assertion is a force for good. You may not wish to defy, but ultimately you do.

2009. The battle between individual, group and society poses questions that still need answering (and in some dusty Cambridge corridors remain as questions yet to be asked) not just among indigenes of South America or the masses who live on a dollar a day but minorities of every country. The lesson of the United States played out in the holocausts of slavery and the near-extermination of native America scream at us about Palestine, and so we march every year.

While we march, others die. I didn't learn that at King's. In the end, however 'radical' King's is within Cambridge, in the wider context it remains at the core from which hail so many of the (wo)men who launched and justified wars, and in this and other ways kill so many millions.

So King's is a mixed memory. An experience I am grateful for, yes, if only because I know what I am rejecting with the benefit of having been there. I don't reject because I desire to self-segregate – although many claim that is what those like me are doing. I reject it because of its irrelevance as a transformative mechanism to those millions who continue to die.

I am a believer and I believe that all those killed in the bloody wars, black ops and coups are martyrs. I do not believe that their deaths will be in vain. Incidentally I also believe they live in eternal bliss. If King's radicalism translates one day into a force that supports the expression and aspirations of those billions disenfranchised, instead of denying them that agency and demonizing them as freedom-haters, then I can say that King's radicalism is worthy of its name. Maybe then I will want to share opportunistically in its glory.

I hope that day comes. But right now, the struggles I see and the ones in which I am involved are still set apart from the world of King's. People laughed, even as recently as three years back, at the thought that today we would be faced with fascists marching on the streets of Britain, and three years at King's didn't warn us that fascism could rise again from its world.

Maybe this assessment is just too bleak. To be honest, I am not sure I care. I may well be scarred by one tutor's assessment (not to me but a friend), as being incapable of understanding English literature because I was a Muslim. If so, then maybe this is all just too personal – except that, I find myself one of many millions who are dismissed in the same way. IHRC was one of the first human rights groups to flag up impending genocide in Darfur. We were accused of supporting Islamist separatists, and later forgotten as one of the early warners. We received hate mail from aggrieved activists asking (without actually bothering to look at our website) why it was we didn't do anything for the oppressed Darfurians.

We struggle still. I survive to write. Others survive to fight.

Goldie's cap

Jonathan Mirsky

Goldsworthy Lowes Dickinson, who entered King's College in 1881, was said to have 'surmised that he must have been a Chinaman in a previous existence'. He was given a Chinese cap by Hsu Chingshu (who came to King's in 1921, and was known later as the famous poet Xu Chi-mo) and wore it when he dined at High Table. Apparently it was Dickinson's *Letters of John Chinaman,* which many readers assumed to be from a genuine Chinese, that influenced Arthur Waley, who came to King's in 1907, the greatest China (and Japan) specialist King's ever produced, although Waley taught himself Chinese years after leaving King's. There is something about Dickinson and Waley that stands out as typical of Kingsmen fascinated by China: few studied Chinese at Cambridge, but all looked at it at different angles from most other Sinologues.

One day in 1961 when Arthur Waley was visiting King's, we sat in the sun outside the Chapel. He knew that I was teaching spoken Chinese at Cambridge and rather sadly said he envied me that I could speak and he couldn't. It was a mystery to me that he never went to China, so taking a big chance, with the greatest Sinologue of his time, I asked him why. Years before, he told me, he had been invited and got as far as Hawaii. He waited a day, got onto another plane, and returned to London. It had occurred to him that the People's Republic would be altogether different from the traditional China whose texts, ranging over 2,000 years, he had studied most of his adult life. 'I was afraid I would be disappointed,' he said. A few weeks later he invited me down to his Bloomsbury flat for tea. When I got there he opened the door and showed me some text. 'Can you help me with this line?' he asked. I told him I didn't recognize the language. He told me it was Uighur, the language of China's main Muslim minority. I have never met a foreigner who knows this language but I'm sure Waley did. We then went down into Gordon Square where Waley settled down with his Uighur while I read the newspaper. After two hours he stood up, thanked me for coming and told me that the great Tibetanist Giuseppe Tucci was arriving any minute from Rome to see him and he mustn't be kept waiting.

There were of course distinguished Kingsmen who read Chinese as undergraduates. Martin Bernal, who entered King's in 1957, moved from a First-class Chinese degree to Vietnamese studies and eventually to his contentious three-volume *Black Athena,* showing the African origins of ancient Greece. Mark Elvin, who entered King's the year before, also a First but in History, began learning Chinese on his own, published at an early age *The Pattern of the Chinese Past,* still regarded as of first-rate importance, on why China never developed real science despite its many other great accomplishments. Years later he wrote another mighty book, *The Retreat of the Elephants,* on the slow ecological degradation of north China over many centuries. Endymion Wilkinson, who entered King's in 1960, another First in Chinese, rose to be a very senior EC official in China.

My own Chinese career began when I was reading History at King's because of a conversation with an elderly American woman who had been a missionary for 40 years in China. 'Jonathan, you should study Chinese,' she advised one day in 1955 when we were lying in a meadow of wild flowers in Switzerland. She said this because my father, AE Mirsky (who had been at King's in the early 1920s getting a PhD in Biochemistry – ironically in the same year as Joseph Needham, who would totally change fields in the 1940s to become the world expert on Chinese science) had been at Peking Union Medical College in the early 1930s and she thought that would inspire me. I asked for advice from Gustav Haloun, the Professor of Chinese at Cambridge, who immediately said I mustn't study at Cambridge but invaluably advised me where to study in America. Fortunately I took his advice. This led to three years of Chinese language study in the US, four more years in Taiwan (Americans couldn't go to China proper) and teaching a summer course in spoken Chinese at Cambridge. I then taught Chinese and Vietnamese history and Chinese language in two American universities and campaigned for Washington to stop pretending the People's Republic of China didn't exist and that the real China, with its capital in Taipei, was on Taiwan with Chiang Kai-shek as its president. In April 1972, just after Richard Nixon held his conversations with Mao, I travelled with a dozen other young China scholars to China where we spent six weeks. Before that trip I was convinced that the Maoist revolution, and even the Cultural Revolution, which was still going on, were good for China. After only a few days there I became convinced that something bad had happened and was still happening and that great efforts were being made by our hosts to cover this up, something at which the Chinese still excel. Most of my colleagues on that trip – who have since changed their minds about China – resented my scepticism and told me that I should be more sympathetic. A few years later, with Mao dead, I met by chance one of our guides who admitted to me, 'We wanted to put rings in your noses and you helped us put them there.'

In 1975 I moved to Britain and became the China correspondent of *The Observer* and later, in 1993, the East Asia editor of *The Times*, from which I resigned in 1998 after my views of China collided with those of the proprietor, Rupert Murdoch.

Goldsworthy Lowes Dickinson by Roger Fry.

My years on *The Observer* were happy ones. Beginning in 1981 I went to Tibet six times and saw plainly what happens in a so-called 'minority area' when China occupies it. This is not merely a Communist problem: the Hans, the ethnic Chinese, have traditionally looked down on non-Hans; when strong, the Hans have defeated their non-Han enemies. Sometimes it has been the reverse, notably with the Mongols and Manchus who established new dynasties.

It was Tiananmen, however, which underlined for me, after many years of reporting from China, what Communist rule meant.

At about 2am on the night of 3–4 June 1989, as I watched the Chinese People's Liberation Army march into Tiananmen Square, I listened to a piece of advice from the man next to me. 'Nothing to worry about,' he said. 'The PLA would never fire on the people.' The night air was filled with shrieks and the yellow light from the lamp poles glistened on a wet red smear where a small tank had just run over a demonstrator. Loudspeakers were ordering us to clear the Square and to watch out for pickpockets. White streaks shot across the sky and sparks flew off the paving stones. 'What are those streaks?' someone asked, and my neighbour said they were blank bullets. 'And the sparks off the stones?' A special kind of blank, he added, with such authority that I believed him. Then he doubled over. When I pulled him up, a red stain was widening on his T-shirt. His friends pulled him away into the screaming crowd, through which I could see three-wheeled carts with dead or wounded demonstrators stretched out on them rushing through the pandemonium. By now the helmeted and flak-jacketed troops trotting along under the walls of the Forbidden City were very close. I turned to leave through the Gate under the gigantic portrait of Mao Zedong; a few days earlier three men from central China had hurled eggshells filled with paint at the portrait and the red, yellow and green ran down the impassive face and over the huge mole. This was so shocking for some of the demonstrators, who earlier had been shouting 'Deng Xiaoping resign!' that they seized the three men and hustled them over to the nearest police post. They went to jail for years. Within an hour a giant crane arrived and an identical Mao portrait replaced the desecrated one.

It was under that new portrait, smooth and impassive, that I was set upon by a squad of the People's Armed Police who had just been assaulted by young men hurling flaming bottles of gasoline. Out of their minds with fear and rage, the police were beating people to the ground with their truncheons and then shooting them with their pistols. They knocked out three of my teeth, fractured my arm, and beat me black and blue. Robert Thomson of the *Financial Times* dragged me away from the men who would have shot me on the ground within seconds.

But does Tiananmen matter any more in China? Some years ago a sensitive young Chinese student gave me a piece of advice. 'Jonathan, listen to me. Tiananmen was long ago. Put it out of your mind. None of us care about that anymore. We just want to get on with our lives. The incident is in the past.'

'The Incident.' *Shijian*. That is one of the official words for what happened in Tiananmen. Or 'the counter-revolutionary uprising'. Sometimes the word 'criminal' is added. Then-President Jiang Zemin dismissed criticism of 1989 as 'much ado about nothing', and some years ago, on the anniversary of 4 June, when a journalist from Hong Kong asked Premier Zhu Rongji about the day he said, 'I've completely forgotten it.'

If what President Jiang and Premier Zhu said was what they really believed it would be fascinatingly pathological. Tiananmen is, after all, a generic name for an uprising that occurred in at least 200 places, in almost all the major cities and in outlying regions where one might have supposed people hardly knew of the events in Tiananmen after Party General Secretary Hu Yaobang died. Deng had already sacked Hu for closing in on corrupt Politburo members and being soft on Tibet. Beijing's students, for whom

Hu was that rarity, an honest official, went into mourning and marched to the Square, where they burst into emotional speeches, extending their remarks over the next days into the shortcomings of the Party. The crowds in the Square, enthusiastically singing the Internationale and the National Anthem, were good-natured and peaceful. But when a *People's Daily* editorial on 26 April condemned the demonstrators as conspirators bent on bringing down the Party and the State and wiping out the economic reforms, the mood in the Square changed to resentment and militancy.

Although it is fashionable in China and among some Western China specialists to dismiss the Tiananmen demonstrators as little more than selfish students, in fact what they were soon demanding was indeed counter-revolutionary: freedom of speech and the press, an end to corruption, and leaders who would discuss what needed to be done. This was overwhelmingly popular in Beijing, from whose streets the police soon largely vanished, ordinary people spoke to foreigners without weighing their words and clapped wherever the students marched. Before long, in Beijing and other places, citizens were blocking motorized military columns to prevent them from reaching the demonstrators.

The nature and scope of this national uprising, according to various sources, the most recent being the memoir of then-Party General Secretary Zhao Ziyang, who died after 16 years of house arrest for advising against a crackdown in the Square, were plain from the many sources of intelligence available to the tiny group of leaders assembled by Deng Xiaoping to consider counter-measures. These 'elders' and a few others were by no means agreed; two or three, including Zhao Ziyang, counselled at least caution with the demonstrators. Against their advice came the words, recorded in the 'Tiananmen Papers', of the 81-year-old retired general and vice-president Wang Zhen: 'Those goddamn bastards … we should send the troops right now to grab those counter-revolutionaries … We've got to do it or the common people will rebel. Anybody who tries to overthrow the Communist Party deserves death and no burial.' This happened; on the morning of 4 June I saw dozens of unarmed people mowed down by the army in front of the Peking Hotel and the bodies of most of those killed in the days after 3–4 June disappeared. There followed a widespread *qingcha* or 'ferreting-out' of one quarter of the Party, at least ten million members, who were considered unreliable or weak. While relatively few students were persecuted, many workers were arrested, tortured and shot. The leaders' nightmare of a union of intellectuals and workers had been made real by the tented 'village' of industrial workers in one corner of the Square. Nothing is more alarming to the Party than the increasingly large and turbulent strikes and demonstrations of badly paid and laid-off industrial workers. Farmers too regularly crowd into country towns to howl against illegal taxes and petty corruption. While there may not be another 'Tiananmen' in Beijing triggered by students, it could take place anywhere, led this time by farmers or workers, against whom the armed forces, uneasy about using force in 1989, might be unwilling to open fire.

I believe that, like much else in China since 1949, Tiananmen was so horrible that many Chinese put it to the back of their minds. I have often asked them about ghastly things I knew had happened to them during the Cultural Revolution and been greeted with a regretful smile and a dismissive wave of the hand. So it appears with Tiananmen. After all, many millions of Chinese and their families were affected by the post-4 June 'ferreting-out'. When Chinese say, echoing the Party, that 'stability' must be maintained and that in retrospect Tiananmen reminds them of the Cultural Revolution, I don't believe them. That chaos of 1966–76 was provoked by Mao and the Party (as the Party admitted in 1981) who were responsible, as well, for the entire 50 years of disasters, including the 1959–61 famine.

Tiananmen remains neuralgic. If the word 'Tiananmen' appears in an internal e-mail (along with others such as Dalai Lama, Tibet, Taiwan or democracy) there may be a knock on the door followed by interrogation and detention. Google, Yahoo and Microsoft have furnished the technology that permits the security services to police the Internet to China. In the West, the first entry for 'Tiananmen Square' on Google shows the famous picture of a man standing in front of a tank. In the Chinese version of Google we see children flying kites in the square. (But early in 2010, Google itself began to have doubts about its Chinese operations and the degree of official interference with its activities.)

There will certainly be a reckoning, and it will not be much ado about nothing. In 1991, the mother of an unemployed 22-year-old youth, Zha Aiguo (Aiguo means 'Love China', a common Cultural Revolution name) who was killed during Tiananmen, visited his grave. As was normal in those days she was detained and taken to a local police station for interrogation. There, she said, she scrawled these words in the dirt: 'Pen and paper will speak in a thousand years. The children and the grandchildren will eventually settle the score.'

Two years after Tiananmen I was told by a Foreign Ministry minder that 'you are no longer welcome in China' and was asked to leave. It seems a long way from Goldsworthy Lowes Dickinson's *Letters of John Chinaman* and Arthur Waley deciding he would be disappointed if he went to China. I can't say I was disappointed but I have seen enough.

'Dear Virginia Woolf'

Kate Newmann

Dear Virginia,

You may not remember that I wrote to you when I came up to King's in 1985 to study English. The first letter, written in response to *A Room of One's Own*, was published in Rupert Hebblethwaite's college magazine, *Pulse*, and I am taking the liberty of enclosing it.

Dear Virginia,

I feel as if I'm going through some sort of crisis, which is all the worse because it won't acknowledge itself as anything – a sort of death. There are a lot of good things about here. Let me tell you about the evening I went to join Animal Rights but ended up at a poetry reading. Overtired, I needed to shut my eyes in oblivion, but avoided being with myself in my room. Ten minutes late, I located the ivy-clad staircase where the Animal Rights people were having their first meeting. Room E8a – I found it – a bedroom with the door open – dirty clothes strewn about. I backed out and two girls who had just cooked a delicious-looking rice thing told me it was in the room opposite. But they, the Animal Rights people, had locked themselves in. The door wouldn't open when I tried it, and there was no response when I knocked, though I could hear voices. The gods didn't want me to be a hunt saboteur presumably.

Dazed, I set off for the poetry reading. A labyrinth of dream-like shadowy arched corridors and bridges over the river and a slow chime of church bells. I asked a man in a gown how to get to the School of Pythagoras –

'I'm going there myself.' (Oh good, at least one person's coming to the reading.) 'Where are you from? Are you a Johnian?'

'Pardon?'

'Where are you from?'

'You mean what college? King's. I thought you wanted to know where my cultural roots were.'

An elderly don (like the one you watched outside the Chapel with a tray on his head, tufts of fur on his shoulder?) dropped back to join our conversation as we wound through dark corridors –

'I remember when Auden came to read. I could not keep him sober – it was really dreadful – he was swaggering about round these corridors … and we got in front of the audience – he was giving a discourse on something – I can't remember what – and do you know, he became instantly sober: he stopped slurring and was most coherent, just for the duration of the talk.'

The two men engaged in conversation, and an elderly lady in a gown waited to talk to me.

'I remember when Auden was here – we all went to have coffee … no – it was a different occasion … and he was discussing someone else's book. He kept making the most stupid, meaningless statements like, Well, one wouldn't have wanted to have known that character – such and such is one of those kind of people who never pays the telephone bill … Well, one wouldn't have wanted to know the hero – the kind of man that never … so by the end of the evening, I thought, "Well really, one wouldn't want to know an eminent poet, whose work one deeply respected, would one?"'

'My aunt knew TS Eliot.'

'Oh, really. What was she called?'

'Eileen Graham. She wasn't here. She lives in Leeds …'

'I never met TS Eliot. I had been invited to have a drink with some friends at one stage, but I had to stay behind and put my first baby to bed … so I was late. And I arrived at the house and my friend clutched my arm in exasperation. You've just missed TS Eliot!'

We had reached the School of Pythagoras. She seated herself beside the elderly man, who smiled pleasantly but distantly. I sensed it wasn't quite the thing to join them, so I sat further along the same row.

This time it was much better. The poet must have read his weaker poems before, to save the good ones for tonight. A couple of times he made me cringe, but he steered absolutely clear of Academicy/ Informed back-up. I wonder (and hope to God not) if he did hear me criticize him. The other poet considers himself quite a guy. Proud to be from the periphery but annunciating loud and clear in public-school-speak. He began with a farty lot of poems — very clever I dare say, but so what. The first was a take-off of all the contemporary poets, given the characters of birds, named by initials: Thughes, Sheaney … The audience loved it. I get the feeling that the art world here feels beholden to the academic, yet academics are afraid to pass genuine judgement on what they see to be popular in the art sphere. A poem, I think, about the war, or prison … Something was 'as welcome as a sandy foreskin' … he boomed this brashly, aggressively almost, in defiance of the decency in the walls and curtains. A sheltered world they live in here — no-man's land all right. To let the place/values impinge on you so much that you feel a constant urge to rebel, is as bad (and either way you are playing into their hands, sacrificing a hair of the head of your vision) as utterly adopting the values being foisted on you, I think. He followed this by a shitty poem about a plastic turd which centred around facile word-play on 'doings' etc. The room guffawed. The old dons smiled and nodded. The people who have spent their lives studying and writing about what other people have written. Who knows if these poets will be famous some time …

'Oh yes, I saw a very amusing reading of his …'

When it came to real poetry — there was some very impressive stuff in among the bumbly bits. Back through starry arches to my room for a bad night's sleep.

Yours sincerely,

Kathleen

Virginia Woolf, with Lytton Strachey (left) and Goldsworthy Lowes Dickinson (right).

Since that letter was written, 24 years have passed, and I'm writing a retrospective consideration of my experience at King's.

It should have been better. I should have been better. For a long time I hid behind the feeling of

I'll not return.
There's nothing there I haven't had to learn,
And I've learnt nothing that I'd care to teach –
Except that I know it was the place's fault. [Philip Hobsbaum]

But that seems too easy. I didn't feel as though I came from the margins – despite the 'You could cut through your accent with a knife,' of an older student; despite the sense of a nebulous, unstated consensus which I never quite understood and to which I couldn't contribute. There was, and is, an emphasis on King's being accessible to students from state schools, and I had attended Friends' School, Lisburn, County Antrim. But there was also a feeling that, as Alan Bennett said of Oxford, this was a chance to be delivered from your surroundings, delivered from who you were. Whereas I, who had spent a year in Crete, surviving on warmth and instinct, was struggling to be myself, and beginning to learn the sober truth of Iolanda King (Martin Luther King's daughter), that it's not so much about trying to change the world, as trying not to let the world change you.

So when a tutor in a seminar about an 18th-century poet (was it Crabbe?) said that the writer became very isolated in the winter when everyone else went home, except the villagers – and they, of course, had inert minds – I couldn't join my contemporaries' nods of assent. I said clumsily, 'I think that's appalling. On those grounds, you would probably write off half of my relatives,' which left me open to her snide conclusion, 'Yes, I very possibly would.'

King's had let me in, but there was a sense in which one ought to be at least *aspiring* to be someone else.

Of course, I did have a room of my own, and a grant, and I didn't make proper use of my time. I didn't want to be in my room on my own, so I began a disastrous relationship with a troubled Cypriot boy who was studying physics in another college, and who had thalassemia, an inherited blood disorder. While I should have been pondering the more complex implications of Barthes, or Empson's ambiguities, I was drawing up sophisticated charts of which foods contained the different B vitamins and folic acid and of what should be consumed concomitantly with what in order to maximize nutrient absorption, or I was shopping for organic chicken, bananas, fresh spinach for him. And once, when he was under severe pressure, I remember spending an entire day cutting out cardboard blobs, which were the outline made by the impact of ball bearings hitting a flat surface, and apparently revealed something crucial about the nature of friction … As Emily Dickinson said, 'To live is so startling, it leaves little time for anything else.'

I did love literature – I still do. But there never seemed enough time to do it justice. I spent hours at a series of lectures about *Paradise Lost* – the room almost empty – which seemed to amount simply to the fact that in some places Milton had, possibly deliberately, created an acrostic – the first letter of each line spelling out SATAN, for example. No mention of how, as he went blind, he used to have his daughters read to him in Latin that they didn't understand.

As someone recently wrote of art, 'Mark Rothko is telling me from the other side that I am not appreciating his paintings in quite the right way.' My emphases didn't seem quite what was required – the misogyny in Forster's description of Leonard Bast's wife; the cruelty in Hemingway's image of a live grasshopper speared onto a fish-hook 'spitting tobacco'; my objection to Yeats' *Leda and the Swan* – that the writing takes its energy from the violation, rather than pulling against it in an undertow … and once, when I pointed out to Tony Tanner that the adults in a Nathaniel Hawthorne novel had left the child standing alone on the other side of the river, he exclaimed in exasperation, 'But you're talking about them as if they're real people!'

It was the mid 1980s, Thatcherite England, where conspiracies were rife and, conveniently, conspiracy theory was completely taboo. There was no room for a moral stance on anything; good and evil, truth and lie, were concepts of equal subjective validity. Even at the time this seemed to me a perfect way of disempowering people, of tying them in self-made intellectual knots, while corruption and power could get on with its work. So on a trivial level, it was no surprise to me when King's College contributed to the protests about the bill which advocated replacing student grants with loans (dubbed the Ger Bill), by keeping us in to cut out badges with pictures of gerbils, to listen to the lecture by the new Provost, and to take part in a pub quiz – so that when the national news showed the student outcry in Cambridge there was only a small handful of young people shouting ineffectually on the corner of Parker's Piece.

Even when I was asked to join the Thursday Club, I didn't think of it as an honour, a privilege to continue in the tradition of EM Forster and the Apostles. I thought it was a joke at my expense to stop me meeting an essay deadline, because they said I'd have to prepare a paper on the history of reggae, and I had three days to do it.

I loved the acoustic of the Chapel, and I sometimes read the Lesson. (Stephen Coles, the Chaplain, is the one lasting friendship from that time.) I loved the forgiveness of old stone, the escape of punting down the Cam, the sugared violets on the chocolate cakes in Fitzbillies bakery. But at weekends especially, the windows took on a lidded indifference, and the whole place seemed to echo the Russian poet Anna Akhmatova. She once said to her friend Lydia Chukovskaya – the one who memorized Akhmatova's poems when it wasn't safe to commit words to paper – when Lydia tentatively mentioned she had written a poem herself, 'YOU?' … the savage civility, the tolling bells unrelenting 'YOU!?' 'YOU?!' 'YOU?!'

It must have been that cold, that lovelessness that echoed through the six people in the University who committed, or attempted to commit suicide the year I did my Finals.

It was the inception of the 21st-century drug culture – the decades of silence and ambivalence on the part of the authorities which have brought things to their current situation. My neighbours, who went for days eating nothing but burnt brown rice to get high, and the syringes in the hostel sink went without mention, while my smuggling of my dog Lindy into Market Hostel resulted in a new written rule about no pets on College property. I saw the drug culture as another conspiracy to separate people from their own potent humanity, and to ensure that the cult of the self would mean the end of any collective action.

And like you, Virginia, I had problems with the servants, though not for the same reasons. Although I came to realize it was a form of policing (bedders had to have access to your room at least three days a week), I thought it iniquitous to have cleaners coming in to empty students' bins: why should their life-hours be of less worth? So I used to clean my room before Eleanor came, and I went out of my way to befriend her, and Richard the strange Irishman who cleaned the lavatories and who would stop me when I was trying to get to the toilets and tell me long sagas about how he gave his money to a Christian group who smuggled bibles into Russia, and of the time he had gone to Ireland but missed his aunt's party because he fell asleep in the train and ended up in Drogheda. When eventually I'd manage to get to the toilet, he'd continue cleaning under the door and you'd find your ankles slapped with a wet mop as you sat in the cubicle.

I *am* grateful. I got to hear Salman Rushdie, Anita Desai, Ted Hughes, James Fenton, Christopher Ricks, Wendy Savage, John Kerrigan, Norman Bryson, John Barrell and

John Carey. Rupert Brooke's mother (or at least the Rupert Brooke Foundation) supported me financially to travel back to Crete twice. I could sit in the fantastic Library which housed everything from *Ancrene Wisse* to Forster's original papers. I could listen to the remarkable Choir.

I did learn some things. On our arrival in King's, the Little Blue Book was a revelation. I hadn't known that cervical cancer, via genital warts, could be sexually transmitted, or of the existence of a gland that made anal sex pleasurable for men. I was introduced to the Apocrypha, and the politics of heresy. I had the chance to give a public reading in the Chetwynd Room with Julietta Harvey. I learned not to be intimidated by the searing silence after you've spoken, as though what you've said is simply so embarrassing that there is no possible response. I learned what a Judas Tree looks like.

And I did return – when the Chapel honoured its radical image and invited my friend, the Reverend Dr Michael Hurley SJ to give the sermon. That night I drank too much from the lazy susan (the small cart that trundled around on the table from one place-setting to the next, with bottles of port and dessert wine) and was nursing my hangover the next morning in the Copper Kettle when I met Australian poet Les Murray and his daughter, and we remained in correspondence.

I returned to give a reading with Irish-language poet Cathal Ó Searcaigh, and we had dinner at high table with Edward Said and his wife.

I returned for the EM Forster day (you were so crushing, Virginia, about the loneliness of an ageing queer) and I had to re-evaluate Forster. Based on the published diaries and letters, I had in my dissertation judged him for leaving his Egyptian lover dying of tuberculosis and taking another lover. During this visit his handwritten diary was propped open at an entry which read: *Also, when the train moved out, you did not watch for the last of me, but turned away with an Egyptian acquaintance … I fear you becoming unreal …*

Most recently, I returned for the day to raise money for an Arts Residency. I was astounded to hear a panel of achieving graduates declare unanimously, 'King's taught me to think.'

And I realized I couldn't do it much better if I were to start now, with everything I know. I could never be grateful enough.

Yours sincerely,

Kathleen

Two brief lives

Charles Nicholl

When I came up to King's in the autumn of 1968 I was billeted, with other freshmen, in the outlying Garden Hostel. Architecturally this is not one of the College's gems, and I think it was for a moment a let-down, turning into the drive in the back of my parents' car, and seeing that big rectangle of post-war red brick which was to be my home for the next nine months. But any disappointment was short lived. My top-floor room was airy and full of light, which is a good antidote to the darker sides of an 18-year-old's psyche; and the hostel was very genially managed by Mr and Mrs George Brownstone. And in a room three doors down the corridor there was Kevin Stratford.

Kevin had startling blue eyes, an elegantly tapering Sergeant Pepper moustache and a pronounced Yorkshire accent. We were somewhat exotic to one another, I suppose, as I was a middle-class boy from the Home Counties and he was a bus-driver's son from Dewsbury. We met on that first afternoon, found that we were both reading English, found that we shared various brandable tastes – Bob Dylan, Otis Redding, cricket, Player's Number 6, post-mod corduroy jackets, etc. ('post-mod' not to be confused with the then-unheard-of 'post-modern'). And we found that we both wanted to be writers.

In my case this aspiration was still vague, but Kevin was already doing what he wanted to do, and what he would continue single-mindedly to do: writing poetry. He was already a very good poet, technically skilled and with a great mix of high-flown and demotic. Here is a bit of one of his schoolboy poems, perhaps one he read out to me that day:

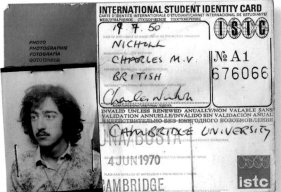

> *Honeysuckle basin blues and trumpets off-tune*
> *I'd hate to see you go in the light of the moon*
> *It's … romantic! That's nice you say*
> *But I'm not listening I can't hear*
> *Bong bong when will it be day?*
> *Bong bong move over dear.*
> ['Lyric', 1965]

His evident admiration of Eliot and Auden and Thom Gunn I shared, but various other poets he admired – Rimbaud, Mallarmé, Rilke, Wallace Stevens – were at that point just names to me. He was always way ahead: he threw these names and texts back over his shoulder and I snaffled them up. He was voracious and eclectic, an avid absorber of influences. Over the three years of our charmed lives at Cambridge his poetry evolved at an astonishing rate, especially when he discovered those mandarins of poetic cool Frank O'Hara and John Ashbury, and the contemporary Cambridge poet Jeremy Prynne. These poets, hard to understand but very beautiful to read, were (in the words of Tony Tanner) 'releasing words from their onerous obligation to "explain" and exploring some of the wonders they can generate when given such liberation'.

Another influence was Samuel Beckett – not so much the plays, then becoming more and more hermetic, but his prose work. I remember Kevin delightedly reading out to me the opening sentences of Beckett's heavyweight philosophical essay, 'Dante … Bruno … Vico … Joyce' (1929): 'The danger is in the neatness of identifications. The conception of Philosophy and Philology as a pair of nigger minstrels out of the Teatro dei Piccoli is soothing, like the contemplation of a carefully folded ham-sandwich.' This was the kind of ironic or playful seriousness he loved and emulated.

Another budding writer who came up to King's this year was Ian MacCormick, who would write under the pen-name Ian Macdonald. Many years later, in an elegiac piece called 'Exiled from Heaven' about the folk singer Nick Drake, he recalled the ambience of that time:

'During the academic year of 1968–9, Cambridge University felt an alien influence from beyond its ancient façade of curtain walls and quiet quadrangles. Sober flagstones peered affrontedly up at kaftans, wooden beads, and waist-length hair. Staid courtyards winced to the strains of *Beggars Banquet*, the "White Album", *Big Pink* and Dr John the Night Tripper drifting through leaded windows.'

Perhaps he overstates the 1960s iconography – my brief fling with kaftans and beads was thankfully over by then – but it catches a mood, exotic from this distance, and is also very characteristic of his wry and elegant style.

He was a quiet, pale man, diffident-seeming but fiercely intelligent. He was already 20, a couple of years older than me, and – like Kevin – had in some indefinable sense 'been around' in a way I felt sure I hadn't. And nothing epitomized Ian's intellectual hip more than a certain afternoon in his room, sometime in the spring of 1969, when what he later called 'a dozen or so loafers' sat listening, in my case for the first time, to Nick Drake – then an undergraduate at Fitzwilliam – playing those bittersweet folk songs which would later feature on his first album, *Five Leaves Left* (a poetic-sounding title which actually, in a typical twist of the day, cited the warning insert in a pack of Rizla cigarette papers, and was thus a submerged drug reference).

Ian went on to an exemplary career as a writer, lyricist and musician. I bumped into him in London from time to time in the early 1970s, when we were both writing for the music press. I must have thought of him, and that afternoon concert he conjured up at King's, when I heard the news that Nick Drake had killed himself. This was in 1974. Drake had made a small reputation with three fine albums (the reputation has since grown exponentially) but had suffered from depression. He died of an overdose of a prescribed antidepressant: the coroner's verdict was suicide, though some have questioned this.

I lost touch with Ian but we followed a similar path – away from the city, and away from journalism into the longer haul of book-writing. In 1990 he published *The New Shostakovich*, a highly esteemed biographical study of the composer; and then four years later came his masterwork, *Revolution in the Head*, a meticulous, learned, socio-musicological charting of the music of the Beatles, song by song, 187 of them from 'Love Me Do' to 'I Me Mine', a meteoric catalogue recorded over just eight years – the soundtrack of our lives in the 1960s.

There were some fine writers then connected with King's – the philosopher Bernard Williams, the poet Clive Wilmer, the literary critic Tony Tanner, who was our tutor – but there was one in particular: EM Forster. A diminutive but venerable figure, then nearing his 90th birthday, he had lived on A staircase since time began, a kind of Legend in Residence. He shuffled through the King's College bar every evening on his way to and from dinner in Hall, and one day Kevin plucked up the courage to waylay him, and we bought him a drink – 'a small glass of port, I think' – and plied him with bright-eyed questions. In my last year, as it happens, I had the room down near the river which Forster himself had had as an undergraduate in the 1890s, and which is probably the room he had in his mind when he wrote the opening scene of *The Longest Journey* (1907), set in Rickie Elliot's Cambridge room.

'Cambridge', Forster wrote in those opening pages, 'had taken and soothed him, and warmed him, and had laughed at him a little, saying that he must not be so tragic yet awhile, for his boyhood had been but a dusty corridor that led to the spacious halls of youth.'

King's offered much in terms of literary tradition, and the matchless beauty of the setting, but it also gave us each other, and what we learned from each other. And perhaps the most vivid memories are of that seemingly improvised everyday culture – the mooching around, the dropping in, the afternoon movies, the late-night discussions – which was the form that learning took. One sees it now in the slightly flat and faded colours of an Instamatic photo. We are drifting out of the gates into King's Parade, en route for coffee at the Whim, or chicken livers and rice at the Corner House, or a pizza at the Eros, or a packet of fags from the melancholy tobacconist Colin Lunn; we are hurrying off to Instantprint with the layout for a magazine or poster, or to browse the latest imports at Andy's record stall in the market, or to consult in the musty shrine of the Arts Cinema such oracles as *Pierrot le Fou* or *Medium Cool* or *Memories of Underdevelopment*. And as likely as not, outside the college gates, we see a burly young man with a shock of blondish hair and a naval surplus overcoat, hawking the far-left *Shilling Paper*, the rabid mouthpiece of some revolutionary splinter group which changes its acronym about once a term. We nod in greeting as we pass, for he is a fellow Kingsman, and though we're hopelessly unpoliticized dilettantes we sometimes buy a copy just to keep up appearances. His name is Charles Clarke, and one of the many things we don't know is that he will one day be Home Secretary.

Kevin Stratford, 1968.

We thought we were special, and of course we were, because every generation at Cambridge is special. But we were not so different. I can think of contemporaries who might have said, 'At Cambridge I ruffled out in my silks, in the habit of malcontent, and seemed so discontent that no place could please me to abide in', but in fact this rebellious student was Robert Greene, who graduated from Clare College in 1583, and who thereafter earned a precarious living in London writings plays and pamphlets, and who died young, as did his fellow Cambridge 'wits', Christopher Marlowe and Thomas Nashe. There are so many traditions at Cambridge you are bound to be part of one of them.

One of the many seeds planted in my mind by Kevin Stratford eventually reached fruition in a book I wrote about the poet Rimbaud. I dedicated it to him, and in a brief epilogue I wrote about his influence on me, both in the particular instance of Rimbaud – I still have the little Larousse 'Pages Choisies' edition he gave me, inscribing himself 'Le Bataleur' (the conjuror, with particular reference to the Tarot card) – and in more general terms of a formative literary friendship.

I say the book was dedicated to him but alas, more precisely, it was dedicated to his memory, for Kevin died of sarcoidosis in his mid-30s, in the early summer of 1984.

Ian MacCormick too is dead. In 2003 he committed suicide at his home in Gloucestershire. As *The Times* obituarist put it: 'He often appeared a troubled individual, the uncertainty of his personal life contrasting starkly with the assured authority of his prose.' That piece on Nick Drake I quoted earlier was one of his last pieces of writing, a conjuring of the ghost of the long-gone 1960s.

A selection of Kevin Stratford's poems, *Songs of the Adept*, edited by his widow Deborah, was published in 1991. It contains a few of the poems he wrote at Cambridge, and I can see and hear him, sitting at an oblique angle on one of those frowsty old armchairs, reading with his soft mischievous voice such poems as 'The Absence of Bread', which evokes a particular summer day on the riverbank in 1970 – bottles of wine, 'shades in swimsuits', a girl 'in a narrow dress and a white scarf' – and ends so beautifully:

Far behind her eyes
Distant boys lose wagers about the heat.

Architecture as a way of life

Robin Osborne

'Courts, cloisters, flocks of churches, gateways, towers'. These make up Wordsworth's Cambridge, together with 'Gowns grave, or gaudy, doctors, students, streets'. King's can boast no cloister (Henry's plan was never executed) and no towers (the 'turrets and pinnacles' Wordsworth saw on King's Chapel don't count). There is a gateway, though one that looked like no other gateway when it was built and which no other gateway has copied. But the most remarkable feature of King's is that is has no courts.

Of course, King's has things that it calls courts – lots of them. But not one conforms to the idea of the court. Courts elsewhere come in a range of shapes and sizes, but small or large, they are all inhabited, not spaces so much as places. Great courts are destinations in their own right, grand piazzas, offering a sense of another side that is just too far away to know for certain, but close enough to ensure acquaintance. Small courts are domestic spaces into which the staircases spill their residents as into a common room. Pass from one court into another, from the great town square to the village green to the domestic yard, from outside to inner sanctum and now you know the college.

None of that holds for King's 'courts'. With only three sides, a station on the river, and a path hugging the buildings, Bodley's Court extends hospitality to too many visitors, and privacy to too many residents, to form a Bodleian community. Long and thin, Webb's Court hides a Provost on one side and the Fellows on another, while bewildered guests attending some function look for a clue to the Beves or Saltmarsh room. No amount of dressing-gowned scurrying to the bathrooms could make Webb's a private space, even if it wasn't a battleground between vans and overgrown shrubs. Chetwynd Court has just the right size for a court, and enough residents eyeing each other up across it to get me invited to tea with second-year philosophers on A staircase who thought I was working too hard for a first year in Keynes. But lack of sunlight, and the decision to give the Keynes Building corridors, instead of staircases, condemned this to be space dead to its residents – if not to the bar.

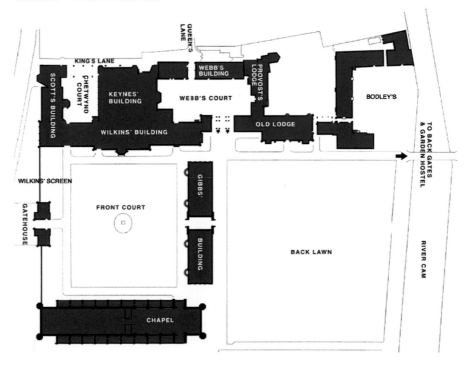

No one even thinks of the back lawn – onto which only the Old Lodge disgorges – as a court. Turn your back on Gibbs arch, and its bicycles, and you have the closely mown lawns at the back of a grand country house, with the river a giant ha-ha separating the park that is Scholars' Piece and the Chapel an overgrown parish church in the grounds. The front lawn shares these pretensions. The locked western door of Hall, and the light use of the eastern passage, restrict comings and goings to the three extreme corners leading to bar, SCR and Chapel – except for the trickle of supervisees scurrying up Gibbs staircases. This lawn is an obstacle to all but Fellows, and Henry's incongruous monument successful in just one thing: the screening of visitors to the bar from chapel-goers (and *vice versa)*. Not even a community of antipathy here.

King's failure to fit Wordsworth's formula, its definition by what it is not, is stamped on everyone inside. But not as strongly as is its dominant topographic feature: the College as thoroughfare. The town has long since had the last laugh in the power struggle which began with Henry's purchase of its centre. King's has gone from heart to artery. If Henry deprived the town of public amenities, the town has taken away the College's privacy. It isn't the impossibility of matching the perpendicular grandeur of Henry's Chapel that cancels thoughts of domesticity, it is the endless traffic.

'Some friends I had, acquaintances who there / Seemed friends, poor simple schoolboys, now hung round / With honour and importance: in a world / Of welcome faces up and down I roved'. Wordsworth's experience of roving among welcome faces has long ceased to be any student's experience of the streets of Cambridge, but in every other college, somewhere, if not everywhere, the welcome faces of friends can be exclusively guaranteed. Not so in King's.

Of course, the sun goes down on those making their way from their cars on Queen's road to their business in the Market Square, and on the tourists redeeming the expense of admission to the Chapel by walking every unbarred path. The College shuts its doors. But by then, the throng of strangers has exacted its price. No one in King's expects to be acquainted with those who amble along, unless they are in the uniform of gardeners, custodians or porters. Joining the commuters on the path, like joining the commuters in the train, induces habits not of greeting but of gaze avoidance.

For those who come from (literally) cloistered backgrounds, King's takes a bit of getting used to. Easier if you were in a vast sixth-form college. King's topography shapes the college community. Radically. This can be no world apart. Hall and Bar offer the only buffer between the intimacy of a room of one's own, and the anonymity and

Top: Webb's Court.

Middle: Gibbs' Arch.

Bottom: Henry's incongruous monument.

Opposite: Wilkins' screen.

uniqueness of the ever-changing crowds whose multifarious life-stories will have only the passage through King's in common. The self-service meals and long bar hours mean that even Hall and Bar offer no stable, 'homely' community.

For visitors, all of this makes King's peculiarly impressive. This is a college that spills its secrets. Arrive at the back gate or turn from Bene't Street into King's Parade and, either way, King's imposes itself on you. If Scholar's Piece affords an aerial perspective, Wilkins' screen teases. Enter the gate, process up the avenue, and all this grandeur is yours. You have come to find a great University and now, finally, it shows itself to be larger than life. The outside proclaims so much, there is no need to enter the buildings. No sense *here* of trespassing on an ever-more private world as court yields to court in staged procession. The path through King's offers instant graduation. There is a single moment of revelation: as you skirt the barrier of Gibbs Building, the urban environment is exchanged for the rural, or the rural for the urban. The grandeur of the country house turns out to be but the other side of a grandeur that might almost be Whitehall.

But that which feeds the fantasies of the visitor is more difficult for a resident. If it is hard to make that Chapel *your* chapel, it is hard to make this space *your* space. How can one not be dwarfed, distracted, lonely? But defences develop fast. Opportunities are quickly taken. Living here turns out to be a readily transferable skill. Most of us live like this. We share our intimate space with a few. Outside that, our neighbourhoods are minimal. The world of faces and bodies among which we move is anchored to no known stories. We know the world from writing and from pictures, not from acquaintance. The separateness of intellectual understanding from practical knowledge is not a feature of the ivory tower, it is a feature of lived life. Learning that, fast, matters. But so do friendships. Real friendships are those formed by the sharing of space more intimate than a court.

The world of Wordsworth's 'acquaintances who there / seemed friends' is a world of nostalgia. Collegiate architecture is the architecture of nostalgia. But not King's. With a cathedral of a chapel, a Gibbs Building of government offices, and the rooms in Keynes borrowed from a tired cheap hotel, what better preparation for the follies of life than this? There can be no nostalgia, for one is never going to leave. One way or another, the experience of King's is a premonition of future life.

Unless you take refuge in another Oxbridge college.

Poster boy

Jan Pieńkowski

Designing theatre posters was my real
education and how I learnt my trade. When
the posters were stolen off the noticeboards
more and more quickly after going up, I knew
I was on the right path.

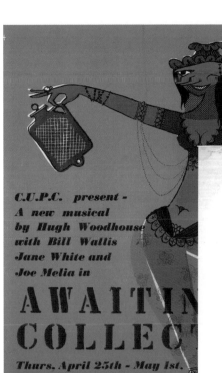

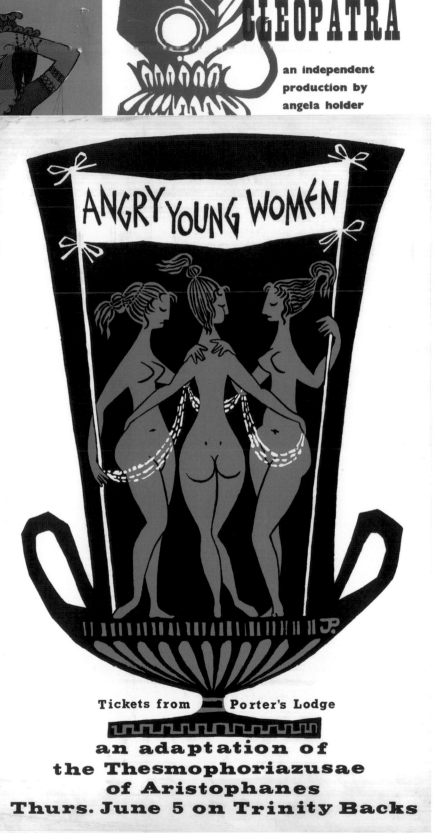

In my first year I shared a house with a South African, an Irish-American, a Punjabi and a Hindu Brahmin – Dilip Adarkar, who became my great friend. We held many parties thanks to our long-suffering landlady, Mrs Hughes – her children insisted on calling me Mr Bing Crosby! At one of these soirées I met Bridget Haines, who became my model for some of the posters while she sang songs from the musicals of the day. Subsequently she hit the headlines when she smuggled a Polish student through the Iron Curtain by lying on top of him on the luggage rack of a train.

P AWN

Out Mon. June 10th. – on sale – Copper Kettle and the colleges

resent—arthur miller's

THE CRUCIBLE

at the A.D.C. theatre park st.
tue. 12th feb.—sat. 16th feb. 8.15
tickets 3/-, 4/-, 5/- from millers

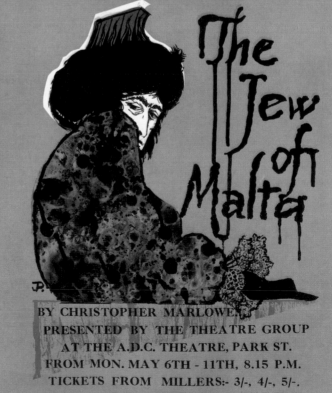

My second-year, next-door neighbour was Nick Tucker. I would repeatedly play 'Cherry Pink' by Eddie Calvert ('The man with the golden trumpet') very loudly until Nick asked me to turn it down; in return he lent me his notes on Marvell – which is probably partly how I got my degree.

Another oracle on the thorny road to undeserved success was Toni Drabble (AS Byatt). She sometimes helped me with an essay. One day, while having tea in her room at Newnham, her new-look cotton frock caught fire on the gas ring. I wrapped her in the hearth rug and sat on her until the fire went out.

Morgan (EM) Forster was my celebrity neighbour in my third year.
We were both blighted by shyness and had desultory conversations on A
staircase, one going up, the other down until they faded out! Eventually
I used to be invited to his room – a veritable Prospero's cave, where we
would discuss Aubrey Beardsley, who was my idol at the time and was to
become a big influence on my graphic work.

Angela Holder rode into my life on a battered bicycle in Silver Street. My first poster for her was *Caesar and Cleopatra* that she was directing at the ADC. Then came Machiavelli's *Mandragola*. The leading lady walked out at dress rehearsal and Angela gallantly played the part to rave reviews. Fortunately she had fair hair too so the poster remained appropriate! The happy ending to this is that Angela and I are still friends and still working together.

Sodom and Gomorrah

Philip Purser

'You will go to King's, of course,' said the headmaster of Birkenhead School, breath tinged with the sherry to which he had resort during morning break. 'It was my college. It has the best site' – he spelled out the word to distinguish it from *sight* – 'of them all. I shall arrange that for you, if needs be with the War Office.'

It was 1943. I was soon to leave school and take up one of the armed forces' short courses which were a feature of university life in the Second World War. The idea may even have come from the universities, fearing that wholesale conscription would leave them with too many empty places. The Navy and the RAF were chiefly concerned to give potential young officers a veneer of sophistication. In their two terms they could read any subject they chose, with perhaps a little extra-curricular tuition in navigation or

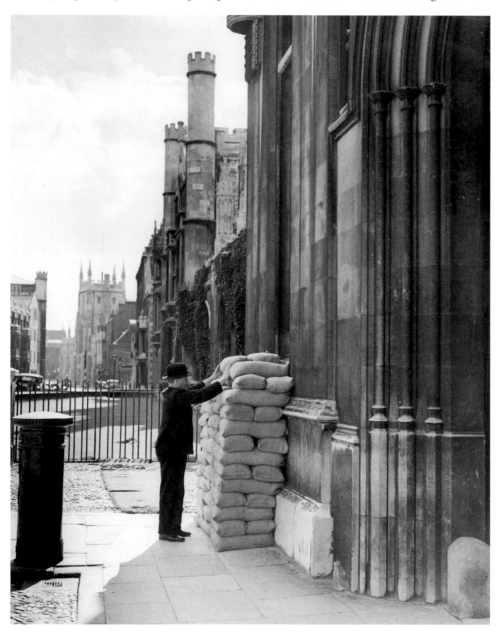

King's prepares for war.

aerodynamics. The army applied the scheme to technical corps only, with related studies. Cambridge specialized in candidates for the Royal Engineers (RE) and, to a lesser extent, the Royal Army Service Corps. There was a set curriculum based on the first years of the Mechanical Sciences Tripos.

That was all right, my grandfather had been a county surveyor, in peacetime my father worked for the Tarmac road firm, and I had been in the Science sixth at school. I should be able to cope. But what was life otherwise going to be like in the most hallowed college of an ancient university?

I had read *David of King's* by EF Benson, with its rival societies, intense games of tennis and funny set-pieces like the donnish madrigal group whose Tintara wine (whatever that was) got spilled everywhere. There were also a few iffy bits with chaps taking a bath together, or exchanging manly embraces. Not so sure about that. But what our Cambridge most certainly did not turn out to be was the empty, blacked-out town, with only one or two monkish figures abroad, which Robert Harris pictured many years later in *Enigma*, his novel about the Bletchley Park code-busters. To be fair, that was in a chapter set early in the war. By 1943, as I shamefully put into the mouth of a character in one of my own novels, the town was more like Sodom and Gomorrah on Saturday night, except that every night was Saturday night.

Well, not quite. But the University was operating four terms a year instead of three, and far from being depleted, the colleges were crammed. In addition there were the London University institutions evacuated to Cambridge for the duration: Bedford College, Queen Mary and LSE (London School of Economics), together supplying a usefully high proportion of female students. Evening brought a roistering inflow from Bomber Command, the United States Army Air Force and the brutal and licentious soldiery of every nationality, all packing into the pubs and picture houses and nooks and corners. A wee Scots ambulance driver was reputed to dispense favours in the back of her ambulance, conveniently parked on Market Hill. Then, a Hungarian second-lieutenant in the Cheshire Regiment … But I'll come to him in due course.

For us of No.7 Royal Engineers short course, arrival at King's was a transformation scene. We had been required to report first to a grim old barracks in Colchester, where we were issued with full uniform, battledress, boots and gaiters, forage cap, socks, webbing belt, the lot. We may even have been marched around and shouted at. We certainly spent at least one night there. And here we were on King's Parade cobbles, clutching suitcases and kitbags, to be politely greeted by the formidable Head Porter, Mr Nightingale, and directed to our sets of rooms.

After scurries around to acquire a broadcloth King's gown, preferably used, the transformation was completed with our first dinner in Hall, and except, perhaps, for a few Etonians, an introduction to the splendour of college life. To hear a Latin grace under that lofty ceiling, to behold the panoply of the High Table, to relax as the gentle rumble of conversation built up, and venture into it yourself — ah, this was life as you had only imagined it, most times wrongly. Next day, I think, we freshmen had to assemble for our group photograph, and a taste of the faintly camp manner King's dons were supposed to display. It fell to the legendary Dadie Rylands to marshal us into three ranks facing the camera, whereupon he declaimed, 'If anyone thinks he is not in the picture, let him *cry out* in horror.'

I was sharing rooms not with another RE cadet but with Doug Norman, a schoolmate from the same rather suburban little resort of Meols, on the Wirral peninsular. He was on the Navy short course. We had S14, Garden Court, was it? — down towards the Backs. Our bedmaker was Mrs Snook. Also from Birkenhead School, indeed the head boy 1942–3, was AC or Archie Moore, but he had a scholarship and would be allowed at least a year of normal studies. So would Dennis Gardner from Calday Grange Grammar, likewise Donald

Higginbottom, whose father edited our local newspaper,
and whose mother wrote a column in it.

I still have my Cambridge Pocket Diary for 1943–4.
At first it records only letters received, letters sent, four or
five a day. But gradually little happenings or future duties
begin to be noted: cuppers matches, Chapel services and
fire-watching, both in College and at the Senior Training
Corps drill hall where we paraded once or twice a week.
The army also dictated the current affairs colloquia which
we were required to attend, usually in the form of an
after-dinner visit to some stuffy old diplomat or empire-
builder who would be clad in evening dress, wielding a
cigar and sipping a brandy, though without offering us
anything. On Wednesday 4 November, after a dentist's
appointment at 4.30, comes the first reference to nicer
dates: *Betty Coming Round.* A few days later it was *Tea-
dance at the Dorothy Café,* and then with her to an Abbot
and Costello film at the Cosmo.

Betty was from LSE, very pretty and lively, in digs
way up Castle Street which doubtless were not approved
Cambridge University lodgings with all their restrictions
and prohibitions. This was soon to be put to the test. We
had been to a formal dance, white tie and tails – yes, really!
Many of us had brought them. My father had insisted that
I should borrow his. When afterwards I walked her back
to the digs, she asked me in. It began to look as if I might
be staying the night. But how to sneak back into College
in the morning without being spotted? The only realistic
possibility was via the Backs, and that meant waiting for
the footbridge gate to be unlocked or sploshing through
the ditch, either recourse likely to attract attention.
Especially if one was in white tie and tails! This was the
thought that finally unmanned me. What if I ruined
Dad's best evening togs? A quick goodbye and I took off,
running, running, running through the streets to make the
Porter's Lodge just as midnight was sounding.

JT Sheppard.

The sequel to this was a strangely formal call on me in S14 by Betty and a solid,
unsmiling but presumably more masterful chap. They were sorry, but he had replaced me
as her boyfriend and felt that I should be told. So, that was that. Ah, but as a raw soldier
six months later I would somehow develop pneumonia and be sent to a Canadian field
hospital near the Essex coast, out of bounds to everyone except local residents because
of the D-Day forces being marshalled there. And who should visit me one day but Betty,
having somehow learned of my plight and bluffed her way into the forbidden zone.

Meanwhile the Christmas break was approaching and the next significant entry in
my diary was on 6 December, just three words: *Bottle of Port.* We had lately gathered that
even a short-term freshman was entitled to buy port from the King's College cellars, and
I had acquired one to take home. It was opened rather sooner, thanks to that anomaly of
a character briefly mentioned earlier, the Hungarian second-lieutenant whose shoulder-
flashes identified him as an officer of the Cheshire Regiment. We had run into him in
one of the pubs we liked, the *Baron of Beef* or the *Spread Eagle.* I was intrigued because
for two years I had belonged to a Home Guard battalion, the 17th, of the same regiment,

worn the same cap-badge, and in the summer of 1942 been attached to a regular battalion for a fortnight's playing at real soldiers. I took him back to our rooms and poured us each a glass of port.

He sipped his, then suddenly put his arm around me. Shock! Horror! Sodom and Gomorrah realized! Fortunately, he was immediately apologetic. 'I thought you must be of that liking,' he said, or something in that vein. It was, of course, naïve of me ever to have invited him in, but part of growing up and growing wiser, I suppose. He continued to be seen around town, often within King's. Rumours began to circulate. How he came to be in Cambridge, what he was supposed to be doing, who he really was I never found out.

Another mysterious presence was that of a group of young officers of the Chinese Navy, rather a long way from the sea but seemingly under the patronage of the then Provost, JT Sheppard. Of course, ordinary visitors strolled round the splendours of the King's College courts as they always have and always will. Sheppard affected old age, though in fact, it was said, he was a mere 52. He was also wont to potter about in comfy and sometimes worn clothes, lending credence to the oft-told story of the American envoy or Canadian general who had assumed him be the gardener, and given him a tip. An extraordinary little vignette of the times I chanced to see, just within the main gates, was a young woman in the khaki uniform of the ATS (the women's branch of the army) being scolded by her mother, I guessed. 'Now do be sensible, Jean,' the latter was snapping, 'if we don't move on now we'll have no time for a cup of tea.' The daughter, if so she were, had her back to me. As she obediently turned to leave I saw that she wore the rank badges and scarlet tabs of a full colonel.

In Hall one evening, I found myself sitting opposite David Rowse. He was good company and, what's more, his father was Herbert Rowse, architect of the Mersey Tunnel, Liverpool Philharmonic Hall and other buildings singled out for praise in my much-thumbed Penguin book on *Modern Architecture*. They lived on the Wirral, too, but in a grand house on a stretch of the Dee a dozen miles upriver from suburban Meols. When David asked me over one Sunday in the Christmas break I was suitably impressed, and not wholly from any social crawling. Looking across the estuary to distant Welsh hills I realized this grassy foreshore was the location of a favourite adventure story of my boyhood, *The House of the Spaniard* by Arthur Behrend. Herbert Rowse turned out to be an agreeable hero, less concerned with architecture just now than with the regular transatlantic broadcast, a kind of *Letter to America*, he was due to make that night.

Once our two terms were over, it was to be half a century before I met David again. He had gone back to King's to read Architecture. He went to only one lecture in this discipline, somehow scraped a Third, but was already convinced that any building he designed would fall down. So how did he pass the time, I wanted to know, if he never went to lectures? 'But I did go to lectures, as long as they had nothing to do with architecture. I just mooched in. History, Philosophy, Archaeology and Anthropology, Science, Literature, the Classics. And hours in the College Library. I *educated* myself.'

What career did he pursue then? All he had resolved was that it should be something on his own account, not working for anyone else. Publishing, perhaps? His cherry-picking from that variety of academic pursuits had given him the idea that there might be a future for specialized magazines, whether related to business or hobbies. He made a modest start with *Autosport* and was eventually running up to a dozen publications, catering for specializations as serious as nuclear energy.

The other architect-to-be I got to know at King's, James Tolson, was a fellow member of the Royal Engineers short course. We began to meet again, after a rather shorter lapse, at its periodic reunions. Rather than going back to Cambridge he had chosen to apply to the esteemed Architectural Association school in London, if now rather regretting this. He had an Italian wife, Anna Maria; their Christmas card one year featured the Pugin engraving of a King's Chapel gable overprinted with the tidings that he remembered fire-watching on this 1515 roof in 1943, while she remembered waiting for the RAF to cross the Alps. It was only when, with advancing age, we began to correspond rather than gather together, that I learned of the social service that James had undertaken throughout our time at King's.

My address in Northamptonshire struck a chord with him. Would it be anywhere near Kingthorne Mill, in Greens Norton, whither old family friends had moved in the early 1940s? He had been to stay there, and renewed his friendship with their son, David Bolton. David was severely handicapped as a consequence of polio in boyhood, but had gained a place at King's, going up the same Michaelmas term as us. The Provost had offered him a ground-floor room in his Lodge, but there would still be a need for someone of his own age to help him in all sorts of ways. Without labouring it, with hardly even a mention that I can remember, that was what Jimmy Tolson did.

Dennis Gardner was meanwhile earning his Rugby Blue, AC Moore and Donald Higginbottom were taking their turn, as scholars, to pronounce the Latin grace in Hall. I contributed nothing, except maybe to help organize a dotty *exeat* one weekend when a gang of us from the Wirral took the train to Oxford to look up contemporaries who had gone to the Other Place, drink a bit too much and sleep on their sofas. We went on the donnish line via Bedford and Bletchley, no doubt picking up or dropping off a code-breaker at the latter stop, but discovered too late that there was no service back on Sunday evening. We had to return by way of Paddington, which happened to be on fire after an air raid, and King's Cross. I suppose this is an example of the memories and impressions which make up my King's album.

They range from the sublime to the subliminal. There is the full vista of the s-i-t-e as my old headmaster had spelled it out, the space, the mellow stone, the greensward. There is, yes, the fire-watching, whether on that fabled Chapel roof or in a cold corner of the Gibbs Building. Buying cigarettes from the buttery or half a pint of beer to take into Hall. The pheasant from College farms to eke out the meagre meat ration, the honey from college bees smeared on a little wedge of dry pastry to serve as pudding. Above all, the Chapel. If you dropped in just to worship you were held there by the music. If you went in only for the songs of Evensong or to listen to the Advent carol service, you felt the soothings of something more.

And for us in S14 that was not the only music. From across the landing would come sweet strains of Monteverdi (or someone) played on fiddle and recorder (or something). A full-course engineer, Victor Robinson, was the occupant. His girlfriend and future wife Frida, daughter of a refugee scientist, would join him to make music. They would sometimes ask me over for coffee when they had finished. It gave me a fleeting insight into the cosmopolitan, Hampsteady world of culture and gentle socialism that many years later I would encounter as a journalist.

I sought to go back to King's on demobilization in 1947, but hadn't done well enough in the exam they gave us at the end of the short course. I would first have to pass the Mechanical Sciences Qualifying Exam. I took a correspondence course while working in a drawing office and failed again. Might I not read something else, such as English? Sorry, no. Instead, St Andrews accepted me unseen, if turning me out after two years with the lowest rank of degree known to man, a War Ordinary. My time there was nevertheless happy and rewarding. King's remains my first love.

The green tie

Charles Saumarez Smith

I was introduced to King's early, when, in July 1954, two months after I was born, my uncle, John Raven, who had just stopped being Lay Dean, got married in the College Chapel and my sister, Helen, who was a bridesmaid, fell in the fountain while the photographs were being taken. John Raven had defected not long before from Trinity, where he had been an undergraduate, and, from that point onwards, because my mother, his older sister, was so besotted by him, King's became, quite erroneously, the family college.

My second introduction to King's was when I was about 12 and my father, who was highly conventional and almost certainly didn't want to talk about sex, gave me EF Benson's *David Blaize* to read – I assume as a substitute for a sex talk and to introduce me to the ethos of sublimated homosexuality which he assumed (rightly) that I would find at Marlborough, the Marchester of Benson's book. Its purpose escaped me. I read it simply as a schoolboy novel, missing its intense homoeroticism, its references to 'beastliness' and obvious anti-semitism, written without irony, pre-Freud, at the height of the First World War, together with its sequel *David at King's*, in which David and his older friend, Frank Maddox, continue their platonic friendship at King's, canoeing up the Cam to Grantchester, attending Saturday evening meetings of the Chitchat Club, and playing real tennis, until David distances himself from the sense of subordination in the relationship just before his finals. I don't know what, aged 12, I made of this. Re-reading it now, I find it ridiculously sententious, but assume that its purpose lay in the warning of David's clerical father that 'You're a handsome boy and an attractive one, and there are hundreds of temptations round you all day, which we needn't talk about because you know what I mean every bit as well as I do'.

My third introduction to King's was reading EM Forster's *The Longest Journey*. A strange, wonderful, rather wild and experimental book about the corruption of suburban values and the lure of the primitive, it begins with a memorable scene of its two protagonists arguing about the ontology of a cow. It, too, has King's as a backdrop and shares some of the same themes: the friendship between Rickie Elliot, who has a hereditary deformity, and the older and cleverer Stewart Ansell, who, interestingly, is also described as Jewish and comes from trade; the hostility towards, and suspicion of, women, who appear as predatory intruders on the all-male college; and the preoccupation with, and argument about, ideas. It introduced me to some of the putative characteristics of college life and to the benefits of intellectual jousting between undergraduates, thinking about and testing ideas about art, morality and literature.

So when, in the garden of my sixth-form history master, I was told by his brother-in-law, who was reading art history at Trinity, that he would have preferred to have gone to King's, where Michael Jaffé presided in his rooms above the arch of the Gibbs Building, I was a soft touch and took the scholarship examination in autumn, 1971. When I went for my interview, the Tutor for Admissions, Keith Tipton, was said to have written OMDB (Over My Dead Body) on my application form because I represented everything that the College was trying not to be. But I made a better impression on Christopher Morris, the History Fellow.

What I realize in looking back on my experience of King's is that, by the time I arrived as an undergraduate in October 1972, I was already aware of it as a moral universe, an idea of collegiate life, of undergraduate and don, which I had constructed in my mind, but which was essentially fictional. It was an Edwardian ideal, which goes back, I presume, to the King's of Oscar Browning, Goldsworthy Lowes Dickinson and John Sheppard,

when dons were still mostly resident, took trouble with their pastoral responsibilities, not necessarily for the right reasons, and when the College was still small and tied into its historic relationship to Eton.

Of course, the King's that I found in 1972 was a massive disillusionment. It was bound to be. It was not an Edwardian moral universe, but a modern college, normalized and democratized by the anthropologist, Edmund Leach, who was Provost in the late 1960s and who was suspicious of, if not positively hostile to, the idea of the collegiate community, based on the privilege of academic tenure, on prize fellowships and bachelor dons. He was interested in research, not undergraduates. I found myself in a claustrophobic room in the then relatively new building designed by Fello Atkinson in the space between King's and Cat's for the conference trade: studiously anonymous, the doors had been painted bright orange and muck green to prevent its inhabitants going mad. I took one look at the King's College bar and retreated to eat my meals in Shades, a subterranean wine bar known to my friends as Hades, on the other side of King's Parade.

But even when I was an undergraduate, there were still a few remaining representatives of what I took to be old King's, including John Saltmarsh, the white-haired medievalist, Philip Radcliffe, the composer, who had been a friend of EM Forster and lived in a barely furnished room down by the river, and, most of all, Dadie Rylands, who strode across the College lawns looking like a 1920s golfer, but who had by the early 1970s retreated to his rooms above the old Provost's Lodge.

Only Peter Avery, the Persian don, kept alive some aspects of the College's old tradition in a grand set of rooms at the bottom of H staircase alongside the Chapel, where, shining pink, polished and round in every way, always smoking without seeming to inhale and, as recorded in his memorial service, allowing the ash to accumulate as he held his cigarette in the air, he would entertain the prettiest and most intellectual and, I now realize, the socially best-connected undergraduates to whisky after dinner and into the small hours of the morning, holding forth in endless monologue about his friends, who included John Heath-Stubbs, the blind poet with whom he had translated the *Rubaiyat of Omar Khayyam* (and whom I once took on a walk through the Cambridge night, bumping cruelly into the back gates), Lady Serena James, who had a house outside Richmond in Yorkshire, and Sir Steven Runciman, the great Byzantinist. He used to take us on long drives up the A1 talking all the way about who owned the estates on either side of the road. Always there was a sense of lives beyond Cambridge, as when he talked of a picnic with boys in the desert outside Isfahan. While I was an undergraduate, he was teaching the SAS Persian. Someone once brought him a small pellet of opium, which he ate, and he is said to have been addicted when he worked for Anglo-Iranian Oil in the 1950s. Like Oscar Browning, he was probably regarded by senior members of the College as slightly preposterous. But we were impressionable and he was life-enhancing. He always managed to convey an impression that their form of scholarship was narrow and possibly pedantic. What was important was success in the world beyond Cambridge. He described his friends as 'our sort of people'.

What were 'our sort of people'? I realize now that we were at the tail end of a tradition at King's of those who Noel Annan described as 'the green ties', which I presume must have referred to the College aesthetes: people who believed in the discussion of ideas; who valued art, history and, perhaps above all, architecture; and who were as likely as not members of the Ten Club, which met during term-time to read plays. This tradition of intellectual aestheticism belonged, I now realize, to a set of ideas and beliefs which had been developed and nurtured in English intellectual life more obviously at King's than elsewhere. They go back to the 1870s by which time Cambridge had been more or less secularized and when Oscar Browning returned to King's from Eton, having been sacked as a master there, established the Political Society, and held court with his vain, pompous and snobbish views, but which were deeply influential on undergraduates. He certainly was a prominent figure among the next generation during the 1880s, which included Roger Fry, CR Ashbee and Goldsworthy Lowes Dickinson. This was the period when King's regarded itself as increasingly special, an elite within an elite, dedicated to a particular form of freedom of thought whereby aesthetics replaced morality, the study of art, literature and music were regarded as at least as important as the Tripos, and friendship more lasting than divinity.

What exactly were the characteristics of this tradition? Some of it was owing to the fact that King's has always been a relatively small college, but high in the league tables, self-consciously intellectual, like Balliol in Oxford (as Rickie Elliot describes it, on arriving back, 'The College, though small, was civilized, and proud of its civilization. It was not sufficient glory to be a Blue there, nor an additional glory to get drunk'). There has certainly been a tradition of intellectual arrogance, a presumption that King's has more clever people than other colleges. It has cultivated the study of the history of art in a way that other colleges have not, for example by electing Michael Jaffé to a prize Fellowship, from which he founded the history of art in the University, and simultaneously having Francis Haskell as a Fellow throughout the 1950s, before he moved to Oxford as Professor of the History of Art there. Both were Old Etonians and Michael Jaffé was an Apostle. It is inescapable that there is a strong tradition of homosexuality, as used to be evident in the obituaries of Kingsmen where a high proportion have always been unmarried and the fact of their sexual preferences was delicately alluded to. And there is a tradition of political liberalism and free thinking, which enabled King's to support Marxists in the 1960s when other colleges would not. Adherence to truth has always been regarded as more important than the smooth compromises necessary to success in a career.

John Saltmarsh.

Many aspects of this tradition are probably now dead. It was merely sputtering when I was an undergraduate, killed off by easy sex, drugs, co-residence and the culture of egalitarianism. I don't necessarily regret this as the tradition is open to every possible accusation of being elitist and intellectually snobbish and, in some respects, perhaps decadent: certainly narcissistic. It was nurtured by a highly unequal society. But I do not think it has been, and perhaps even now is, without value, since it involved the careful questioning of received values and a premium placed on particular aspects of intellectual creativity, most especially originality of thought. At its height, it produced, alongside the poetry of Rupert Brooke, many of the most prominent members of the Bloomsbury Group – Roger Fry, Morgan Forster and Maynard Keynes – which, as a movement, may be said also to have suffered from the most conspicuous defects of this tradition, being certainly highly self-conscious and, in many respects, rather too pleased with itself.

I fully recognize that it is impossible to defend this tradition of sublimated homoeroticism and the pursuit of youth, which privileged and romanticized a particular style of good looks and literary intelligence, and possibly stimulated breadth of knowledge, rather than depth, the cultivation of intelligence for its own sake. In a more egalitarian age, this aspect of the history of the College may feel slightly uncomfortable, to be easily forgotten. But this should not lead one to ignore that it was this form of sublimated homoeroticism, conveniently described by the green tie, which gave to King's much of its distinctive character – indeed, contributed much to the greatest works of art and literature, if not scholarship, which members of the College have produced.

'I wrote a few novels …'

Mohammad Shaheen

I arrived at King's on a grey Sunday evening in November 1968 from Leeds University. The porter helped me with my luggage (the porters are always kind and helpful) as we climbed that staircase combining the beautiful old dining Hall with the new sandwiched Keynes building. Only one step makes you move from the old world of tradition to that of the comfortable new one. K20 was my room. Some found the Keynes rooms claustrophobic but not me. A really claustrophobic room was the one I had been living in for over a year in Henry Price Building in Leeds, which I had just left behind that morning. Comparing that room, like a train compartment, to my room in Keynes made me feel that I was moving to a five-star hotel room, with my own bathroom and wash-basin, not a shared flexible tube with the neighbour as in Leeds. Perhaps this is what made me stay in Keynes building for over three years without grumbling.

Immediately afterwards I dashed to the College bar hunting for something to eat. I found there was no food service in the dining hall on a Sunday and I joined an old man who was sitting alone on a cushioned seat around a small table. I thought he might be a father of a boy at the College who came down from London with his son and decided to stay overnight in Cambridge. 'What are you reading?' he asked after we both gulped down some of the sausages and beans on our plates. 'English,' I replied. 'I am interested in English literature myself,' he said, 'I wrote a few novels and a book of criticism,' and he then added, 'I am Edward Morgan Forster.' I was overwhelmed by embarrassment, for I thought the great old novelist of the century had already departed.

Back to K20 where I spent the night partly reflecting on my new situation. It was obvious to me that Cambridge was such a privileged place, but I did not look back in anger at the year I spent at Leeds University. I had won a British Council scholarship for a higher degree in English literature which eventually would qualify me to go back to the English Department at the University of Jordan where I have been since then. What made me think of leaving Leeds was not the legendary accommodation of Henry Price, nor the choking autumn smog, but the obnoxious British Council officer who told me when I first met her that she fought in the June 1967 war, three months before my arrival at Leeds, and continued to glorify and even brag about the triumph of Israel, with or without

Shaheen with Forster.

an occasion. Yet you cannot leave Yorkshire without reminiscences. The simple locals and the spontaneity they have: they talk everywhere, not only in formal meetings and places: 'Cum up, luv, luts of seats oopstairs,' the bus conductor would say! And who can forget the beauty of the dales!

I kept bumping into Forster every now and then especially on Sunday morning when he used to come for breakfast, and I had the privilege of attending the chamber concert presented in celebration of his 90th birthday on 22 November 1969, where King's Hall was fully packed. 'It is time to depart,' I heard him say on the following Sunday. In June 1970, Forster died.

Comparison, however, between Leeds and Cambridge may not be fair; it ought to be rather between Leeds or Cambridge on the one hand,

and the fragile house on the border with Israel where I previously lived until June 1967. How could I help expressing my deep gratitude to the British Council who brought me to England and to those Cambridge people who facilitated my transfer to King's? John Northam, secretary of the degree committee of the English Faculty, Gillian Beer, my supervisor, Bob Young, Tutor for graduate students at King's, Tony Tanner, Admissions Tutor at King's, and Patrick Parrinder, assistant lecturer and Fellow at King's, all became

EM Forster in 1970, shortly before his death, photographed by Mohammad Shaheen.

lifelong friends after I had left King's. On her retirement, a few years ago, Gillian Beer said to those who attended the occasion, 'I grew up with Mohammad.' Dame Gillian Beer was quite junior when I arrived at her very small office in the faculty library building on my first visit to Cambridge.

Life at King's in the early 1970s was quite eventful. It was the time when King's introduced co-education and I still remember Provost Edmund Leach's words directed at the other colleges, when he defended his long report: 'In a few years you will follow suit.' In fact they actually did in less time than anticipated. I attended seminars of all sorts in the College. In one, Leach talked about structuralism, stretching his legendary arms in front of him and saying, 'Here are the rules on the table, it is the way you play them.' He concluded, 'Forster's magical phrase "only connect" is remembered for its articulate sense of connectedness.' I have been quoting Leach's words every time I introduce the subject to my students at the University of Jordan.

I asked Leach once to give a talk to the Arab Society in Cambridge on any subject relevant to the current Arab–Israeli conflict. He was first reluctant because of the negative reception by rabbis in London of his book *The Genesis of Myth*, and his article published in the *New York Review of Books* round about the same time, in which he pointed out that terrorism started in Palestine in the 1940s by Jewish gangs, not in Northern Ireland. Eventually he accepted my invitation and gave a unique lecture in the Chetwynd Room with the title 'An Anthropological View of the Palestinian Problem'.

He neither satisfied the Jews nor pleased the Arabs, perhaps because the talk was not straight politics supporting one side or the other. However it was most interesting, for it was not the kind of talk you come across in the mass media or books written on the question. I later spent years looking for the text of the talk until I found it in King's Modern Archives, catalogued partly under my name. This is how the talk began:

'I must start by giving some kind of explanation of the viewpoint from which I shall be talking tonight. I am here simply because Mr Shaheen happens to be a member of King's College and as the saying goes 'he twisted my arm'. I have no very appropriate qualifications. My knowledge of Arab society is marginal. I have at one time or another visited most of the Arab countries but only very briefly and a long time ago. The last time I was in Palestine was in 1938. My interest in the present Arab–Israeli conflict is wholly negative – I wish it did not exist – and pessimistic: I can see little likelihood of it ceasing to exist. But conflict of this kind is a phenomenon of sociology as well as a phenomenon of history and as such it is grist for a social anthropologist's analysis. It is as social anthropologist not as Middle East expert that I am addressing you this evening.'

Leach concluded his talk with a most prophetic note:

'I am not offering you pie in the sky: as I have tried to make clear, all history and sociological experience is stacked up against any 'solution' to the present Palestine conflict. On the contrary, all the evidence points to the conflict being indefinitely prolonged. No military solution would ever be a solution in more than a purely temporary sense. But that being so, men of good will must necessarily think about long-term solutions rather than short-term solutions and any kind of long-term solution implies the disappearance of frontiers. All kinds of frontiers … the frontiers of kinship, of territory, of religion, of language, of nationality … a merging of interests for the common economic good. Idealist nonsense of course, but in this particular case the alternatives are idealism or suicide, so you might as well be idealistic.'

King's has become over the years a legacy for me beyond time and place. It has shaped my whole career. Forster wrote that 'in Art life expands'. In King's life expands, too. Zadie Smith's celebrated recent novel *White Teeth,* written under the inspiration of Forster, is evidence of that. A King's woman, this time, thanks to Provost Leach and his co-education project. 'Only connect' is central to my legacy from King's.

'It's vulgar to win'

Eleanor (Leo) Sharpston

I arrived at King's in October 1973 full, in equal measure, of excitement and trepidation – and I spent my first term in a state of complete incomprehension. Although I was British and spoke English as my mother tongue, I'd grown up in Brazil, Switzerland, France and Austria. My reference points were European; my instinctive social and cultural parameters those of a polite young Viennese girl; my comfort food, when I was homesick, a nice bowl of goulash soup. I could not get my head around Cambridge, or King's. Bemusedly, I made my way through the endless series of 'squashes' in Freshers' Week, with their ever-flowing alcohol and excited contemporaries trying so hard to upstage each other in being cool and sophisticated. With something closely approximating terror, I realized that (unless I could somehow manage to retune my ear to Scots dialect) my economics theory supervisor – a bearded PhD student from Aberdeen called George – was going to go on asking me questions that I could neither clearly hear nor easily understand; and that he would think me a complete idiot if I always asked him to repeat the question three times before venturing a reply. (Having explained to him that I was part-deaf, I got them in rather louder Aberdonian, which did at least help.) I resigned myself to being always cold (in College, in the lecture rooms, on the river) and to people looking strangely at me when, as a logical Continental, I reacted by putting on a sensible number of layers of clothing. I even worked out, after a few embarrassing incidents, that 'half seven' did not, in Cambridge, mean 18.30 as it would in Vienna.

King's attitude to sport somehow typified the whole mystifying set-up. Oxbridge college tribalism would (I had naively supposed) imply fierce interest in successful sporting performance, combined with equally fierce antagonism from college Tutors who felt that one should have been working instead. I experienced neither. I got sucked into the boat club (the women had already proudly proclaimed their independence by being 'Queen Margaret of Anjou Boat Club' – QMABC – rather than 'KCBC'). I rowed, coached, captained, tried out for University squad against a background of benign indifference from the College authorities and gentle amusement from my non-rowing friends. College crews – male and female – sometimes did unexpectedly well. More often, perhaps (given our relaxed attitude to life) they did predictably badly. No problem: as the boat club song puts it, in deliberate self-parody, 'It's vulgar to actually win'. The (smallish) group of King's sportsmen in fact included people who were genuinely very talented – Rachel Scarth, whom I bank-tubbed as a novice rower, leapfrogged over us all to become President of CUWBC – but no one made any particular fuss. And we were a stage army. When Janet Downs founded Cambridge University Women's Football Club, she naturally recruited me to play left half. The College rugby team asked me to turn out once for a cuppers match when they were three men short an hour before kick-off. Over the course of a single year, oscillating between College and University sport, Leo-the-rower became a skier, a footballer, a squash player, a cricketer and half the first couple of the otherwise male College tennis team. No one gave a monkey's, one way or the other.

Gradually, King's – as distinct from Cambridge – wrapped itself around me, absorbed me and claimed me. There was a lot going for it.

First and most importantly, King's was prepared – unlike the English boarding school that I had run away from three times and finally left just before I turned 16 – to engage with me as a thinking and (potentially) responsible person. College treated my forays into serious sport (University rowing), journalism (editing *Stop Press*), theatre, music and student politics with amazing tolerance. No one seemed to think it odd when, trying to

Kenneth Polack.

combine three all-night sessions on the trot working on the paper with rowing in a First Mays Four for QMABC, I arranged for my crew to call by the dilapidated offices in Round Church Street to wake me (after an hour's nap) for the outing and then turned up (very ill-prepared and half-comatose) for a supervision as a mixture of wet rower and weary student editor. The nearest to a shot across the bows that I experienced was a very gentle word from Tess Adkins, my personal Tutor, who explained to me half-way through my second year that it really would be helpful if I would arrange actually to pass prelims, as otherwise she would have to make out a case to College Council why I should nevertheless be allowed to return into residence next academic year.

Next, College gave me an unbelievable amount of intellectual space to explore. Only King's would, over the space of four years, have allowed someone who came up on Classics to read Economics, then Modern and Medieval Languages (French and Spanish, with some classics thrown in), then Economics again and finally Law. As it turned out, that particular home-brewed cocktail was almost the perfect background for tackling EU law and laid the foundations for everything that happened afterwards.

In the quietest, most undemonstrative way possible, College was also tremendously supportive. In part, this was because there was (relatively) much less distance between dons and students than was then common in an Oxbridge college. My year of Economics finalists was horrified when Professor Wynne Godley turned received macro-economic wisdom upside down with a blockbuster article in the *Economic Journal* in April 1976, a bare six weeks before Tripos. We read it. None of us understood it. So we sandbagged Wynne in the College bar. Mildly, he apologized ('I wrote it in rather a hurry and it may not be as clear as it should be') and offered to meet us a couple of times to talk us through the new theory, the objections to it and his answers to the objections. I'm sure I owe him my First.

In dealing, in private practice, with lawyers who hadn't passed through King's, I realized how important the blend of rigour and principled context was that I'd learnt from Ken Polack, together with the humanity and tolerance that were (more generally) hallmarks of King's. It seemed entirely natural, on being offered a University lectureship in 1992, to ask the Faculty of Law to wait while I enquired whether I might be able to come back to College as a Fellow (and, as events sadly turned out, as Ken's successor). The Faculty spluttered, but acquiesced.

The King's I returned to was less sure of itself. It worried about the viability of having our very own interdisciplinary research centre; about research exercises generally; and the feedback from student questionnaires. It agonized over whether we could afford to build and renovate (and then, taking a deep breath, did both). It chased its own tail in Governing Body meetings. And yet … and yet: there was enough of the essential core still there to be worth fighting for. The College community is small enough that it is still possible to believe – to hope – that one can make a difference. There are enough other idealists still left in the place. And even though College can (and does) make some amazingly stupid decisions, one can usually rely on the cock-up theory of history, rather than the conspiracy theory, as the explanation.

Potts of King's.

MCMXXX

By Anna Trench.

Douglas Potts was a distinctly abnormal boy. His dress was eccentric and grew more so.

John FitzGerald Newman met Potts in his first term and became very friendly with him.

To amuse themselves they started a jazz band.

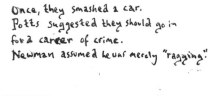

They drove around the villages bearing picturesque names for themselves. Pott used the name Victor Morel. He said it was his trade name.

Once, they smashed a car. Potts suggested they should go in for a career of crime. Newman assumed he was merely "ragging."

> I can't face my people...
>
> Nor can I.
>
> I'm leaving.
>
> I'm coming with you.

David Cyril George Gattiker, a first-year undergraduate at Christ's, had a Webley automatic.
One night, Potts came into Gattiker's room with about eight undergraduates.
The majority were intoxicated or pretending to be so.
Potts took Gattiker's revolver.

Potts and Newman's conduct brought them into contact with the college authorities, and a propensity for running into debt brought them into bad odour with Cambridge tradesmen.

202

Potts and Newman left Cambridge and went to London by motor-bike.
They had no particular idea where they were going to.
They sold the motor-bike in the evening and received a cheque for £22 10s.

They did not sleep anywhere that night but sat for half an hour on the steps of St. Martin-in-the-Fields.
They had no intention of returning to Cambridge.

The £22 10s. went rather quickly.
Potts pawned his onyx cufflinks.
For several nights they walked along the Embankment.
Potts carried the pistol in his hip pocket.
He produced it in front of people.
He wanted to give the impression that he was desperate.

A few days later, between 2 and 3 o'clock in the morning, Potts and Newman met Miss Madge Miller. Some friends of hers at Cambridge had given them her address. She gave them some Russian tea—she had no milk and no money either. They went to bed in the spare room.

The following morning Potts and Newman left, saying they were going to meet a friend named Desmond for luncheon at the Savoy, and that he might give them some money.
They had no luck with Desmond.

Miss Miller borrowed some money from a friend and cooked them dinner and took them to the pictures. On their return to the flat they played poker for matches.

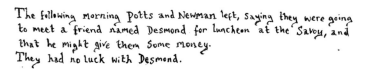

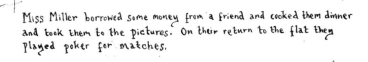

Potts and Newman were in London for ten days. On the last day they met some Cambridge friends who persuaded them to return.

Upon his return from London, Potts's tutor, Mr. Wollaston, met him in the street at Cambridge and walked back with him to King's college, where they both went into Mr. Wollaston's rooms in Gibbs building.

Potts, you will have to come with me to the police station.

While they were there, Detective Sergeant Willis arrived. A conversation, not a very pleasant one, took place. Sergeant Willis had a warrant for the arrest of Potts.

After a fairly long retirement, the jury returned in the case of Potts a verdict of suicide during temporary insanity, and in the cases of Mr. Wollaston and Sergeant Willis verdicts of murder by Potts during temporary insanity.

[All characters, names and incidents in this story are entirely factual.

Text taken from the Coroner's Report published in the Times June 7th, 1930.]

Travelling light

Tansy Troy

As far away from King's as I can go

I wanted out of this walled kingdom. The pressure, the parties, meeting my Director of Studies one blazing hot day on the way to the river and having to blag on about how much revision I was doing; suddenly, I realized that I couldn't endure a final year in this head-space. *Get me as far away from King's as I can go!* I screamed silently. As luck would have it, I was invited to a séance at the Spiritual Society the very next week. The medium prophesied that I would travel far. She presented me with a metaphysical bunch of deep pink peonies. I took this as a sign that I should visit the Senior Tutor and beg a year out.

'Where will you go?' he asked gravely.

'Japan,' I decided on the spot. It was the furthest place I could think of.

'And what will you do there?'

'Paint, write, maybe teach a bit. Find out what the hell I'm here for.'

The Senior Tutor still looked grave. 'What's to say you'll ever come back?'

I was as solemn as he. 'I'll come back. I give you my word,' I promised.

In a temple, high in the Japanese mountains, I lost myself in a maze of walkways, tiptoeing past wrathful demon guards half as high as a house, their daggers held aloft, ready to annihilate me if I didn't sort out my negative karma. In the most sacred central shrine of all, a small Buddha sat. On the ceiling above his head flew 108 phoenixes. On the golden screens around him were painted deepest pink peonies.

'So what did you get up to?' asked my Tutor, Pippa, in the autumn term.

'I taught a hundred small Japanese children English through painting. I've discovered what makes me happy.'

'I may not be able to provide the children, but we can go and paint together.'

Pippa and I attended sessions all that year, painting out all manner of dreams and dragons, demons and visions. When Finals loomed, I asked, 'D'you think I'd be able to take my paintbox into the Prac. Crit. exam? I mean, a picture might answer a question completely.'

Luckily, Pippa's partner, Frank, had the Book of Rules at his command.

'Nowhere does it say you're forbidden to take a paintbox in. Go for it.'

After so many days of spouting relentless words, I was relieved to work in another expressive medium. The final paper, the final question, a passage from Shakespeare's *Richard III*; and 'Illustrate your answer', the question added helpfully. For the last hour, I painted away, a glum-looking king on his throne, meditating upon the state of his monarchy.

Pippa phoned before the results were posted. 'You've caused something of a battle royal.'

'What?'

'Well, we've never had to give a mark for a painting in the English Faculty before. One of the examiners thought it was genius and gave it a First, but the other, a medievalist, thought it the greatest outrage he'd ever seen. He failed you.'

'Oh my *god*, Pippa!'

'Don't panic, they're still wrangling. At least you've caused a stir.'

'Yeah, but I didn't do it to *fail*!'

'You won't fail. They'll compromise. Your other papers were all fine.'

Her intuition proved correct. Some years later, I happened upon a Practical Criticism paper and was happy to note it was highly illustrated throughout – for those more visually inclined.

The suitcase in Portugal Place

Oh god. No way. Not me. This couldn't be happening. I was falling, falling … damn it, I was in love. In love with a Fellow, of all original things. I was back in Cambridge to research my second novel and wanted to be among the gypsies and showmen on Midsummer Common. I duly dragged Pippa to have her palm read, went round with sketch and note books, jotting down as much as I could.

'Ere, you an Inspector?' One of the Romanichal matrons faced me squarely, hands on hips.

I laughed. 'No! I'm researching a novel.'

'Oh yeah.' She was far from convinced.

'What are these for?' I asked, pointing to the great metal jugs she sold.

The woman stared at me indulgently. 'Water,' she said, gesturing with her thumb and opening her large mouth. 'Water. Fer drinkin'.'

At the same fair, I struck up a friendship with Bill, a 70-year-old horse dealer, brown as a berry and fit as a man half his age. As I sat round the open fire with his family, drinking smoky chai and playing with his grandchildren, I wondered whether this was my path, if I should run away with them. Bill held my shoulders and looked deep into my eyes.

'If I were 20 years younger and not tied to the apron strings of my Missus, swear ter god I'd take yer with me.'

Making my way back through the fields, I remembered the voice of the fortune-teller. *Look in the grass fer gold*, she'd said. *You'll find gold terday*. Moments later, half-hidden among some weeds, I spied a handful of change fallen from some stray pocket. There were pound coins, shiny gold in the clutch. They had some power of foresight, these travellers of the Road.

'Well, let her come and see me then,' boomed Peter when the Porters delivered my message. 'She's clearly not one who's after m'money.'

I was admitted to Mr Peter Avery's haven of sacred knowledge one late afternoon as the sun threw white shards of light through the smoke haze of his room. He told me how he had been posted to Kandy, Ceylon during the Second World War, the same place as my grandfather. Perhaps it was the replenished glass of port that did it, but my eyes began welling up. Out poured the whole reason for writing my first novel, a homage to the beloved memory of my grandfather; and oh! How Peter's gruff paternalism reminded me of him!

'You know, I'm getting awfully peckish,' he said at last. 'Must be well after nine.' With a mock-turtle sigh, 'The Buttery seems to have forgotten me again.'

I fumbled in my satchel. 'It's not much,' I faltered, 'but I made myself some sandwiches and forgot to eat them. Would you care to share them?'

We munched away in silent companionship.

'I declare that was the finest supper I've had in a long time,' he said, dusting his lips with a large, pristine napkin.

'I hope it was all right,' I mumbled.

'Those unexpected feasts always bring the greatest joy.'

We adopted each other from that moment on.

But what of my unsuspecting heart, through all these meetings with remarkable men? What of the semi-permanent state of flux and torment, the prayers on bended knee in the Chapel I had barely visited during my entire student days? Suddenly, it seemed the choristers would reach such feverish pitch that the hallowed ceiling would burst asunder and this love I felt be shouted out on high.

In the Chapel's dim gloom, I asked for some sense of sanity to return to my frenzied heart. The wise voice of Peter as he lit the candles on his mantelpiece: 'Oh there's the tolling of the bell, dear. You'd better be off.'

I would kiss his freckled cheek and fly, heart in mouth, a moth on the summer evening, as eager for sugar as Hafiz's parrot, so enamoured of the Seller of Sweets.

It was ridiculous, though; an affair never to be, as all-enveloping as the emotion may feel. *Let me go, oh king of King's!* This time, I was on my knees.

Walking back to Alice's on her birthday, I stopped outside a house in Portugal Place. There, left among the rubbish, a Persian rug, rolled up; and a huge leather suitcase missing only a handle. I heaved them home, one under each arm.

'Alice!' I cried, bursting through the door. 'It's a sign, we're saved! You can fly back to Guadeloupe on the magic carpet and as for me – I'm going to start packing for India as soon as I've fixed a handle on this stalwart old case.'

Dharamsala: a hoonda in the woods

Pock! Pock! The only sound, as I climbed the mountain road, top-heavy rhododendrons falling; and the invisible trace of white butterflies, stark against the sombre pines. It felt strange, being back on this road, so familiar, though I had not walked it for 15 years. As a child, I'd come back alone from Tibetan restaurants in the village to our guest house, skipping over scorpions, playing fearful games of hide-and-seek with the silver-haired gibbons; but I'd always been safe, protected by the deep greenness of the forest. Now, I walked with a growing sense of unease.

Half a mile further and a man in white salwar kamis seemed to be collecting some plant from the hedge. Probably harvesting something, I thought. As I walked past him, he pointed to his wrist: 'Time? Time?' he asked.

I shook my head. 'No watch,' I said, pointing to my own.

Then I frowned. Who the hell needed to know the time in the middle of the forest? I looked back over my shoulder. The man was now hurtling towards me, eyes wild. The plants he had been picking, I discovered, were nettles. Now, the *hoonda* (thug) was whipping me with them, round my head, neck, wrenching my headscarf from my short-cropped head, practically scalping me in the process.

I was too astounded to scream or even panic. What was with this guy? And did he know how much effort it had taken me to get here, to get back on this road? I was beside myself.

'STOP!' I cried out. 'You're hurting me. Why are you hurting me?' The frenzy in the man's eyes flickered briefly through unease, fear. He wrestled me to the ground and dragged me along the road on my stomach. My glasses fell off. I was clutching my bag for all it was worth. Inside, everything. He pulled and pulled, stepping down off the road and into steep, prickly jungle. I held on, he tugged harder. One final wrench and snap! The strap of my bag broke. Like a villain in a cartoon, the hoonda lost his balance and toppled through the furze, backwards somersaulting through the trees.

I picked up my precious bag and ran; ran for life, soul, novels, for finding my path and holding my ground. At last, two young Tibetans on motorbikes came roaring along.

'Stop!' I gasped. 'Stop!' Breathlessly, I recounted the tale.

'This is very auspicious,' they said when I came to the end. 'When something bad could have happened, but doesn't, we Tibetans say it is a very auspicious event.'

Masking the fear in Palestine

In the courtyard of the Al Aqsa mosque, marvelling at that great gold dome which almost outshines the sun, I discovered that Nandita, who had persuaded the British Council to fund this research journey to schools the other side of the Wall, was a Kingswoman too. I decided to make masks with the children of Abu Dis and with Sofia to help me bargain, went on a shopping spree at the local stationers. Ribbons, sequins, fabric, paints, brushes, crayons, beads: the shopkeeper was delighted.

'Can we make animal masks?' I asked back at school. During the ensuing chaos, I glanced anxiously at the Palestinian teachers, wondering if they would consider this one step too far, too much liberation, the madness of the kids bordering on irreligious. To my relief, they were smiling, enjoying themselves as much as the children.

'They are having such fun,' said Sofia. 'We love to see them this happy.'

In a land where terror is rife, I learnt to understand the importance of a glimmer of happiness. Towards the end of our journey, Nandita determined to smuggle the Palestinian teachers on a bus for a day out in Jericho and the Dead Sea. She hired a coach with Hebrew writing across the side, persuaded a trembling Christian driver to take us, and we sat in the window seats, our friends veiled and hidden by our sides. One checkpoint, two checkpoints, three checkpoints, each as nerve-wracking as the last. Our driver pulled over to the side of the road and devoured cigarettes, in tears.

At last, the full moon rising over the Dead Sea. The haunting strains of Arabic song as we floated in the shallows: how, in this raging land, was it possible to feel such peace?

As our bags were duly searched by Israeli security, I heard a tiny mewling. Looking down, I spied a kitten, trying to climb into the soldier's outsize boots. Distracted, he reached down and picked up the animal in a palm twice its size, put it on his shoulder and allowed it to clamber round his neck.

'All day, he is trying to get into my boot,' he grinned, amiably. The scene reminded me of another in Brussels, when the Dalai Lama had been teaching there. Security, black-shirted and thick-booted, was tight. As the crowds waited to wave farewell to His Holiness, a small boy reached between the legs of one of the guards to retrieve a twig for his game in the dust.

Three deaths; and the birth of a daughter of King's

As teachers, of course we shouldn't have favourites: but how could I resist young Tsetun, a boy of six who had trekked across the Himalayas the year before, in order to receive a Tibetan education? Always in trouble with his other *gelas* (teachers), he reminded me of a Tibetan Just William, his catapult ever at the ready, his knees constantly scuffed, his head bearing the knocks and blows of recent adventurous mishaps. When the *mela* (funfair) came to the shores of Dal Lake, I paid for his rides on the big wheel, turned not by a motor, but the strong arm of a mustachioed gypsy, his eye as fierce as a tiger's.

After school, Tsetun would seek me out, craving paints and brushes to depict epic Himalayan battles, snow covered in blood. In our final lesson together, we made dragonfly puppets. That afternoon, a swarm of real dragonflies swooped across the playground.

It was my last day at the Children's Village. I wondered why there were no teachers in the staffroom when I went to make my goodbyes. Seeking them out in the classroom, I found the whole school chanting mantras.

'What's going on?' I asked. With tears in her eyes, Kunchog explained to me that a child had just died. My own eyes filled with horror.

'Who?'

'Tsetun.'

I fell to my knees. In his usual way, he had been playing dangerously, hitching a lift on the tailgate of the dustcart. The cart, unaware of his presence, had stalled, reversed, thrown Tsetun to the ground and crushed his skull.

Hurtling down the mountain, eyes wide open with shock, I couldn't stop asking why. A watery rainbow appeared above us. Oh small warrior of light, fight with all your courage the demons and strange visions you're bound to encounter on your journey to the next place.

Jenny came to save me when I felt too afraid to walk the quiet mountain paths of Dharamsala after my meeting with the hoonda.

'Oh rot! Nothing to worry about. I've walked these paths a million times.' We spent the next five months exploring together, eating handfuls of sweet currants in the nooks and clefts of mountains. When Jenny died of cancer two years later, she left a substantial legacy to KINSHIP, the small charity I had set up in Tsetun's honour, to create exciting, safe play-spaces for children in need. The first project was at Tsetun's school. When last we checked, the kids were playing dangerously in the space, enjoying themselves to the full.

Peter Avery passed away after years of ill health, a release, in his own words, from 'a cage too gilt for the bird'. His coffin, enshrouded in cloth rich with heraldic beasts, was borne aloft into the late autumn sunshine from King's Chapel to the skylark voices of the Choir. Later in the Fellows' Garden, I sat under a tree, listening for his irreplaceable voice.

'If you remember nothing else, remember this,' he seemed to say. 'A loaf of bread, a flask of wine, and thou beside me, singing in the wilderness: and the wilderness is paradise enow.'

Today, I am in Ladakh, climbing a sacred mountain to caves thousands of feet above the campsite. It is 5am. I have had no breakfast. No matter, it's time to go, says Tashi.

'I may have to go slow,' I tell him.

'That's fine,' he says, racing off to scale a sheer rock face. 'Just follow the easy path.'

So it is that I begin an extraordinary climb alone, through ravines and crevices, up stepladders over which waterfalls gush, up and up, pausing every 50 steps for my pounding heart to resume a normal pace, for my legs to grow solid again. Eventually, in my own time, I reach the caves. They are smooth and worn round as cubby holes. I am tempted to curl up like a cat and sleep until the others come careering back from even higher caves.

This adventure has made me aware of being alone in vast space and silence, wilderness. I am daunted by the epic crags above me, soothed by the water-mellowed rocks. I feel happy, despite the altitude and challenge of the way. At this moment, I am a true daughter of King's, treading an unknown path in a place that hasn't yet made it into the guidebooks, so remote and rare.

The gift of a year

Noel Williams

'If I catch you dossing round this house again, boy, I'll throw you through that window. If you touch that girl again, if I even see your face here, you're through that window. No doubt.'

It's October 1974. I've the arrogance of 21 years' ignorance. I've a cascade of hair that would make Charles II jealous. I'm told any girl would kill for the curl of my eyelashes. I'm draped in my dad's RAF greatcoat. I spend my days idly wondering which rules to bend and which to condescend to. I'm fresh and cocky after my overnight hitch from King's to my girlfriend, Carrol, in Headington, Oxford. And now I'm in fear of my life. He means it.

I try to face down this hateful man, but it's not easy when you're – not to put too fine a point on it – a coward. I know the theory of the bar-brawl: fist his nose with your index knuckle proud, to split the septum; grind your instep down his shin, to scrape away a peel of skin; turn your back to deliver a mule kick to the balls – tactics to spawn pain and blood in equal measure. I do know the theory. Somehow, however, I suspect putting it into practice might not be that straightforward. He is so much bigger than me that he appears to have extra dimensions. His body may've been shaped mostly by Guinness and the sausage sandwich, but he knows how to handle pickaxe, shovel and broken beer glass, too.

But it's his Dublin accent I really find threatening. I'm in my final year at King's, but in 1974, the year of Ross McWhirter's assassination, the M62 bombing and 29 dead in Birmingham pubs, the Irish accent sends me back ten years into the short trousers of trepidation and trembling.

What he – I'll call him Mike – saw in the greasy greatcoat that blocked the TV was elitism and privilege. He saw a dosser sponging off the cash he laboured for in long days among scaffolding and ditches. He saw a middle-class snob too enthusiastically engaged in acts of undoubted reprehension with his recently acquired stepdaughter.

What I saw, on the other hand, was a brute without culture, a patriarchal

Tess Adkins.

throwback with no compassion or sense of family or beauty, for whom life was beer, betting, sex and work-avoidance. Moreover, I saw a caveman who aimed to destroy a love stronger than anything Tristan had felt for Iseult or Dante for Beatrice.

So there we were, idiots posturing on both sides of the coffee table.

I retreated to Cambridge. I was appalled, fearful, lovelorn. My work would certainly have suffered badly, if I'd actually been doing any. But Wordsworth and Aristotle were unimportant now. It was clear to me what I had to do. I had to quit King's, rescue Carrol from the ogre, free her from the tower, put on my woodcutter's garb and somehow figure a way to make a life for us together.

I loved Cambridge then. I love Cambridge now. To a working-class scholarship boy, King's, the University, the city and all it offered were a revelation and a release: a heady mix of liberation, confusion, joy, frustration, astonishment, epiphany, dreaming, desire, enlightenment and loneliness; a place of opening doors and invisible walls; a place which gave more than I could possibly take, and excited every sensibility. Yet, without Carrol, it was empty.

My personal Tutor was a new Geography Fellow, one Tess Adkins. She was young and pretty inexperienced, I think, as a tutor. I told her I was leaving College, forced to give it up. A little uncomfortably, I explained why. I knew adolescent infatuation raised more weary eyebrows among Fellows than botox would ever be likely to. Tess rather surprised me, therefore, by being hugely sympathetic. Even more surprising, she was anxious that I shouldn't go. She claimed I had promise, that it would be a waste to throw away the two years and the 2.1 I'd so far managed. She also seemed to know about me, which surprised me, too. Others in the College, she said, thought I had a good chance of finishing the Tripos with a First.

Despite this sudden inflation of my self-esteem, I explained passionately that I had no choice in the matter. I don't think I used words like 'intertwined' or 'at first sight' or 'forever' or 'destiny'. But I may have. I was like that. We belonged together. We couldn't be apart.

Our romance made Romeo and Juliet look like Tom and Jerry. Well, I don't suppose I said that, but I'm pretty sure I was melodramatically poetic in my account of my firmly made decision. Almost instantly Tess began to unmake it for me.

This interview with Tess sits in my memory as a turning point in my life only slightly less profound than the moment Carrol and I met. Two hours after our first words, we kissed under the stars (just to be clear, that's Carrol and me, not Tess and me). We still haven't come up for air nearly 40 years later. Yet, as Carrol turned me on my head, so Tess inverted my life, too. I maintained stolidly I was compelled to stay with Carrol, so I had to give up King's. Tess took the opposite tack: clearly I had to stay at King's, so what would it take to bring Carrol to me?

I still am unable to believe the extraordinary compassion of the College, and particularly of Tess, as well as her energy and kindness, in finding and allowing a solution that enabled me to stay in College, live with Carrol, achieve my First and, moreover, do so through a year of beauty, joy and learning which remains unsurpassed in any of my remaining years.

Tess found, offered, and then arranged for us to live in, a furnished flat over Mowbray's Bookshop on King's Parade itself which King's kept for married (we weren't) postgraduate (I wasn't) students.

Carrol was 17. She would have to leave school. Her family was as poor as you can get. She was the eldest of six. Her mum had been abandoned by her dad when the youngest boy was born with Down's syndrome. They lived off Social Security, seven people in a three-bedroomed council house; a family to whom jam was a luxury and a typical meal was mashed potato with an egg beaten into it.

My family was rather better off. My parents, too, were divorced. But my father held down two jobs to ensure that my two brothers and I could transcend our Sheffield working-class origins. I'd then been fortunate enough to win a scholarship to an excellent school in Oxford, though I always was something of an outsider there, a clever but peculiar poor relation, generally out of uniform and out of my depth. People like Carrol and I simply did not get chances like this: to live together, to be in love, to sit at the edge of privilege and put our toes in the waters of culture, to begin to build a proper, joint life when, really, we expected only obstruction and disappointment. Such generous understanding and institutional kindness from the College seemed to me almost beyond what might be imagined. Certainly outside the realm of the possible.

Naturally, we had to live as if married. Tess accepted quite simply our commitment to marry when we could. But we couldn't do that at once, because Carrol needed her dad's permission, and no one knew where he'd absconded to, six years previously. He was a lorry driver. He could be anywhere. I also undertook not to trumpet my undergraduate status, for clearly I was being given something that no one else in College was likely to have.

So it wasn't plain sailing. We had to skulk a little. We avoided our neighbours, just in case they asked awkwardly postgraduate-type questions about madrigals or Wittgenstein or whether we'd be at Biffy's do after the ADC premiere.

Carrol left her mother worried, though, fortunately, her mum loved and trusted me. She also left five siblings saddened, and wasn't pleased to abandon them to their new stepfather, either. But her smile as she stepped off the coach and we lugged a single cardboard suitcase down Petty Cury was one of perplexing escape into bewildered fulfilment.

She had to find work in order to make sure we could live as well as pay the rent, which was rather more expensive than for a student bedsit. King's wasn't quite *that* compassionate. First she worked in the dire cheese department of the International Supermarket in Market Square, paring mould from various discoloured Red Leicesters and Gorgonzolas.

After a few weeks of cheese-related discomforts, she gravitated to shop assistant for Primavera, a King's Parade shop for tourists and art lovers. Here she flourished, tending the pottery of Susie Cooper, Lucy Rie and Ray Finch, and serving Italians and Japanese with art postcards of Nolde paintings and weird wooden artefacts from Indonesia. In a few months she became manager. The owners, Mr and Mrs Rothschild (not *the* Rothschilds, but rich and busy people nevertheless) found her a godsend in their world of flighty students and coachloads of potential shoplifters. However, though we lived four flights of stairs and ten seconds of pavement from the shop, she was generally late. I expect she'd blame me.

We'd fantasized about life together, but neither of us was that well equipped for the business of managing electricity meters, shoestring budgets, meals without ingredients, housekeeping. It hardly mattered. The flat had four rooms, mice, a double bed, woodworm, a single gas heater, wall panelling, proper bookshelves, St Edward's Church immediately behind us, the Chapel, the Parade, the College and a smooth green lawn ahead and, throughout, a sense of rightness, a sense of belonging.

This year that King's gave us was the foundation of our entire lives together, setting up a marriage that endured because fed by a thousand unrepeatable memories: rumpled awakening to the bells of Great St Mary's; leaning on the sash window to watch the streaming scarlet and white of the Choir; punts skidding through the gap next to Gibbs; a procession passing beneath our window, the fire-eater's gouts of flame raging up towards us; nipping in to Primavera for a quick kiss every morning on the way to the University Library (I tried to time my arrival to coincide with the first warm cheese scones in the library cafe); our one May Ball, a night I remember as silk and silver; wading waist-deep upriver through the dangerous grip of turgid floods because it was the only way to move the punt (no, I don't know why I didn't drown); skateless skating on the frozen millpond; a kiss preserved on King's bridge by the BBC, as reported by Carrol's gleeful sisters; dancing through the streets in vampire garb; writing poems (generally execrable, occasionally fine) under the willows; arm in arm to Grantchester, Carrol barefoot or in platforms, in sexy frills, maxis, Indian cotton. These were days of patchouli and perfection.

In March 1975, having tracked down her father, we married, but not in the Chapel. We felt our 15 guests from distinctly downmarket postcodes might look and feel somewhat out of place. I'd have liked to, but no one else had my pretensions.

Tess came to the reception, in the flat, to sample the luxuries of cherry wine and communal rice salad. I don't think she ever understood how profoundly she and King's affected our lives. In fact, when I made a cursory email contact with her a couple of years ago, she'd no memory of her compassion or King's generosity at all. I don't think she'd erased me from memory as a difficult problem eliminated. I think I was lost in the years of College kindnesses, the institutional assumption that fostering student well-being is the necessary responsibility of real educators. So ingrained is this ethos in the natural operations of the place, that no one notices how deeply and irrevocably lives are changed each time a new student steps into Keynes or settles down for that first frightening tutorial in Gibbs.

I don't know what sort of fist we'd have made of our lives without that gift of a year. Perhaps we'd have found things too hard for love to conquer. Perhaps I'd have resented giving up King's, and learned bitterness. I might never have found an academic career, or a career as writer, and condemned myself to some sort of nine-to-five mindlessness to compensate for having dragged Carrol from her school to uncertain poverty. Perhaps we'd have arrived at none of the pleasures, blessings and achievements our years have brought, without the idyll of that first.

Reconsidering the Backs: a fragment

Sarah Wood

October 1992, Front Court

Going through the gatehouse with Mum and Dad, clutching two black bin bags and a
copy of Catherine Belsey's *Critical Practice*, it wasn't clear to me that I could ever feel at
home somewhere like this. Coming from a comprehensive school and a dyed-in-the-wool
Labour family, I'd chosen to read English at King's because of its reputation for being
informal, left-leaning, and less beholden to archaic customs and formalities. Yet the King's
that greeted me on that overcast and drizzly afternoon – the implacable stone frontage of
the Gibbs building (*Caution: Slippery Paths*), held at arm's length by a sheet of hallowed
lawn (*Please Keep off the Grass*) and flanked by a line of bayonet-tipped buttresses (*Choral
Service: Please Queue from Here*) bespoke an architectural pomp and circumstance that made
me want to turn and run.

Freshers' Week brought little reassurance: Latin phrases were effortlessly dropped into
small talk about canapés; French philosophers were brought to bear on the controversial issue
of which Freshers' parties to attend, and accomplished raconteurs had honed to perfection
entertaining vignettes about unmanageable luggage carts. Gauche and gaffe-prone, I felt
myself fixed by scornful eyes and saw myself pinned and wriggling on the wall. When I didn't
understand a single word that anybody said at our first seminar (*What is Style, anyway?*), I bolted
back to my room and began to pack my clothes. I was a fraud and a fake, a fool dressed in
scholar's clothing, about to be exposed by those who really
knew their Derrida from their De Man. How could I
have presumed? And how could I begin?

Well, I may not have known my Barthes from
my Baudrillard, but I did know my Tanner (my
Tony Tanner that is), so I began by looking behind
the grand facades for the backside of the place. In
Tanner's seminal essay on Nathaniel Hawthorne,
published in *Scenes of Nature, Signs of Men*, he echoes
Hawthorne's idea that there is 'more truth to native
and characteristic tendencies, and vastly greater
suggestiveness, in the back view of a residence […]
than in its front,' since the latter is 'meant for the
world's eye, and is therefore a veil and a concealment.'
Not unlike the writing of Hawthorne and Henry
James, Tanner's own criticism consistently looks
'behind and beneath for the suggestive idea,'
examining the significance of back passages (be
they topographical or anatomical), back stories
(etymological, historical, or narratological), back
waters, back doors and underbellies, rendering
visible and meaningful the unseen, ostensibly banal
but potentially illuminating worlds that lie behind,
beneath, and between what's on public display.

So this ruled out 'The Backs' straight off. For sure,
they presented a softer, more bucolic aspect of King's
than austere Front Court, but they never actually
felt like the back of the College. Artfully contrived,

formally and aesthetically satisfying, irresistibly photogenic, they were off-limits to people and emptied of everyday objects; Scholars' Piece belonged to the cows, while the back lawn lay beautiful but soulless by the Cam, aloof from the life of the College, a flat and vacuous face to be gazed at rather than used.

The Backs presented an unforgettable picture, but I wonder if you remember the brown-tiled corridor behind the kitchen? It wraps around the buttery by the Hall and opens out into the loading bay. If I had to point to the true back of the College, it would be here in the loading bay, and daft as it seems, I walked this brown-tiled corridor at least a dozen times a day in my first year at King's. There was something reassuringly material about the churning of dishwashers, the jangle and clatter of cutlery, the whistling of kitchen porters accompanied by the whirring hum of air-conditioning units – a strangely calming cacophony of white noise to cloak my footsteps as I ventured down from 118 Keynes and bolted in and out of the buttery. I rarely entered the sombre, frowning Hall itself (*Members of the College and their Guests Only*), but the row of surplus dinner tables, scrubbed and stacked in the corridor, have stuck in my mind ever since, like a fleck of hardened food that defies detergent and cleaves to the tabletop when the meal itself has long since been digested and expurged. Blown along the draughty corridor, the smells were distinctive, too, and reminded me of long, hot summers spent waiting tables, stacking dishwashers and mopping restaurant floors. Suspended between a lunch that was and a dinner soon to be, the savory waft of chops and gravy mingled with dishwasher steam, seasoned by occasional blasts of beer and vomit, belching upwards from the Cellar. Sickly-sweet and sticky at midnight, the floor tiles reeked of bleach by morning. A world away from the etiolated atmosphere of the College Library, here was somewhere I could belong.

Well away from the spaces on public display, the loading bay enjoyed a rather different aspect from the so-called Backs. Where the Backs had the River Cam and the grand Gibbs Arch, the loading bay boasted only mop water and a delivery hatch (*Strictly Deliveries Only*), a gaping hole in the wall that afforded an outlook onto the blackened brick walls and wheelie bins of King's Lane (*Flatten ALL cardboard before putting in the cage*). While the Backs were scrupulously emptied of everyday paraphernalia and appeared untouched or unchanged by the passage of time and the processes of decay, the loading bay was filled with the detritus of college life, unloved objects that attested to the processes of production, consumption and excretion: kegs of Carlsberg, damp wooden pallets, plastic bread crates and six-foot tray trolleys, stacked or strewn, filled or empty, depending on the time of day, revealing the College as a visceral, vital, and materially grounded world. In contrast to the waistcoated, seemingly 24/7 custodians of the Porter's Lodge out front, the kitchen porters would come and go around the back, slipping outside for a smoke, chatting about last night's telly and this evening's plans, reminding this overly-anxious and agoraphobic first year that there was actually life beyond The College, that the overwhelming undergraduate experience was not forever nor need even be a 24/7 existence, hermetically sealed and separated from the world outside its walls.

So, where to from the loading bay? Well, if you continued along the brown-tiled corridor it would lead you into Webbs Courtyard, to the laundry, the Library and the back gate to King's Lane. This was the short cut to the city for students who dreaded the prospect of running the gauntlet of Front Court, a kind of emergency exit for those of us who felt unable to prepare a face to meet the faces one would inevitably meet. I would frequently steel myself for the Front Court route to King's Parade only to lose my nerve at the last moment and double back down the brown-tiled corridor, consumed with self-doubt and burning with shame at my own pusillanimity. Having scurried along the familiar back passage and come out into Webbs, I would slide my key into the back gate lock, slip out unnoticed through the wicket door (*Leave the Door as you Found it: LOCKED*) and find relief in the anonymity of the crowds that flowed through the city streets.

List of Contributors

Samson Abramsky is Christopher Strachey Professor of Computing and a Fellow of Wolfson College, Oxford. He has held chairs at Imperial College, and at the University of Edinburgh and is a Fellow of the Royal Society. He has played a leading role in the development of game semantics, and its applications to the semantics of programming languages, and has recently been working on new methods for quantum information and computation.

Sebastian Ahnert joined King's as a Fellow in 2009. He is a Royal Society University Research Fellow in the Theory of Condensed Matter at the Cavendish Laboratory and his research covers several topics at the interface between theoretical physics and biology.

Stephen Bann is Emeritus Professor of History of Art and a Senior Research Fellow at Bristol University. Among his recent books are *Paul Delaroche: History Painted* (1997), *Parallel Lines: French printmakers, painters and photographers in nineteenth-century France* (2001), and *Ways around Modernism* (2007). He was a Guest Curator for the exhibition of the work of Paul Delaroche at the National Gallery in London in 2010.

Patrick Bateson retired from the Provostship in 2003 and now lives in East Suffolk. He is President of the Zoological Society of London and remains active as a writer and speaker. He published in January 2010 the report of his *Inquiry into Dog Breeding* and his most recent book *Plasticity, Robustness, Development and Evolution* will be published in 2011. He was knighted in 2003.

Martin Bell joined the BBC in 1962 and worked as a reporter and correspondent until 1997. His assignments included 90 countries and 11 wars from Biafra to Bosnia and Vietnam to El Salvador. In 1997 he was elected to Parliament as the first elected Independent since 1951. He has also worked as a UNICEF Ambassador in Tajikistan, Burundi, Kosovo, Malawi, Iraq, DRC, Darfur, Afghanistan and Somalia. He was awarded the OBE in 1993.

Peter Cave is a philosopher, lecturer and author, and chairs the UK's Humanist Philosophers, becoming involved in public debates on philosophical, religious and socio-political matters. He has scripted and presented humorous philosophy programmes for BBC Radio 4. Among his books are the best-selling *Can a Robot Be Human?* as well as *What's Wrong with Eating People?* and *Do Llamas Fall in Love?*

Suranga Chandratillake worked for a variety of technology companies after reading Computer Science at King's, and then founded blinkx, an Internet video search company, in 2004 and took it public in 2007. He lives with his family in San Francisco.

Anthony Clarke was called to the Bar, Middle Temple, in 1965 and he spent 27 years specializing in maritime and commercial law. He has been a High Court Judge, a member of the Court of Appeal, the Admiralty Judge and Master of the Rolls. He was awarded a life peerage in 2009 and appointed as a Justice of the Supreme Court.

Stephen Cleobury came to King's in 1982 as Director of Music, having previously held posts at Westminster Abbey and Westminster Cathedral. He has been Chief Conductor of the BBC Singers, and Conductor of the Cambridge University Musical Society.

Lily Cole is a third-year undergraduate at King's, reading History of Art. She also models and acts.

James Cox has been a journalist all his working life, in newspapers, radio and television, concentrating on political coverage and commentary. During his career in the BBC he was the New York correspondent, a lobby correspondent at Westminster and political editor of *Newsnight*. He ended up as main presenter of Radio 4's *The World This Weekend* and continues to write and broadcast and, freed from the BBC's political constraints, is an active member of the Liberal Democrats.

Michael Craig-Martin has established an international career as an artist, with work in many collections including the Tate and MoMA in New York. He taught at Goldsmiths College for many years, eventually becoming the first Millard Professor. He was a Trustee of the Tate through the 1990s and was involved in the creation of Tate Modern. He is currently a Trustee of the Art Fund, an RA, and a CBE.

Eleanor Curtis is a photographer and writer, working both internationally and in the UK. She specializes in black-and-white film and print photography. She has worked for a variety of UK broadsheets and wire on the Middle East and Angola, and has written four publications on architecture and design. Her most recent publication is a photographic study entitled *St George's Chapel, Windsor Castle* (2008).

Tam Dalyell started work as a teacher at a comprehensive school, where he was seconded to be Director of Studies on the ship-school *Dunera*. Elected in 1962 as MP for West Lothian, he served turbulently for 43 years, becoming Father of the House of Commons, 2001–2005 and Member of the National Executive of the Labour Party for 37 years. He has also been a weekly columnist at *New Scientist* and Rector of the University of Edinburgh.

Iain Fenlon became a Fellow of King's in 1976. Except for visiting appointments at All Souls, Harvard, Bologna and the Ecole Normale Superieure in Paris, he has remained in Cambridge ever since, and has been Professor of Historical Musicology since 2005. His most recent books are *The Ceremonial City: History, Memory and Myth in Renaissance Venice* (2007), and *Piazza San Marco* (2009).

Anthony Figgis joined the Foreign Office after leaving King's. His postings included Belgrade, Bahrain and Madrid. He was Ambassador to Austria from 1996 to 2000, and Marshal of the Diplomatic Corps from 2001 to 2008. He became Chairman of the Royal Over-Seas League in 2009.

Richard Fortey is a palaeontologist, and one of the world authorities on trilobites. For most of his working life he was employed in the Natural History Museum in London, and he has published several hundred scientific papers in international journals. He is a Fellow of the Royal Society and Visiting Professor in Palaeobiology at Oxford University. He is also known for his popular science writing, and his book, *Life: an unauthorised biography* (1996) has been translated into 12 languages.

Richard Hamblyn is currently writer in residence at the Environment Institute, University College London. He has written *The Invention of Clouds*, which won the 2001 Los Angeles Times Science Book Prize; *Terra: Tales of the Earth*, a study of natural disasters; and *The Cloud Book*, published in association with the Met Office. His most recent book, *Data Soliloquies*, co-written with the digital artist Martin John Callanan, is a collection of essays and artworks on the theme of visualizing climate change.

Geoffrey Harcourt is Emeritus Reader in the History of Economic Theory at Cambridge; Emeritus Fellow of Jesus College, Cambridge; and Professor Emeritus at the University of Adelaide.

Ross Harrison was elected a Fellow of King's in 1975, and was a member of the University's Department of Philosophy, starting as a Lecturer and ending as Professor of Philosophy. He then decamped to the University of London and became the Quain Professor of Jurisprudence at University College. He was elected Provost of King's in 2006.

John Higgins taught at the University of Geneva between 1980 and 1985 where he was also founder and Director of the Cultural Studies Group. In 1986, he moved to the English Department at the University of Cape Town where he remains as a Professor. He was founding editor of the journal *Pretexts: literary and cultural studies* and his study *Raymond Williams: Literature, Marxism and Cultural Materialism* won the UCT Book Award in 2000 and the Altron National Book Award in 2002.

Simon Hoggart joined *The Guardian* in 1968, later becoming the American correspondent for *The Observer*, and occasional guest commentator on National Public Radio's *Weekend Edition Saturday*. Hoggart then became the parliamentary sketch writer for *The Guardian* in 1993. He also writes a wine column for *The Spectator*.

David Ignatius is a columnist for the *Washington Post*, whose articles are syndicated internationally. He is the author of seven novels, including *Body of Lies*, which was made into a film by Ridley Scott.

Martin Jacques completed his doctorate, and took a teaching post at Bristol University. Before long he abandoned academia to become editor of *Marxism Today*. He became a prolific contributor to the mainstream media, including as a columnist for the *Sunday Times* and *The Times* and making TV programmes for the BBC. He invented the think-tank Demos. From 1993 he took a growing interest in East Asia and in 2009 he published *When China Rules the World: the Rise of the Middle Kingdom and the End of the Western World*, which has become a global best-seller.

Peter Jones has been Fellow and Librarian at King's since 1985. He is the Coordinator of the College's Summer Schools (running since 2006), and teaches a summer course called 'Bloomsbury and English culture in the 20th century.' Currently he is working as part of a team on the history of 'Generation to Reproduction' in the Department of History & Philosophy of Science.

Tony Judt was a Fellow of King's from 1972–8 before moving first to UC Berkeley (where he taught modern history) and thence to Oxford, where he taught Politics. In 1987 he joined New York University, where he was University Professor and Director of the Remarque Institute, which he founded in 1995. He was a Fellow of the American Academy of Arts & Sciences and a Corresponding Fellow of the British Academy. He was the author of *Postwar: A History of Europe Since 1945*. Tony Judt died as a result of motor neurone disease in August 2010.

Ben Leapman has reported on politics, home affairs, crime and economics for several newspapers including the *Evening Standard* and *Northern Echo*. He is currently the deputy news editor of *The Sunday Telegraph*.

Colin MacCabe became a Research Fellow at Emmanuel in 1974 and a Teaching Fellow at King's between 1976 and 1981. He is currently Distinguished Professor of English and Film at the University of Pittsburgh and Professor of English and Humanities at Birkbeck, University of London. He is also Associate Director of the London Consortium and editor of *Critical Quarterly*. He has produced more that 10 feature films and over 30 hours of documentaries on the history of the cinema.

Alan Macfarlane is Emeritus Professor of Anthropological Science and a Life Fellow of King's College. He became a Fellow of the British Academy in 1986. He has written 17 published books, the latest of which is *Reflections on Cambridge*, and has spent the last 20 years filming interviews with leading thinkers in Cambridge and placing them on the Internet (www.alanmacfarlane.com/ancestors/index).

Lucy McMahon graduated in Philosophy and is studying for an MPhil in Development Studies.

Alison Maitland is a writer, speaker and conference moderator specializing in work and management. A former *Financial Times* journalist, she is co-author of *Why Women Mean Business*.

Arzu Merali is a mother, writer and activist based in northwest London. Her writing focuses on human rights, Islam and social justice. Her work has appeared in various media, including *Cultures of Resistance, The Guardian, New Internationalist, Q-News* and *Hecate*. She is co-editor of the recent volume, *Towards a New Liberation Theology: Reflections on Palestine*. She is one of the founders of the Islamic Human Rights Commission.

Jonathan Mirsky is a journalist and historian specializing in Chinese affairs. He was East Asia editor of *The Times* in the 1990s based in Hong Kong, but resigned after accusing the paper of failing to pursue stories critical of China that might affect the interests of Rupert Murdoch, proprietor of *The Times*. In 1990 he was the British editors' 'International Journalist of the Year' for his coverage of the Tiananmen uprising.

Kate Newmann is a poet and writer. She compiled the *Dictionary of Ulster Biography*, which was published by Queen's University, Belfast in 1994. She has won several poetry prizes and in 2009 was shortlisted for the National Poetry Competition. She has held various residencies for the Arts Council of Northern Ireland and the Down Lisburn Health Trust, and in 2007 was writer-in-residence for the Louis MacNeice Centenary Celebration in Carrickfergus, County Antrim. She is co-director of the Summer Palace Press.

Charles Nicholl has worked as a journalist in London and South America and written a dozen books of history, biography and travel, including *The Reckoning*, about the death of Christopher Marlowe; a biography of Leonardo da Vinci, *The Flights of the Mind*; and *The Lodger: Shakespeare on Silver Street*. He was awarded the Hawthornden Prize in 1999, and is a Fellow of the Royal Society of Literature.

Robin Osborne is currently Senior Tutor at King's, where he was an undergraduate and graduate student and Junior Research Fellow. He returned to King's in 2001 as Professor of Ancient History. His books range over Greek history, the history of Greek art, and Greek archaeology. He is a Fellow of the British Academy and currently Chairman of the Council of University Classical Departments.

Martin Parr is a member of the Magnum Photographic Corporation and one of Britain's leading photographers. He has exhibited all over the world, and carried out photographic commissions for a wide range of national and international publications. He has also published more than a dozen books of photography, many of which have become collectors' items.

Jan Pieńkowski was a book designer at William Collins and Jonathan Cape before becoming a writer and illustrator. He was the creator of the very successful *Meg and Mog* books for children, copies of which he has donated to the King's Library. He has just completed an illustrated version of the Old Testament called 'In the beginning…'

Philip Purser was a full-time journalist throughout the 1950s, latterly on the *News Chronicle*. On the death of that paper in 1960 he became the television critic of the *Sunday Telegraph*, and remained in that role for 26 years. He branched out into book-writing in 1962 with several thrillers, a comic novel, a volume of bogus reminiscences, two biographies and a memoir. He has also written plays for radio and television.

Karl Sabbagh, editor of *A Book of King's*, worked in the BBC for 14 years before becoming director of a medical foundation. He then returned to full-time documentary production, eventually forming his own company, Skyscraper Productions. He is now an author, with ten published books on science, engineering, architecture, and Palestine.

Charles Saumarez Smith went from King's to Harvard to study at the Fogg Art Museum and to the Warburg Institute to do a PhD. Since then, he has been a Fellow of Christ's College (now an Honorary Fellow), worked at the Victoria and Albert Museum, where he was Head of Research, and been Director of the National Portrait Gallery and the National Gallery. He is now Secretary and Chief Executive of the Royal Academy.

Mohammad Shaheen was awarded a PhD at King's in 1974 and then taught the novel and literary theory at the University of Jordan, becoming Professor of English Literature. His most recent books are *E.M. Forster: The Politics of Imperialism* and a translation of the poetry of the Palestinian poet, Mahmoud Darwish, *Almond Blossoms and Beyond*.

Eleanor (Leo) Sharpston spent 25 years in practice at the Bar, combining that, from 1992 onwards, with a Fellowship at King's. In 2006, she became a member of the Court of Justice of the European Union, the EU's supreme court, where she serves as an Advocate General.

Anna Trench is a recent graduate of King's. She edited *Varsity* and drew illustrations and cartoons for the newspaper and other publications. She also played football for the University.

Tansy Troy lives and works in London, teaching Music and Creative Arts to primary school children. During the summer holidays, she travels to the Himalayas, where she enjoys high altitude adventures.

Noel Williams gained a PhD in English Language at Sheffield, then in 1979 took a temporary job in Communications at Sheffield Polytechnic. He is now Professor of Communications at Sheffield Hallam University, and remains academically eclectic, working on (among other things) creative writing, folklore, artificial intelligence, technical communication and interactive fiction.

Sarah Wood read English at King's from 1992–5 and American Literature (MPhil) in 1996–7, under the supervision of Professor Tony Tanner. She undertook doctoral research at UCL and her thesis was published as *Broken Heads and Bloated Tales: Quixotic Fictions of the USA 1792–1815* (Oxford University Press, 2005). Sarah was awarded a Leverhulme Research Fellowship at Sussex University before quitting academia to join the rat race. She co-founded and is currently a director of Unruly Media, a digital ad agency and leading exponent of viral video seeding, based in Shoreditch, London.

List of Subscribers

This book has been made possible through the generosity of the following subscribers.

The Revd Stephen Abbott	1962	Brian FC Clark	1955	George French		1943
Samson Abramsky	1972	Ralph Clark	1947	Colin Noel Garrett		1961
Travis M Adams	1955	Angus Clarke	1973	David Gaunt		1953
AP Aitman	1989	Adam Clayton	1991	Molly Elizabeth Gavriel		2009
J Alcraft	1952	Nick Clayton	1975	Trevor and Pauline Gazard	1971 and	1973
Mansoor Ali	1975	Stephen Cleobury	1982	Noel Gibbard		1941
Ralph Allwood	1972	Dr Crispin Cobb	1962	Michael Gibbon		1986
Jane Anderson	1980	Dr J Cocker	1944	Dr LA Glyptis		1997
Dr SR Anderson	1986	PMS Corley	1954	Peter DH Godfrey		1941
Julian Arkell	1953	Mr J Cox	1957	The Revd Dr Joseph Goetz		1966
William Arnold	1971	Dr Timothy J Crist	1973	Sir Nicholas Goodison		1955
Paul Aylieff	1983	Simon Crookall	1979	Jane and Mike Grabiner	1972 and	1969
Professor Derek Baker	1959	Professor Pierre Lalive d'Epinay	1948	John R Grace		1965
Gordon and Elizabeth Ball	1992	Martyn Daldorph	1963	JF Grant		1954
Peter Barley	1987	Tam Dalyell	1952	Ian Gray		
Alastair John Bealby	2006	Mr John ML Davenport	1955	Brian Greenwood		1956
John Beard	1970	Sophie Davies-Patrick	1991	Jefferson C Grieves		1951
Martin Bell	1959	Martin Davies	1984	Mr Ashley Grote		2001
Richard A Bell	1989	Siân Davies	1975	Pramod K Gupta		1955
Robert Belton	1942	Revd Prebendary John Deakin	1945	Peter Hall		1961
Mrs Deborah Bennett (née Bartlett)	1987	Stanley Dixon	1953	Paul Hallas		1976
John Bentley	1966	Tien Xuan Doe	1986	Mr Sebastian Halliday		1957
Professor Alan Bilsborough	1962	Tony Doggart	1958	Rachel Hammersley		1993
Mark Birch	1990	John Dorken	1962	Dr CS Handscomb		2000
Dr Christopher A Birt	1960	Mr G Down	1949	Neil Hardwick		1966
Mr David Blythe	1958	Joëlle du Lac	2006	Alexander Hardy		1992
Jonathan M Bonello, PhD	1995	John Duckett	1955	TS Harrison		1964
Christopher Borroni-Bird	1983	Toby Hart Dyke	1981	William Hassett		2003
John Bowley	1988	Michael Eaton MBE	1973	Bill and Debbie (née Thornton) Hawkins		
Lewis Braithwaite	1958	M Edwardes-Evans	1948		1979 and	1978
Mr Peter Braithwaite	1961	Dr Robert M Edwards	1992	Dr K Hayakawa		1975
Kelvin Bray	1953	Dr Keith RF Elliott	1967	JD Hayward		1990
Julie P Bressor	2009	Mr JG Ellis	1975	Brian Head		1955
The Revd John William Bridgen	1959	Chris Elston	1957	Dr Linda Helen (née Thornton)		1985
Lucy Jago Briggs	1985	Patrick Richard Emerson	2002	DH Higgins		1956
Donald G Browne		Matthew Evans	2006	Valerie Higham		1977
Dr Tej Bunnag MVO	1962	Alison Falconer	1985	Eric Hobsbawm		1936
Mr Charles Burney	1949	IW Farminer	1968	Richard J Holloway		1954
David W Burton		Kit Farrow	1958	David Howdon		1994
Adrian Cadbury	1949	Lewis H Ferguson	1966	Spencer Hudson		1948
Michael Cahill	1980	Dr Nick Fieller	1966	Emyr Hughes		1963
C Cain	1958	Paul Filer	1976	John Hughes		1967
Dr Michael E Callender	1967	Donald J Firth	1953	Dr Tony Hulme		1961
Katie Canell (née Mintern)	1993	CJN Fletcher	1958	Luke H Humphry		2003
Peter Cave	1972	David Forrester	1963	Dr Daniel Imhof		2001
S Chandratillake	1997	Mr JP Forrester	1967	Paul E Jack		1967
Dr Robert Chen	1983	Lee A Forstrom	1963	H Lionel Jackson		1945
Russell Cheng	1965	Michael Foyle	1953	Christopher Jagger		1987
Charles Marcus Clapham	1961	Dr Roger P Freedman	1959	Jason James		1983

Name	Year
Allison Jenkins	1987
Elizabeth Johnson (née Robinson)	1972
Mr H Johnson	1957
Dr Dafydd E Jones	1999
Peter Jones	1973
Bjarni B Jònsson	1957
Yohei Kanayama	1983
Alan Kaufman	1965
Sarah Khan	1998
Dr Shahab Q Khokhar	1998
Anne Marie King	1999
Anthony Knowles	1944
His Honour Judge Graham Knowles QC	1986
Dr Stefan G Koeberle	1987
Richard Kurti	1981
James Lancelot	1971
Ave Lauren	2008
Richard Lea	1967
William Lee	1982
George Leggatt	1976
Leong Wai Leng	1975
Dr VL Lew	1974
Beverley Lewis	1976
JB Lewis	1964
Chi-Fu Lin	1986
David G Lindsay	1962
Dr Claire Lorrain	1985
Mark Lowe	1954
Martin Lucas-Smith	1997
Peter Lund	1975
Sally Lund	1972
Helen Macaulay	2004
Anne-Marie Macmahon	1976
George Magnus	1956
Paul Makepeace	1993
Moni Malek	1978
Professor John Mann	1961
DE Marshall	1960
Dr Nicholas Marston	2001
Richard Martin	1957
TJW Martin	1945
Rt Hon. Michael Mates	1952
George McGregor	1957
Revd Dr AJ McGuire	1969
Malcolm McKenzie	1977
John DA Meredith	1955
Myles F Minchin	1941
Dr Jonathan Mirsky	1954
John Keith Mitchell	1948
Joy Mitra	1961
Mr Gerard Mizrahi	1970
M J Moore	1960
Allison Morehead	1997
CJE Morris	1944
JM Moss	1954
Linda Murgatroyd	1973
Dr PJD Naish	1951
Lucian Nethsingha	1956
Paul Nicholson	1993
Dr Christos Nifadopoulos	1997
Patrick A Nott	1958
Professor JF Nye	1941
Ilka Oevermann	1990
Mr Anthony Parker	1966
John Morris Parker	1952
M St. John Parker	1959
Stephen Parks	1961
Joanna Pearson	1985
Robin Pegna	1964
Michael Pelham	1944
James Peschek	1946
Nicholas Phillips	1958
Dr RJW Phillips	1972
Rory Phillips QC	1980
Mr Richard Pike	1957
Mr Hugh GL Playfair	1954
Geoffrey Plow	1975
Mr Richard Podger	1958
Dr JHB Poole	1968
Dr Jose Mauricio Prado	2009
Dr Martin Press	1962
Mrs Joanne Preston	
Dr Emma-Jane Price	1995
Dr Catherine W Proescholdt	1979
Bruce Pullan	1961
PA Ratcliffe	1960
Jane Readman	
Oliver Rinne	2007
Paul Rivers	1979
HRM Roberts	1951
Jessica Robertson	2009
Dr DGC Rogers	1967
Alan Rogerson	1965
DH Roose	1955
James Ross	2003
Victoria P Rostow	1978
Mr NA Routledge	1946
David Rowse	1943
Lord David Sainsbury	1959
Katharine Sawyer	1974
Eric Scott	1951
Professor Anthony Seaton	1956
Timothy Joseph Senior	2000
Professor JR Shackleton	1966
Kamalesh Sharma	1962
Denis Castle Shaw	1959
Peter Sheldrake	1963
WG Sherman	1950
Guy Shuttleworth	1945
Andrew Simms	1971
The Revd Duncan Sladden	1947
Lucy Slater	1978
Olav Slaymaker	1958
Mr Adrian Smith	1960
Michael JCC Smith	1982
Dr PA Smith	1992
Penelope Smith	1974
Robin C Smith	1968
Simon Standage	1959
Peter Stansky	1953
Andrew James Stevens	1996
Mike Stewardson	1957
Fenella Strange	1973
Martin Strangwood	1981
Peter Stredder	1968
Adrian M Suggett	1985
John Sunderland	1964
Richard Tapper	1961
Mr NM Taylor	1967
Professor Rodney Eatock Taylor	1962
C Tello	1961
Dr A Thomas	1968
Martin Thomas	1968
Dr Alwyn R Thompson	1962
Stephen Ashley Thompson	1991
JM Tiffany	1959
CR Tiné	1998
Deri Tomos	1970
M Tooke	1974
Jonathan Treasure	1967
Anthony J Turner	1966
Robert Turner	1938
Piers Tyrrell	1946
Dr Eboo Versi	1978
Albert von dem Bussche-Ippenburg	2003
Edward Vulliamy	1961
RW Wallbank	1949
Dr Lynda Ware	1972
Professor Joseph Watson	1962
Dr Alan Wells	1948
George WS Wen	1971
Mr EJ Wihl	1943
Hugh E Wilkinson	1946
Bryn Williams	1982
Dr D Gareth Williams	1965
David Owen Williams	1960
Patricia Williams	
David K Williamson	1964
Donald W Willis	1945
Keith Dudley Wilson	1954
Deborah L Wince-Smith	1973
William H Woolverton	1973
JB Young	1977
Sir Erik Christopher Zeeman	
Rosemary Zeeman	

Index

Picture Acknowledgements

Sebastian Ahnert 13; Stephen Bann (courtesy) 17, 18; Antony Barrington-Brown (photographer) 69; The Bridgeman Library 14; Peter Brookes/ The Times, nisyndication.com 68; Cold Spring Harbor Laboratory 84; Michael Craig-Martin 66; Eleanor Curtis 5, 7, 32, 101, 114–9, 124, 149, 160, 180–1, 214; Anthony Figgis 79; Richard Fortey 83; Getty Images 31, 161, 188; King's College, Cambridge 40, 103, 127; Edward Leigh (photographer) 107, 131, 133, 201, 210; National Portrait Gallery, London 167, 172, 190; Charles Nicholl 176, 178; PK Pal (courtesy) 56; Martin Parr 2, 20, 35, 42–9, 50, 55, 60, 87, 88–97, 100, 111, 135, 137–47, 152, 156, 194, 213; Jan Pieńkowski 182–7; Ramsey & Muspratt (photographer) 102, 196; Peter Schrank/ The Independent 7; Karl Sabbagh 6, 23, 59, 62; Mohammad Shaheen 197, 198; Susan Tomes 157; Anna Trench 202–4; Tansy Troy 209; Kate Whitely 75

©2010 King's College, Cambridge and Third Millennium Publishing Limited

First published in 2010 by Third Millennium Publishing Limited, a subsidiary of Third Millennium Information Limited.

2–5 Benjamin Street, London, United Kingdom EC1M 5QL
www.tmiltd.com

ISBN 978 1 906507 36 7

British Library Cataloguing in Publication Data:
A CIP catalogue record for this book is available from the British Library.

Edited by Karl Sabbagh
Designed by Matthew Wilson
Production by Bonnie Murray
Reprographics by Studio Fasoli, Italy
Printed by Gorenjski Tisk, Slovenia